NEW ORLEANS

"New Orleans' Enterprises"
by David H. Jones

Produced in cooperation with
The Chamber/New Orleans
and the River Region

Windsor Publications, Inc.
Chatsworth, California

NEW ORLEANS

AMERICA'S INTERNATIONAL CITY

A Contemporary Portrait by Mel Leavitt and David H. Jones

Windsor Publications, Inc.—Book Division
Managing Editor: KAREN STORY
Design Director: ALEXANDER D'ANCA
Photo Director: SUSAN L. WELLS
Executive Editor: PAMELA SCHROEDER

Staff for *New Orleans: America's International City*
Manuscript Editor: TERI DAVIS GREENBERG
Photo Editor: LARRY MOLMUD
Production Editor: JEFFREY REEVES
Editor, Corporate Profiles: MELISSA WELLS
Production Editor, Corporate Profiles: DOREEN NAKAKIHARA
Proofreader: MARY JO SCHARF
Customer Service Manager: PHYLLIS FELDMAN-SCHROEDER
Editorial Assistants: DOMINIQUE JONES, KIM KIEVMAN,
MICHAEL NUGWYNNE, KATHY B. PEYSER, THERESA J. SOLIS
Publisher's Representative, Corporate Profiles:
ROB OTTENHEIMER
Layout Artist, Corporate Profiles: BONNIE FELT
Designer: ELLEN IFRAH

Windsor Publications, Inc.
ELLIOT MARTIN, Chairman of the Board
JAMES L. FISH III, Chief Operating Officer
MICHELE SYLVESTRO, Vice President/Sales-Marketing
MAC BUHLER, Vice President/Acquisitions

Library of Congress Cataloging-in-Publication Data
Leavitt, Mel, 1927-
    New Orleans, America's international city : a con-
temporary portrait / by Mel Leavitt and David H.
Jones. — 1st ed.
        p.   cm.
    Includes bibliographical references and index.
    ISBN: 0-89781-425-8
    1. New Orleans (La.)—Civilization. 2. New Orleans
(La.)—Description—Views. 3. New Orleans
(La.)—Economic conditions. 4. New Orleans
(La.)—Industries. I. Jones, David H. (David Hiram),
1957-   . II. Title.
F379.N55L43 1990
976.3'35063—dc20   90-12769
                                                  CIP

Right: The old state capitol in Baton Rouge is in the Gothic-revival architectural style of the mid-nineteenth century. Now a museum, it reflects the wealth and high fashion that existed during the economic boom days in Louisiana prior to the Civil War. Photo by Philip Gould

Page 10/11: Photo by Bob Rowan/Progressive Image Photography

Page 152/153: Photo by Philip Gould

CONTENTS

PART TWO

NEW ORLEANS' ENTERPRISES

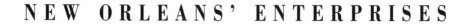

12 THE MARKETPLACE

New Orleans' location, culture, and favorable business climate make The Big Easy a great city to visit or call home. **page 155**

The Louisiana Superdome, 156; Blaine Kern Artists, Inc., 160; New Orleans Convention Center, 163; The New Orleans Hilton Riverside and Towers, 164; New Orleans Marriott, 166; Windsor Court Hotel, 168; Delta Queen Steamboat Co., 169; Hotel Inter-Continental New Orleans, 170; Weiner Cort Furniture Rental, 171; Antoine's, 172

13 THE GREAT NATURAL RESOURCE

New Orleans and the River Region have been blessed with abundant reserves of natural gas and oil, creating a thriving petrochemical industry. **page 175**

Freeport-McMoRan Inc., 176; McDermott International, Inc., 180; Texaco USA, 184; The Louisiana Land and Exploration Company, 186; Taylor Energy Company, 188; Chevron Corporation, 189; Walk, Haydel & Associates, Inc., 190

14 THE PORT

Millions of tons of cargo cross the wharves of the Port of New Orleans each year, placing the city at the forefront of U.S. port activity. **page 193**

International Shipholding Corporation, 194; Bisso Towboat Company, Inc., 196; Lykes Lines, 198; Cooper/T. Smith Stevedoring, 200; International-Matex Tank Terminals, 201

15 NETWORKS

New Orleans' network of energy, communication, and transportation providers contributes to its status as a major metropolitan center. **page 203**

Entergy Corporation and LP&L/NOPSI, 204; South Central Bell, 208; Delta Air Lines, Inc., 210; WVUE-TV, 212

16 BUSINESS AND PROFESSIONS

Greater New Orleans' business and professional community brings a wealth of ability, expertise, and service to the area. **page 215**

17 INDUSTRY

New Orleans' location and qualified work force draw manufacturers, distributors, and high-tech industries to the area. **page 243**

18 QUALITY OF LIFE

Medical and educational institutions contribute to the quality of life for New Orleans area residents. **page 257**

19 FROM THE GROUND UP

Developers, contractors, and realtors all help to shape the New Orleans of tomorrow. **page 269**

PART ONE

• • •

AMERICA'S
INTERNATIONAL
CITY

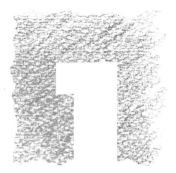

INTRODUCTION

Genius is nothing but a greater

aptitude for patience.

George **L**ouis **L**e**C**lerc de **B**uffon

Southeast Louisiana abounds in holiday traditions. One is the building of huge bonfires along the Mississippi River in the river parishes on Christmas Eve to help lead Santa Claus in his travels through the area. Photo by Philip Gould

AN AIR OF INGENUITY SURROUNDS THE CITY OF New Orleans. It is more than just a relaxed connection to its long and colorful history. And it goes far beyond common characteristics used to describe most American cities. In fact, the city's sheer originality transcends mere words. Its unique ambience flows straight to the heart, embraces the soul, and enlivens the senses. It affects how people think, how they interact. It affects composition and life-style. In effect, the genuine inventiveness of this city becomes the quintessence of life itself.

Some cities were built as work centers, while others were built as resorts. Either work or play, the choice is yours. But, as America's most international city, New Orleans successfully and quite creatively combines these elements into one seamless, continuous celebration of life. That's because New Orleans, as is true of other international cities, personifies the patience to exist in contemporary society, making progress when necessary, while continuing to respect and honor the ancestral threads of Old World charm that form the very fabric of this cosmopolitan urban center of the New South.

From outside Orleans Parish, one approaches through exotic, sometimes primordial, terrain, whether through the low-lying marshlands crisscrossed with bayous and dotted with cypress knees; over the seventh-largest lake in the nation, Lake Pontchartrain; across the mighty Mississippi; or through the new suburbs fresh and alive with new money and even newer ideas. If approaching from the west, the city rises up to meet you. Not too large, mind you, New Orleans can be taken in by the eye in one sweeping vista. It is built on a human scale. That is why some call it "The Big Easy." The Superdome anchors the vision, stabilizes it, orients the visitor.

It's the universally recognized Goodyear Blimp view of the city—a picture postcard. The steel-and-glass skyscrapers, all constructed in recent years, nestle in a tight, planned pattern of growth down Poydras Street Corridor, surrounding the Superdome like a space-age gem in a high-tech setting.

Off a down ramp and soon you're speeding down a wide boulevard illuminated in electric light and flanked by banners proclaiming the next special event, for New Orleans is a special-event city. It is special, made to order.

Facing page: The proliferation of modern, towering buildings in New Orleans has created a striking silhouette more like big-city Texas than Louisiana. Unlike Houston and Dallas, the tall buildings in New Orleans are set wide enough apart that the skyline does not overpower the horizon. Photo by Bob Rowan/Progressive Image Photography

Above: Not only on Mardi Gras can a person see a clown on a streetcar, but on any other day, fully costumed clowns can be seen "going to work" as street performers in the French Quarter. Photo by Bob Rowan/Progressive Image Photography

Food, whether it is prepared at home, at a corner neighborhood cafe, or in one of the world's finest restaurants, is considered by many people the real heart of New Orleans. Every conversation, sooner or later, turns to food. Photo by Bob Rowan/Progressive Image Photography

Thus far our journey has been strictly American, with some Southern influence thrown in for good measure. But once across Canal Street, you're immediately thrown into the funky, mesmerizing, kaleidoscopic, churning, artistic, serene, hard-edged, soft-light aesthetics of the French Quarter. As a veteran traveler, you immediately sense adventure and a wonderful tingle begins. The initial tingle will never be achieved again, but it will also never be forgotten. New Orleans is that unforgettable.

The people extend their hands in welcome. They smile. They surround you in good cheer. The *joie de vivre* is a virtue learned early in every New Orleanian's life. The camaraderie is contagious; it is the glue, the stuff of celebration, the binding element in the living fabric that is New Orleans. There exists an interwoven mixture of cultures and ethnic backgrounds mixed to new heights and given to a hospitality known only in the southernmost regions of the world. It is almost perplexing, this good cheer. Never, ever, have you been treated this way. Still, for those patient enough, the experience is just beginning to take hold. Prepare your senses for sights and sounds and tastes and a feeling like you have never before experienced in your life. Relax. Yank off the tie, slip into something light and comfortable. Although a formal town, New Orleans takes its formality in an easy stride. It makes exceptions for visitors, providing a needed jacket for those times required, excusing the occasional faux pas.

Who knows what will strike your fancy and stick in your memory—the history, the food, the blending of jazz, all the elements of being, of celebrating the contagious aspects of this sometimes frivolous city, of conducting business in an informal way like it used to be, open and honest.

New Orleans is a historian's dream come true. Founded by the French-Canadian Jean Baptiste Lemoyne, Sieur de Bienville, in 1718, it became a French colony. Bienville chose the site of the new town on a slightly higher level of ground nestling in the great sweeping curve of the Mississippi River (the "Crescent City") just a little more than a hundred miles from its mouth. Named for the Duc d'Orleans, regent to the child-king Louis XV, the town was first formally called Nouvelle Orleans. Since that time New Orleans has accepted its circumstances matter of factly, and it has transformed itself many times over. Under French, Spanish, and American flags, New Orleans has absorbed and retained diverse ethnic influences benefiting from a rather large influx of distinctly Irish, Italian, German, Hispanic, and African cultures. The diversity and unique nature of the music and food and the festivals can be directly attributed to this melting pot, a veritable gumbo of mixed traditions.

The city of New Orleans, long known for its natural resources and splendid geographic location, continues to impress its admirers and astonish its skeptics with a seemingly endless supply of optimism and resourcefulness. As the only city in America that lies below sea level, New Orleans has designed and maintains one of the most extensive and powerful pumping and drainage systems in the world. Skyscrapers, once

thought to be genuine folly because of the unstable soil prevalent throughout the region, now tower spectacularly overhead in remarkable shapes and sizes. Needless to say, class-A office space is not a problem in this forward-thinking mecca.

As you dig beneath the sleek exterior of the new New Orleans, you find that the city serves as the offshore and administrative oil industry while Louisiana handles more than 60 percent of the U.S. offshore oil production. The New Orleans Port area, now number one in the country in total ton-

nage handled, anticipates further growth in the coming decade. Since the late 1960s New Orleans has invested heavily in tourism-related developments, including the Louisiana Superdome, Rouse Company's Riverwalk, DeBartolo's Poydras Center, a $40-million world-class aquarium, a three-phase convention center that consists of more square footage on one level than any other convention center in America, and an ever-improving streetcar system that now includes a riverfront route.

Still further in your search for the true New Orleans, you find that transportation equipment manufacturing activity is the single most significant manufacturing activity in the New Orleans area, with 31 percent of the region's manufacturing work force employed in either shipbuilding or aerospace industries. The food industry has been growing steadily in the region, building on natural assets and the area's strong ties with the culinary arts. Currently the food manufacturing sector is the third-largest manufacturing sector in the city. In addition, the region produces 26 per-

All people require a periodic escape from the realities of everyday life. New Orleans understands human nature, and has its own built-in escape mechanism—the annual Mardi Gras season. Photo by Philip Gould

cent of the national domestic seafood catch. Tons of crab, oyster, craw-fish, shrimp, fresh tuna, alligator, and red snapper come from Louisiana waters.

As one of the best places to live in America, New Orleans receives high ratings in health care and medical services, an industry that accounts for more than 37,000 jobs in direct employment. The metropolitan area has 35 hospitals, including five teaching hospitals, two medical schools, a school of nursing, and the state's only schools of allied health professions and dentistry. In addition, Children's Hospital in New Orleans is the only full-service pediatric facility between Texas and Alabama that is dedicated solely to the health care of children.

Because of its geographic compactness, New Orleans and the surrounding River Region offer a surprising wealth of life-styles all within reasonable commute times of the downtown area. Whether it's the hustle and bustle of the Central Business District or the quiet of the suburbs, the variety of the region's life-styles leaves nothing to the imagination.

Facing page: The French Quarter, with Jackson Square at its heart, is one of the most exciting areas in the United States. For many Southerners, it is a very desirable weekend destination. Photo by Philip Gould

For those who care about future generations, new legislation is now aggressively addressing the issues and putting public education at the top of the state's agenda. The reforms enacted in 1990 put into immediate effect a three-year program to bring teacher salaries up to the Southern average. In addition, the new act limits teacher certificates to five-year renewable certificates.

New Orleans Public schools serve the needs of urban children, ranging from special education to advanced college courses offered through high schools. Benjamin Franklin High School, a magnet school and college preparatory public school, is recognized nationwide for its unusually high number of National Merit Scholars. The New Orleans Center for the Creative Arts is a special school for talented youth, graduating students such as Grammy Award winners Wynton Marsalis and Harry Connick, Jr.

In New Orleans education is recognized as the single most important factor in shaping the future economic and social well-being of its citizens, and it is treated as such. The area's 13 colleges and universities, 11 in Orleans Parish alone, educate a diverse population of students from around the world. Of the 11, there are two seminaries, one medical center, one community college, and 7 four-year institutions. New Orleans' Tulane University is recognized for its School of Tropical Medicine as well as its excellent law and medical schools. Next door, Loyola University offers an extensive curriculum, recognized for its excellence, especially in the fields of communications and journalism, law and

Above: New Orleans is not only a grand old town for humans, but it's a nice place for dogs, too. Where else but New Orleans could a noted pooch like Spuds McKenzie be crowned king of a major Mardi Gras parade. Photo by Bob Rowan/Progressive Image Photography

A wide array of regional produce is available throughout the area at a variety of markets and stands. Photo by Bob Rowan/Progressive Image Photography

medicine. The University of New Orleans on the lakefront offers a broad undergraduate program and an excellent extension program.

As you probe deeper and deeper into the essence of this oddly unique center, you begin to find that, just as the great Mississippi River makes an indelible imprint on life in the Crescent City, so too have the culture and heritage made similar impressions on the imagination of the world. Other regions have attempted to duplicate the cuisine only to find something lacking—that "something" being the generations of experience in the kitchen combined with the freshest of ingredients. New Orleans is synonymous with music—Dixieland and progressive jazz, rhythm and blues, Cajun and Caribbean soul, and the special New Orleans sound captured by the inimitable Dr. John and the ever-popular Neville Brothers. World-class film directors have now come to respect New Orleans for its unique look. Directors such as David Lynch, Walter Hill, Joel Cohen, and Taylor Hackford have just recently used New Orleans as the backdrop to their feature films. And area novelists and other book people overwhelmingly agree that New Orleans is in the midst of a literary renaissance to rival that of the 1920s and 1930s. During those glory years Sherwood Anderson made his home in the French Quarter, William Faulkner dropped in during 1925, F. Scott Fitzgerald lived in a boarding house on Prytania Street, and Lyle Saxon was den mother to the WPA writers, one of whom was Tennessee Williams. Today major novelists such as Anne Rice, Richard Ford, and Lucian Truscott IV, among others, call New Orleans home.

New Orleans can also boast the oldest theater company in America, Le Petit Theatre. There's also the Contemporary Arts Center, which stages theater productions as well as exceptional contemporary art exhibits. For the traditional art lover, there's also the beautiful New Orleans Museum of Art, which is located in City Park. Add to this plethora of cultural diversity a world-famous zoo—the Audubon Park and Zoological Gardens—along with the New Orleans Symphony, the New Orleans Opera Association, a ballet company, and a network of national parks and state museums, including the Louisiana State Museum. Among all these cultural gems also exist significantly historic buildings such as the Cabildo, where the face of the nation was changed forever with the signing of the Louisiana Purchase. And there are the festivals such as the French Quarter Festival, which annually attracts thousands of locals and tourists alike, treating them to the "world's largest jazz brunch" and filling Jackson Square with food and music. There is also the Louisiana Jazz and Heritage Festival, claimed by many to be one of the world's great festivals, which draws more than 300,000 visitors during two weekends in late April and early May. Live music on more than five stages simultaneously delights the music enthusiasts, while everyone enjoys sampling native Louisiana cuisine and roaming among the hundreds of fine craft booths.

Finally, in a class by itself, is Mardi Gras, or Carnival, as the season is called. Outclassing all other festivals and celebrations locally, it is an international draw for tourists, many of whom return annually. Few people know that the Carnival season actually begins on January 6 and ends on midnight of Mardi Gras day or Fat Tuesday. All through the season, Carnival organizations called krewes hold their masqued balls and stage their parades nightly. The larger and more famous organizations, such as Bacchus and Endymion, feature movie stars and celebrities as royalty. The chosen few have included Tony Bennett, Dolly Parton, Charlton Heston, Bob Hope, William Shatner, John Goodman, and many, many more.

It is in Mardi Gras that we come full circle in our brief tour of New Orleans. Mardi Gras provides a fitting metaphor for the city, its history, and inhabitants. For Mardi Gras is full of action, color, music, marching bands, masqued balls, and mystery. It is a joyous occasion. For local families it is a rich, unforgettable experience, full of tradition and memories. For those visiting it is an awesome spectacle of the highest order. Huge crowds, mixed and mingled throngs of every conceivable race and ethnic background, celebrate life with a kind of quiet exuberance. It is a time when people can be something that they are not or can become something that they want to be. It is a celebration unique in its format, global in scale, and unique in its execution. And it takes the ingenuity and patience of an international city like New Orleans to make it special.

In New Orleans, rain, especially in the summer, is a part of life. It can actually be quite pleasant to sit on a comfortable step under a gallery in the French Quarter while waiting out a sudden downpour. Photo by Bob Rowan/Progressive Image Photography

THE NATION'S MOST UNIQUE CITY

New Orleans is blessed with an aura that is indefinable and probably indescribable. It is, one senses, that of a woman of a certain mature age, experience, bemused, her youthful blush slightly faded, but her sensuality, her attraction undiminished.

James Kilpatrick

Dispensers of beignets and café au lait at the French Market's Café du Monde take a break between orders. Eating out is an important part of life in New Orleans—not only does it provide pleasure for diners, but employment for a large segment of the population. Photo by Philip Gould

NEW ORLEANS IS AN INTENSELY PERSONAL CITY. ITS people delight in walking and talking, visiting and dining, the sound of music and laughter. It is a city of small places, secret pleasures, discovered treasures. It may be one of the few large metropolises where people can mingle freely, linger at their own pace, smile and chat with strangers, and stroll through history at their leisure while actually feeling its living presence.

Recent polls show that visitors and newcomers heartily agree on what specific qualities they like about New Orleans: the old world charm, the food and the many fine restaurants, the hospitality and friend-liness of the people, the fascinating architecture, the music, the small-town atmosphere with big-city convenience, the wide choice of activities (especially for families), the many festivals and parades, the character and variety of the neighborhoods, and the quality of life—the ease in making friends and the balance between career and personal life.

New Orleans' people are its most valuable resource. They define the infectious charm, the indomitable spirit of an improbable city built on an implausible site. They have developed their own special cuisine, their own special architecture, their own grand festivals, and their own infec-tious musical idiom. Orleanians are a breed apart.

Although a compact city, the Crescent City still has many open areas perfect for a leisurely stroll. Often this is within sight of downtown office towers. Photo by Philip Gould

Mediterranean by disposition, Anglo-French-Hispanic and Afro-Caribbean by heritage, the city is primarily all-American in the fullest sense. It is a jambalaya of many races, a projection of America. Ancestral ties with other races and other nations long ago moved Orleanians to put out the welcome mat to one and all, making New Orleans "America's International City."

Today, as in its past, this international city is really two cities. One is more than two centuries old, historically and architecturally eclectic, yet alive—a European masterpiece unlike anything else in the United States. Tenderly preserved, the fabled French Quarter (Vieux Carre) maintains its timeless grace. The other city lies just across Canal Street, a monument to Anglo-American enterprise and the "melting pot" origins of this unique American metropolis. Once called the American Sector, this part of the city represents the Central Business District (CBD) of New Orleans, the core of the Middle South's banking and commerce.

Stoop sitting, or watching the world go by from one's front steps, is an old New Orleans custom. In more crowded areas, like the French Quarter, the custom takes on a different character with similar enjoyable results. Photo by Philip Gould

PRESERVING THE CITY'S HERITAGE

To preserve the city's personality and a feeling of neighborhood, more than 60 active neighborhood associations have grown up throughout New Orleans during the past two decades. They are vigorously involved in protecting the integrity of their turf through building codes, security measures, and revitalization plans aimed at keeping the city livable.

During the 1920s the Vieux Carre, abandoned by the French Creole inhabitants, became a decaying slum. Sicilian immigrants arrived by the thousands and welcomed any housing, no matter how run down, sleeping as many as eight to a room. Goats wandered the balconies of the Pontalbas, and chickens strutted about Jackson Square.

In time the hard-working Italian-Americans reestablished the French Market. Soon they dominated the produce industry so much that the Vieux Carre was temporarily called the Italian Quarter. Second and third generations moved into professions, leaving their immigrant surroundings behind. The historic Vieux was threatened with extinction. A parking lot marked the spot where the grand old French Opera House once stood before fire gutted it in 1919. Another parking lot, overgrown with banana trees, showed no evidence of the majestic St. Louis Hotel, which was razed in 1918.

Then, in the early 1950s, the decaying Vieux Carre rediscovered itself. A magnificent hotel patterned after the historic St. Louis arose on the same property, carefully scaled to the size and authenticity of its progenitor. The Royal Orleans was soon followed by the Royal Sonesta on Bourbon Street. An elegant restoration of the old Morphy residence (Brennan's Restaurant) reawakened Rue Royale.

Property values soared. Preservation fever revived the moribund Old Square. A city-appointed regulatory group, the Vieux Carre Commission, created in 1936 by state constitutional amendment, was given broader powers in the 1950s to assure and to protect the integrity of the French Quarter. It approved all new plans for renovation and repair and established stringent building codes designed to preserve what architects call the *tout ensemble*. The VCC became a model for preservationist groups. The 1939 organization of the French Quarter Association and the Garden District Association established a blueprint by allowing neighborhoods to maintain their own property and also protect the character and appearance of their area.

Today New Orleans community activist organizations are combined under the umbrella of the Preservation Resource Center (PRC), which also serves as a clearinghouse for information and joint effort.

In 1956 preservationists and progressives, both a strong presence in New Orleans and usually at odds with one another, united to save the French Quarter from destruction. That year the federal government announced plans to build a mammoth six-lane expressway, 100 feet wide and elevated 40 feet, a great, rumbling concrete high-rise designed to slash across the face of the French Quarter following the river levee. Unified under the battle cry: "Stop the Highwaymen," the preservationists and progressives made sure that the expressway never got off the drawing board. Most important, the experience alerted New Orleans to the fact that, in this time-tempered city, progress and preservation walk hand-in-hand.

New Orleans' well-organized preservation movement does more than encourage restoration and renovation; it also insures that the city's uniqueness, its very heart and soul, will remain intact. In New Orleans preservation *is* progress, and it is absolutely vital to its civic and economic well-being.

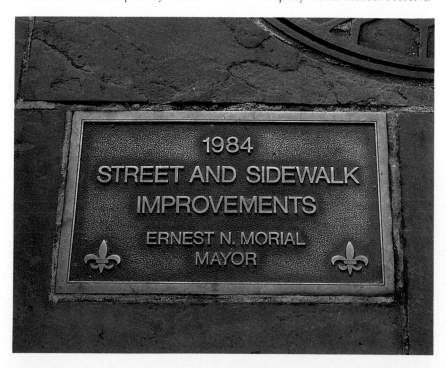

New construction and improvements can also mean preservation. In 1984, Canal Street and French Quarter streets were repaved. The new look followed old traditions with the use of brick and flagstone, in order to revive a nineteenth-century look. Small French Quarter hotels and bed and breakfasts in restored buildings are also a method of preservation while serving the growing tourist industry. Photo by Bob Rowan/Progressive Image Photography

Its modern high-rise steel-and-glass structures stand in dramatic contrast to the venerable Vieux Carre with its shaded, sequestered patios and its iron grillwork—its nineteenth-century grace.

For three centuries New Orleans has guarded the gateway to the mighty Mississippi River and the vast bounty of Middle America's harvest and trade. Situated five feet below sea level, it is virtually an island in the middle of a huge oak-cypress delta swamp, squeezed between Lake Pontchartrain to the north and the sinuous, brawling Mississippi.

The configuration of the city was tightly controlled by its cramped location for two centuries. Most other major cities, less confined and built on strong, stable foundations of rock or clay, were able to expand outward with relative ease. New Orleans was forced to grow into itself, compacting into a series of once-isolated neighborhood "islands" adrift on a sea of marsh.

Through a series of remarkable engineering feats, this city, lying below sea level, managed to drain and reclaim the swamp, bridge both the lake and the river, and develop a belated suburban sprawl now as thickly populated as the city limits. Since 1940 the population of Greater New Orleans has almost tripled, while it declined within the limits of the city proper.

In Jefferson Parish modern skyscrapers and spacious shopping malls rise up within a continuous residential community numbering 400,000 citizens. In the 1950s it was mainly rural country where raising dairy cat-

New Orleans is surrounded by swamps and water, which has made expansion difficult. As a result, many handsome, old houses have survived and been maintained for several generations. Photo by Philip Gould

tle and hunting rabbits were popular activities. And a small enclave called Kenner (now a bustling city of 70,000) was once the truck garden capital of the South.

In addition, the Pontchartrain Causeway overleapt the lake, creating comfortable and secluded bedroom communities in the piney woods of Slidell, Covington, and Mandeville, once isolated weekend and summer retreats.

The metropolitan area spread downriver to Chalmette, Arabi, and Meraux, while across the Mississippi, the river hamlets in Algiers, Gretna, Westwego, and Harvey became the base of a new West Bank complex. There, layer upon layer of new residential subdivisions have been developed with service industries, malls, and a population of 200,000.

Greater New Orleans was once composed of 10 separate townships and 3 separate independent municipalities. A three-year study, "Neigh-

Left and facing page: With numerous well-maintained, old neighborhoods in New Orleans, many lovely architectural styles from bygone days can be seen throughout the city. Victorian houses, with all of their ornamentation, can be found in abundance. Photos by Philip Gould

borhood Profiles," commissioned by the City of New Orleans in 1979, named an astounding 71 separate neighborhood entities. About one-third were postwar subdivisions, creatures of the suburban explosion and the white flight characteristic of many American cities. In many cases these postwar suburbs appear, at first glance, to be clones, faceless and identical to other American cities. Yet that pervasive feeling of neighborhood so characteristic of New Orleans continues to survive. All over metropolitan New Orleans, businesses have moved to the suburbs but have still maintained the "ambience, character, and often the clientele of their old neighborhoods" according to the 1983 edition of the *WPA Guide to New Orleans*.

The oldest and most posh of New Orleans' "newer" neighborhoods is a wealthy enclave called Metairie Park and Gardens. Originally laid out in the 1920s, when buyers received a bonus membership in the exclusive Tudor-style Metairie Country Club, this architectural showplace contains an eclectic mixture of million-dollar mansions ranging in style from Gothic to Southern Colonial to Art Deco.

Old and new stand side by side in New Orleans. Nineteenth-century buildings in the French Quarter are in the shadow of modern skyscrapers. An old-fashioned streetcar travels along the new riverfront car line. Photo by Bob Rowan/Progressive Image Photography

One of the proudest accomplishments of post-World War II development is the string of fashionable neighborhoods along the lakefront, built on land reclaimed from Lake Pontchartrain. Lake Vista, Lakeview, Lakeshore, Lake Terrace, and Lake Oaks all represent limited access communities with close proximity to lakefront marinas, seafood restaurants, small shopping malls, and the wide range of recreational facilities in nearby City Park. Yet each is within a 20-minute drive of the Central Business District.

At least 40 old New Orleans neighborhoods, some dating back to 1807, still exist and have maintained an historical character and distinctiveness, with 10 of them National Historic Districts and/or listed on the *National Register.* One of these neighborhoods, Carrollton, first greets the Mississippi on its downward rush from the hinterlands. Originally subdivided from the huge Macarty plantation in 1837, it lies eight miles from the center of the Old Square (Vieux Carre). So remote at a time when nothing but swamp intervened, it became a separate municipality. From 1853 to 1874 it served as the seat of government for adjoining Jefferson Parish. It was settled heavily by German immigrants, some of whom called it Karlton, and was not annexed by the City of New Orleans until 1874.

Downtown the Creole faubourgs (suburbs) of Treme, Marigny, and New Marigny (Seventh Ward) attached themselves to the primarily French-speaking French Quarter (the First Municipality) along with an

Orleanians are less prone to abandon an old house for something new in a suburban subdivision. With so many old houses available in New Orleans, common weekend pastimes include lovingly restoring and maintaining one's home. Photo by Philip Gould

One of the top destinations in New Orleans for tourists, architectural historians, and locals alike is the beautiful Garden District, which was named for its many trees and large gardens. A guided tour, or just a quiet stroll through its streets, evokes at every turn a feeling of what American urban life was like during the second half of the nineteenth century. Photo by Philip Gould

enclave known as Little Saxony, which was heavily populated by German emigres. To this day natives still refer to themselves as living Uptown or Downtown with a touch of implied superiority, regardless of race or social or economic status. The rest of New Orleans is called Backatown and is mostly the part of town that was once swamp, but since has been drained, filled, and developed.

The Uptown District, one of the largest National Historic Districts in the United States, contains more than 10,700 structures. It was the residential garden spot of New Orleans in the late nineteenth and early twentieth centuries and includes the university section and the campuses of Tulane, Loyola, and Newcomb, as well as Audubon Park and its nationally renowned zoo. Every socioeconomic group is represented in the Uptown District, and its rich diversity of architecture is a constant source of fascination to visitors and natives alike. Here past and present meld in a style of living that transcends history while encapsulating it.

At one time ornate riverboats lined the wharves of New Orleans. The riverboat era may be gone, but its aura is still present in the romantic architecture of several "riverboat houses" that still stand in the city along the banks of Old Man River. Photo by Philip Gould

Magnificent Greek Revival, Italianate, and Queen Anne-style homes overlooking immaculate lawns and gardens stand proudly, intermixed with Creole cottages and shotgun, Art Nouveau, and Colonial Revival homes.

The Garden District is a national treasure with perhaps the largest concentration of genuine antebellum homes in America. It dates back to the 1830s, New Orleans' "Golden Age," when only New York City was richer or more commercially powerful. It became known as the Garden District because its mansions, built on double lots in land-poor New Orleans, were elegantly landscaped and set back behind broad lawns and extravagant gardens. Today giant live oaks two centuries old shade its quiet streets, and the seductive aroma of oleander, jasmine, and sweet olive permeate the night air. Like most of New Orleans, there is a feeling of semitropical languor, for the city is not only timeless, but is is also evergreen.

The largest local historic district, Esplanade Ridge, is downtown, just below the Vieux Carre. Once the Creole grand promenade, this historic area now includes Treme and Marigny. Treme, which was the city's first public suburb (1807), contained the largest concentration of free people of color in the United States. Marigny, named for Bernard de Marigny (known as the "last of the Creole aristocrats") and wedged in between Esplanade and Elysian Fields and the river, is an outstanding example of restored Creole cottage architecture.

The spacious old mansions of Esplanade Ridge, many dating back more than 100 years, were homes for the French *creme de la creme.* Many classic Greek Revival and Italianate-style town houses have been rescued from demolition and elegantly renovated. In many cases they have been subdivided into apartments. Esplanade Avenue, with its ancient oaks, is one of the city's most fascinating and historic streets.

New Orleans' obsession with the preservation of its unique culture, its varied architecture, and historic landmarks once was considered by so-called progressives as a symptom of succumbing to the romantic past. Today, however, restoration and renovation have become almost stylish, and it has been said that New Orleans does not live *in* the past so much as it lives *with* the past. Past and present coexist comfortably. It is this pride of heritage and the city's longtime isolation from the mainland that have made the people of New Orleans intensely aware of their uniqueness.

New Orleans is a very street-oriented city. Whether attending one of the region's many festivals, going to a parade, just strolling in the French Quarter, or feeding pigeons in a park, Orleanians can always find outdoor diversions. Photo by Bob Rowan/Progressive Image Photography

A LOOK BACK

The nation that controls New Orleans and the mouth of the Mississippi will control the destiny of North America.

Napoleon Bonaparte

The fall of New Orleans to the Union Navy in 1862 cut the Confederacy in half and led to the eventual Union control of the Mississippi River during the Civil War. Courtesy, The Historic New Orleans Collection

I N 1718 FRENCH-CANADIAN NAVAL OFFICER JEAN BAPTISTE Lemoyne, Sieur de Bienville, founded New Orleans on what he called the Mississippi River's "great crescent." There, upon a natural levee created by the Mississippi and overlooking the downstream approach of foreign vessels, he located his first settlement, the Vieux Carre.

New Orleans was, from the beginning, an international city. The French and Spanish governed it for almost a century before it became part of the United States. Napoleon Bonaparte, who had once sought to make New Orleans headquarters for the French North American empire, sold the "Isle of Orleans" to the infant United States in 1803 as part of the Louisiana Purchase. The United States, which paid only about four cents an acre, also acquired enough additional territory in the bargain to create 13 new American states.

Napoleon's comment at the time of the Louisiana Purchase was prophetic: "I have given England a maritime rival that sooner or later will humble her pride." His prophecy was certified 13 years later on January 8, 1815, on the plains of Chalmette just below the city of New Orleans. There, in the Battle of New Orleans, General Andrew Jackson and his hastily recruited assemblage of rough-cut Kentucky and Tennessee sharpshooters, Creole dandies, free men of color, and Jean Lafitte's free-booters repulsed an army of 10,000 British regulars who outnumbered them roughly five to one. In this battle, called by historian Hugh Wilkinson "the single most consequential battle in American history," the British suffered a staggering defeat and lost more than 2,000 men. Jackson counted no more than 12 dead.

The Battle of New Orleans dramatically unified a struggling young nation and confirmed its revolution. It broke America's bonds with Europe and proved to be the downfall of Britain's colonial ambitions in the New World. The Mississippi Valley was secured.

The Battle of New Orleans also made an American folk hero of Andrew Jackson. He became President and set the stage for a peaceful populist revolution. What had been primarily a republic ruled by aristocrats gave way to a new concept of egalitarian rule—Jacksonian democracy.

For decades following the Louisiana Purchase, New Orleans bristled with discontent, caught up in an uneasy detente between the original French and Creole inhabitants

New Orleans' first suburb was Faubourg St. Marie, established in 1788. It was soon followed by others up and down the Mississippi River. The new suburbs were created as plantations were subdivided by their owners to accommodate new housing. Some neighborhoods are still named for their original plantation owners. Courtesy, The Historic New Orleans Collection

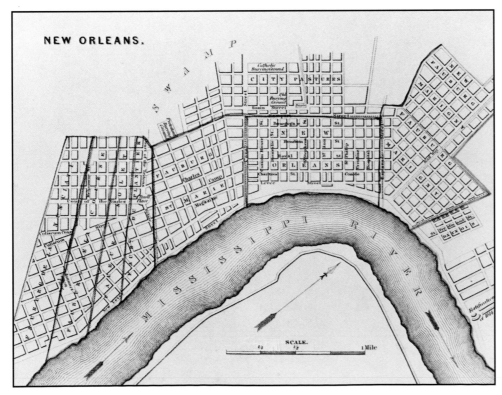

and the nouveau riche Anglo newcomers. Les Americaines, as the Creoles called them, were primarily merchants and entrepreneurs. They claimed the Uptown above Canal Street, an area variously known as the Quagmire, the American Sector, and the Second City, and aggressively set out to seek their fortunes.

The Second City was a marshy backwash until the steamboat turned it into the citadel of Southern commerce. One area known simply as "The Swamp" was so sleazy and ungovernable that the police refused to enter it. (This haven for lusty, thirsty riverboat men was the city's first tourist attraction.) In 1805 the area above Canal Street was a welter of mud wallows, plank walkways, small shacks, and pigsties. A cluster of warehouses ran up the river. Several large plantations produced indigo and, later, sugarcane. One was run by the Jesuits, who introduced orange trees.

The competition between the French-speaking Creoles, the "natives" and founders, and Les Americaines, the "foreigners" or usurpers, was heated and, at times, bloody. It was not unusual for 10 duels to be fought on a single Sunday under the oaks in City Park. The Creoles considered the Americans crude of manner, boisterous, and materialistic. The Frenchmen clung tenaciously to their Gallic customs and living style and

THE PIRATE PATRIOT

The Battle of New Orleans made a legend of Jean Lafitte. His 1,000 buccaneers occupied a small island fortress called Grand Terre, guarding the entrance to Barataria Bay and the labyrinthine swamp bayous beyond it. Lafitte called it his "back door to New Orleans." He made a handsome living with his fleet of 100 seagoing marauders and shallow-draft swamp craft, smuggling contraband and slaves into the nation's second most lucrative market.

The suave rogue-gallant spoke four languages fluently and dealt openly with some of the wealthiest and most influential merchants in New Orleans. Lafitte angrily rejected charges that he was a pirate. He carried a "letter of marque" from the Republic of Cartagena (Venezuela) authorizing him to run down any Spanish ship entering the Caribbean and sink it (after confiscating its cargo). He was, in a sense, the naval wing of the spreading South American revolution against Spain. One of his "hellish banditti," Rene Beluche, later became commodore of the Venezuelan navy.

The so-called "Terror of the Gulf" took pains not to bother American shipping and actually checked much of his booty through U.S. Customs. However, since the importation of slaves was declared illegal in 1807, Lafitte's confiscated slaves were channeled by way of Grand Terre through the back door and the swamp.

Lafitte, his men, and especially their vitally needed powder and flints were indispensable in routing the British during the Battle of New Orleans. Andrew Jackson arranged presidential pardons for the lot, and many became American citizens. Lafitte grew restless, however, and set up another buccaneer outpost on Galveston Island.

When a crew of his renegades plundered an American ship, Lafitte was blamed. Given 30 days to abandon Galveston, he burned his base and sailed away, never to return. Down Barataria way natives say: "Lafitte's treasure is buried in everybody's backyard." Where Lafitte is buried, no one knows.

Pirate Jean Lafitte's reputation has been greatly enhanced; he has been a hero of both books and movies, and is often depicted as elegant and dapper, although much of what has come down about him has been colored by romance. Courtesy, The Historic New Orleans Collection

The New Orleans Cotton Exchange was established in 1873 when "King Cotton" was at its height. Constructed in 1920, this was the second Cotton Exchange on this site, replacing an ornate structure that had been built in 1883. The Cotton Exchange was disestablished as cotton growing has moved to the western United States and overseas. Courtesy, The Historic New Orleans Collection

the French language. Most Creoles refused to speak English. Many sent their sons away to France to be educated. They built separate banks, hotels, restaurants, and theaters.

Yet, each time the Creoles looked across Canal Street, the industrious Anglos were building something bigger, newer, and better. The St. Charles Hotel went up in 1835. Advertised as the most palatial hotel in America, it stood four stories high and had elegant Grecian columns and a dome so prominent that it was visible for miles. Downriver the French Creoles countered with the St. Louis Hotel, which they referred to, tongue in cheek, as "the most palatial hotel in America, even in New Orleans." It, too, featured a grand rotunda under which was operated the world's largest slave auction block. (Reflecting its Mardi Gras traditions, New Orleans was the only city to auction off its slaves in costume.)

Uptown the Anglos built the opulent St. Charles Theater, equipped with 4,500 seats and featuring a two-ton, crystal chandelier. Its flamboyant owner, an English actor-producer named James Caldwell, modestly termed it the first "Palace of Drama." Not to be outdone, the Creoles constructed a marble and granite masterpiece, the fabled Old French Opera House, which became the social center of

The ornate New Orleans Stock Exchange building symbolized the city's dominant position at the time as the financial capital of the South. The facade of the building is now incorporated into the front of a bank building on Canal Street. Courtesy, The Historic New Orleans Collection

the *creme de la creme*. There were four balconies, including screened boxes for the "freed color" and women *enceinte* (pregnant) plus a segregated tier for the blacks.

Uptown and Downtown were divided by a median strip that ran up the middle of Canal Street. It was called the Neutral Ground. To this day, all medians on New Orleans' boulevards are referred to as neutral grounds.

Unable to compromise, much less cooperate, the people of New Orleans embarked on a rare experiment. They officially divided the city into two separate governments, one Anglo and one French. Each had its own mayor, its own council, and its own currency. The Second City or American Sector, which became the Second Municipality in 1835, remained a semi-autonomous state until 1852. It was so independent and so prosperous that an English visitor, Alexander MacKay, was prompted to write in 1852:

CANAL STREET—THE NEUTRAL GROUND

Canal Street is undoubtedly one of the most famous main streets in the world. At 171 feet wide, it is also one of the widest. Not part of the original city street plan of 1721, Canal was kind of an afterthought, a fringe area to the old French town, a promenade. Cows and carriages vied for running room.

Until "Les Americaines" arrived, Canal Street marked the outskirts of the Vieux Carre. Once envisioned as a waterway connecting the Mississippi River and Lake Pontchartrain, Canal Street evolved into a "neutral ground" dividing competing French and Anglo societies, separating Uptown from Downtown. Gradually Canal evolved into the retail and merchandising heart of New Orleans.

The Canal Street levee became the city's doorstep to world commerce and the scene of more than a few major historical events. The first commercial steamboat, Robert Fulton's *New Orleans,* landed there on January 12, 1812, ushering in the city's golden era. Then, on June 30, 1870, two riverboat giants, the *Natchez* and the *Robert E. Lee,* set out from there for St. Louis in history's most famous match race.

In 1874 a bizarre battle, complete with cannon and Gatling guns, was fought downtown at Canal Place between the rebellious forces of the White League and the Union-supported Metropolitan Police (mostly black). In the 45-minute skirmish, watched by local citizens from balconies and barricaded side streets, the carpetbagger forces were routed.

For two centuries "all roads led to Canal," the city's lifeline. "I'm goin to Canal" was a common expression for those going to shop, work, play, or meet people. All but one of the city's 27 streetcar lines terminated at Canal. And each Mardi Gras, one million costumed and masked revelers converged on Canal Street.

These days the Boston Club at 824 Canal, built in 1844 as a residence and considered the most exclusive private club in the city, is the site of the official reviewing stand where the Queen of Carnival toasts her King every Mardi Gras. The club stands in isolated splendor among a jumble of small shops and discount stores that have invaded a once-stately merchant's row. One by one the larger, more upscale retailers have aban-

doned Canal, closing down or fleeing to the wealthier suburbs. Only Maison Blanche, established in 1909, remains among the venerable downtown stores that once made the street the cynosure of smart shoppers.

Yet, rumors of Canal's demise are greatly exaggerated. Today this one-time promenade for local patricians is undergoing a noticeable transition. The Rivergate project touched it off in 1968 with construction of the 33-story World Trade Center and the Rivergate exhibition hall behind it. The Marriott Hotel followed in 1972, inspiring a series of major hotel constructions including the International, the Sheraton, and the Meridien.

Furthermore, lower Canal Street has been declared a National Historic District and owes much of its rebirth to the determination and vision of developer Joseph Cannizzaro. His Canal Place complex embraces a combination shopping center/business center/hotel adjacent to the French Quarter. Cannizzaro lured new, prestigious retailers such as Brooks Brothers and Saks to New Orleans and then wrapped an upscale hotel, the Westin, around the entire package.

Canal Street, shown here in the 1880s, was the dividing line between the French and American cities, and while it was planned to be a canal, one was never built. By the 1850s the street had evolved from a residential street into the city's premier shopping district, a status it held for over a century. Courtesy, The Historic New Orleans Collection

In crossing Canal Street, you seem bound from one century to another. You might also fancy that you had crossed the boundary line between two hostile nations . . . New Orleans is literally two cities—one French, one American.

A third municipality was added downstream from the French Quarter—the forlorn faubourg (suburb)—developed by Bernard Marigny, a millionaire playboy credited with fighting 27 duels, naming 66 streets, and inventing the dice game Craps.

For 17 years the three municipalities coexisted, their officials meeting as a "Council of the Whole" once annually each December in strictly ceremonial fashion. And though two virulent epidemics, one in 1835 and another in 1853, wiped out nearly 20,000 New Orleans inhabitants, the city still prospered.

The French called the era before the Civil War the "Belle Epoque." The Anglos preferred the "Golden Age." Either way, there is no parallel in American history. New Orleans grew into the second-largest and second-richest city in America, and by 1860, as the Civil War loomed, the Second Municipality boasted the biggest banking industry in the South. One bank began printing currency with "Ten" in English on one side of its $10 notes and "Dix" (French) on the other side. These novelties became known as "Dixies," and New Orleans as the capital of "Dixieland."

In addition, New Orleans became the nation's busiest port in the years preceding the Civil War as its shipping tonnage exceeded that of New York.

New Orleans was occupied by Union Army troops from 1862 to 1865. Never has any other American city been controlled by enemy forces for so long a time. The federal presence, supported by troops, was felt for 12 more years during Reconstruction.

The city's politics were so chaotic that historian Joe Gray Taylor was moved to write:

In every election between 1868 and 1878 there was so much fraud, intimidation and skullduggery that it is impossible to say who won a majority of the votes actually cast—or who would have won had an honest election been held.

By 1874 the State of Louisiana was bankrupt. Its debt was a staggering $53 million. State funds were systematically plundered by carpetbagger opportunists and local scalawags who manipulated the newly enfranchised black voters in collusion with federal authorities. During a two-year period, 37,000 property seizures took place in New Orleans and 30,000 Orleanians left town.

By the time federal troops were withdrawn on April 24, 1877, New Orleans had become virtually an open city, prey for unscrupulous gamblers and vice lords.

With Reconstruction came the rising challenge of railroad traffic. The increase in east-west trade via the Erie Canal and the Great Lakes threat-

Elected in 1928, Huey P. Long was Louisiana's most powerful governor. Many people thought that Long could have been elected president of the United States had he not been cut down by an assassin's bullet in 1935 when he was serving in the United States Senate. Many public projects were completed during the Long years such as bridges, roads, and the skyscraper state capitol building where Long was shot. Courtesy, The Historic New Orleans Collection

ened New Orleans' major industry—the port. Old Man River kept right on rolling, but he no longer commanded American transportation and commerce.

New Orleans fared better than other Southern cities during Reconstruction, but it did not begin to really recover until the turn of the century. Cotton continued to represent more than 50 percent of its export revenue. Coffee, sugar, and bananas accounted for roughly two-thirds of its import dollar.

King Cotton deserved a monument, and New Orleans businessmen, an audacious breed, made certain he got one. In 1889, after two years of construction, the grandiose Cotton Exchange was dedicated. It was, by far, the costliest and most ornate building in New Orleans, the center of a thriving financial district that ranked close behind New York, Chicago, and San Francisco. It cost $380,000 and lasted 40 years. Local citizens remembered it primarily because it was the first building in their swampy city to have a subterranean cellar. Soon there was a building called the Produce Market Exchange, then a Board of Trade, then a Cotton and Maritime Association, followed by a Dock Board and a Port Authority.

By 1906, when the local stock exchange moved into handsome new headquarters at 740 Gravier, the center of wealth and power in the city (and much of the South) was concentrated within a few city blocks in the Central Business District.

Dramatic changes began to occur. The Mississippi was finally controlled at its strategic entrance to the Gulf. An ingenious system of jetties cleared the passes and maintained a constant 30-foot-deep channel for oceangoing ships. Captain James Eads was the man responsible for opening New Orleans' port to the world.

Another engineer, A. Baldwin Wood, finally conquered the city's longtime nemesis, the pestilent, mosquito-infested swamp. His huge pumps, tied in with a network of underground drainage conduits, made the old system of open canals and drainage ditches obsolete. It put an end to the virulent epidemics of yellow fever, cholera, and malaria that scourged the city for a century and opened the way for extensive landfill and real estate development.

The steamboat era was now only a romantic memory. Cargo ships and barges transformed the levee, and New Orleans became a rail center and kick-off point for the Southwestern United States. Yet there still was no metropolitan link between the east bank of the river and the west, the central city of Algiers. For the time being, ingenuity triumphed. Entire trains were uncoupled, transferred to river barges as large as football fields, and floated across the Mississippi. There they were reassembled and sent on rumbling cross-country.

Through all the changes the city managed to retain its reputation for foot-loose, fancy-free fun and games. The corrupt Louisiana State Lottery, which virtually ran state politics from 1868 to 1890, was replaced by a new breed of small businessmen—bookies and numbers runners. In addition, an organized, legalized red-light district called Storyville was established, designed to confine pleasures of the flesh to a single 36-block area.

During the early years of the twentieth century, New Orleans gained a reputation as one of the nation's most tightly organized political "Rings." First, Martin "Papa" Behrman, a former grocer from Algiers across the river, was elected mayor of New Orleans five times. He dominated city politics for a quarter century until he died in office in 1926. Then, two years later, a fire-breathing "messiah," Huey P. Long, broke the stranglehold, leading his "poor-white revolution," only to become what one historian calls "America's first dictator."

A widening political schism developed between hedonistic New Orleans and puritanical North Louisiana. Lacking a genuine two-party

DeLesseps S. "Chep" Morrison was elected mayor in 1946 and led the city's first reform government in over a quarter of a century. During his administration he helped bring in new industries and initiated many important municipal improvements such as expressways, a network of overpasses, and a new civic center. Courtesy, The Historic New Orleans Collection

system, the state split into two hostile Democratic party factions—Longs versus anti-Longs. One was big-city cosmopolitan, primarily Catholic, laissez-faire, and relatively prosperous. The other was essentially rural, dirt-poor, puritanical, and fundamentalist Protestant. South Louisiana and its teeming port, New Orleans, sat on most of the state's resources—oil, gas, sulphur, salt, and sugarcane. North Louisiana had few resources but more votes.

In this symbolic battle of the "haves" and "have nots," Huey and Earl Long and their legions of misbegotten developed the most extensive welfare state in the country. Then, in 1935, Huey Long was assassinated in the corridor of the Louisiana State Capitol in Baton Rouge.

Shortly before his death, Huey Long exclaimed: "God help Loozyana if I die . . . These rascals of mine will steal this state blind." Long's statement was pure prophecy. The scramble for power began the day after his funeral, which was attended by 100,000. They filed by his open coffin inside the skyscraper state capitol that he built 32 stories high "so it'll be one story higher than anything in Dixie."

Judge Richard Leche, a tractable man with a taste for the good life, succeeded Huey as governor. Huey's bellicose little brother, Earl, who called himself "The Last of the Red Hot Poppas," grudgingly settled for lieutenant governor. The legatees of Long's populist revolution were so entrenched that, cloaked in the martyr's mantle, they undertook a startling political coup. Huey's henchmen actually forced New Orleans mayor Semmes Walmsley, a longtime antagonist, to resign. In return, Leche guaranteed a return of the "home rule" powers Huey had stripped from the city with the aid of his captive legislature.

Lacking any organized opposition, Robert Maestri (Long's local "money man") was appointed (some say "anointed") to serve out Walmsley's last two years. The infamous "Louisiana Hayride" rolled on, unchecked. The "statehouse gang" pushed through the legislature a constitutional amendment that extended realtor Maestri's term as mayor to six years.

Because state officials had made peace politically with President Franklin Roosevelt, a flood of federal money poured into Baton Rouge. What followed during the next four years was described by reporter-historian Harnett Kane as "the most systematic theft of an American state in American history." Huey's "rascals" bled Louisiana dry, tapping state funds, federal funds, and LSU funds and brazenly using state vehicles, personnel, and materials for personal pleasure or profit. "Double-

dipping," "phantom payrolls," even phantom buildings and property, were among the various scams that landed seven of them in federal prison, including Governor Leche and LSU's president, James Monroe Smith.

Unabashed, in 1940 Dick Leche told reporters as he stepped aboard the train for the Atlanta penitentiary, "Boys, when I took the oath of office I didn't take any damned vow of poverty." Louisiana voters, fed up with chicanery, elected reform governor Sam Jones. The Long machine was temporarily stalled. Then, in 1948, "Uncle Earl" Long grabbed up the Populist banner and became governor for the first of three tempestuous terms.

Down in New Orleans, Bob Maestri prepared to face opposition for only the second time in 10 years.

In 1948 a handsome, charismatic war hero, 34-year-old Delesseps "Chep" Morrison, entered the political arena as a reform candidate. He was perfectly cast for the role. The articulate former lieutenant colonel made his first campaign appearances in uniform, adorned with service ribbons and citations. Backed by a small army of female volunteers wielding kitchen brooms, he vowed a "clean sweep" of City Hall and the end of 46 years of machine politics.

Morrison won and then won again and again. From 1948 to 1961 he was unbeatable as mayor. In the process he developed his own machine, the CCDA (Crescent City Democratic Association) and went about freeing New Orleans from its geographical isolation and physical obsolescence.

Where five separate railroad terminals once clogged passenger and freight delivery, a modern Union passenger terminal was built in 1954. Countless railroad crossings and rail lines running down the neutral grounds of boulevards were eliminated, bypassed, or rerouted. At one point it was said Morrison dedicated a new overpass every six months.

Union Station served the passenger needs of the Illinois Central Railroad from the 1890s until 1950 when it was replaced by a new union station which combined the services of all the city's railroads. Old Union Station, now demolished, was the only building in New Orleans designed by noted architect Louis Sullivan. Courtesy, The Historic New Orleans Collection

The citywide New Orleans Recreation Department (NORD) developed an impressive variety of programs for children and adults in sports, crafts, drama, and the arts. It became a model for the nation.

For the first time the metropolitan area and the north shore were directly connected as the world's longest overwater span, the 24-mile-long Lake Pontchartrain Causeway, was completed in 1957. The following year downtown was finally directly connected to the West Bank by the Greater Mississippi River Bridge, a monument to creative engineering and a marshland construction coup.

Though a demonstrably effective mayor and unbeatable on his own turf, Chep Morrison was drubbed three times in his run for governor by Earl Long's populist brigade, only to be appointed Ambassador to the OAS (Organization of American States) by President John F. Kennedy.

Four months after his last attempt for the governorship, Morrison's light plane crashed in Mexico. He was only 52 when he died on May 22, 1964.

Victor Schiro, a Morrison protege and city councilman-at-large, inherited the mayor's office when Morrison resigned in 1961 to become the OAS Ambassador. For seven years Schiro presided over a remarkably calm period of desegregation and the beginning of New Orleans' greatest industrial boom since the antebellum "Belle Epoque."

Under Schiro, the first blacks were appointed heads of significant boards and commissions, offices they had not held since the days of federally enforced Reconstruction. At Michoud, in New Orleans East, NASA set up shop to produce the Saturn-1 booster rockets that eventually lifted man on his way to the moon.

In 1967 the New Orleans Saints "came marching in" with a flourish; a black speedster named Jon Gilliam ran back the first kick-off of the first NFL game of the city's first pro season 93 yards to score.

Despite a succession of losing seasons for the Saints, New Orleans fans supported the team with religious fervor. Some, who thought their only reward would be in heaven, finally found it in the Superdome. Under the rejuvenated leadership of local auto tycoon Tom Benson, the Saints hired a brilliant young coach, Jim Mora, and became perennial contenders in the last half of the 1980s.

Racially and economically two "new-style" political leaders seized the moment of transition in the 1960s and 1970s. "Moon" Landrieu twice ran successfully for mayor with strong black support. John McKeithen, a former Earl Long floor leader, abandoned the earlier path of many upstate "segs" and began preaching racial understanding and embarked on an industrial crusade.

McKeithen, an unknown quantity when elected in 1964, became the first governor to reconcile historic differences between the state and its richest, largest city. On November 4, 1967, voters approved a second term for McKeithen and an unprecedented constitutional amendment to build an all-weather, all-purpose stadium.

The Superdome became McKeithen's and New Orleans' vision of the future. Billed as "The World's Largest Room," the Superdome triggered a startling rejuvenation of the city's Central Business District once it was completed in 1975. Within five years, eight new high-rise buildings averaging 17 stories in height and costing $193 million arose.

By 1979 South Louisiana's boom in offshore development and the Port of New Orleans' rise to number one status in the nation gave the city of New Orleans a new, modernist stance. The voters elected the first black mayor, Ernest "Dutch" Morial, and then gave him a second four-year mandate in 1982. Blacks were integrated into government at all levels—the city council, the school board, the police department, and at City Hall. In addition, between 1977 and 1985 private investment rose at a rate of $500 million a year.

The 1984 World's Fair was a financial disappointment, yet it ironically spurred another era of development—the renaissance of the riverfront and the reclaimed and renovated Warehouse District.

When the bottom fell out of the oil business, and the price per barrel plummeted from $34 to $10, the state found itself in the midst of an almost overnight depression due greatly to its overdependence on oil revenues. The 1980s, however, ended on an upbeat note. A new reform movement led by Governor "Buddy" Roemer and Mayor Sidney Barthelemy tightened budgets and set out to restructure the political-economic system along lines of fiscal responsibility, industrial inducement, and educational excellence.

As the 1990s began, New Orleans once again was the nation's leading port in tonnage, a trimmed-down energy business once again was venturing boldly into offshore drilling, and tourism continued its phenomenal growth with the new 100-acre Woldenburg Park complex and Aquarium in place. The newly accessible Riverfront "Golden Mile" gave promise of doubling the number of visitors by the year 2000.

Like its patron and its source, the Mississippi, New Orleans "just keeps rolling along."

Louisiana was among the first states to legalize boxing. For several years in the early 1890s, New Orleans became a center of the sport, and several important boxing matches were held here, including one of the most famous ever fought, when "Gentleman Jim" Corbett knocked out world champion John L. Sullivan at the Olympic Club. Courtesy, The Historic New Orleans Collection

GATEWAY TO THE AMERICAS

There is on the Globe one single spot . . . It is New Orleans, through which the produce of three-eighths of our territory must pass.

Thomas Jefferson

New Orleans exists because of the Mississippi River. It was founded because France needed a trade center at the mouth of the great river. The city has grown and prospered because of its location ever since. Photo by Philip Gould

Below: Until the twentieth century, the New Orleans riverfront was lined with miles of wide-plank wharves. Today many changes have altered this area, but the Moonwalk, across from Jackson Square in the French Quarter, evokes the feeling of the old harbor. Photo by Philip Gould

Facing page: The Mississippi River at New Orleans is so vast that to bridge it requires not only great technology, but also years of construction. Bridges must rise high above the water, to allow passage of all sizes of ships. Photo by Philip Gould

THE BROAD, BROWN, MUDDY, MEANDERING MISSISSIPPI River is New Orleans' reason for being. Without it there would be no city, no world port, no possible excuse for a city existing in the middle of an oak-cypress delta swamp. The river is its source, its lifeline, the vital connection to one-half the continuous American states, and, through its port, to the oceans, seas, seaports, and capitals of the world.

Geological evidence indicates that the "Father of Waters" was a cantankerous sort, periodically changing course during the past 5,000 years. Time and again it left behind former channels with their own overlapping deltas and natural levees. It literally constructed a series of elevated islands in the swamp, including the site Bienville chose for his "City on the Crescent." In addition, the state of Louisiana, once a huge embayment off the Gulf of Mexico, was virtually created by the Mississippi. Every 1,000 pounds of river water carries at least two pounds of silt and soil. (This is enough to fill a 150-mile-long freight train each day.)

The river begins modestly as a mere trickle in northern Minnesota, so narrow you can step across it easily. Swelled by the waters of some 1,500 tributaries, the Mississippi winds its way southward, gathering strength as it passes St. Louis and Memphis and Baton Rouge, 2,340 miles to the open Gulf. It is the third largest river in the world (next to the Amazon and the Congo), draining 40 percent of the subcontinent, a mighty avenue of commerce linking the American hinterland with markets as far away as Japan and the Soviet Union. By the time it reaches New Orleans, the Mississippi is 217 feet deep and 2,200 feet wide, pouring an estimated 300 billion gallons of water past the foot of Canal Street every day. (This is double the amount of water used daily by the entire United States.)

The vast Mississippi River watershed of more than one million square miles was opened up to fantastic trade opportunities on January 12, 1812, when the first successful steamboat, the *New Orleans,* negotiated the Ohio and Mississippi rivers from Pittsburgh to New Orleans. The coming of the steamboat caused New Orleans, with its favored gateway position near the river's end, to flourish and to prosper. Despite an unfortunate tendency to catch fire or explode, the "floating volcanoes" became the major carriers of Middle America's wealth and Louisiana's harvest. Grain, cotton, and sugar formed the backbone of the city's new riches. As *La Gazette* of June 12, 1818, noted: "In the beginning steamboats were a curiosity. But they soon ceased to be a novelty . . . and became commonplace on the New Orleans levee . . . the recognized agent of commerce in the Valley." The treasures of Europe and Africa were deposited on the public docks and, upstream, on the private docks of the great plantations. Steamboats brought manufactured merchandise and the luxuries of life—delicate china, crystal chandeliers, priceless works of art, exquisitely carved furniture, and more.

Luxurious pleasure boats or "floating palaces" shared the river with commercial packets loaded with so much cotton that only the pilothouse and smoke stacks were visible. When showboats made their appearance on the river, they introduced melodrama and vaudeville to their passen-

Large oceangoing vessels are served daily by the Port of New Orleans; but without the Eads Jetties built in 1879 at the mouth of the Mississippi River, the passage would not be deep enough to accommodate ships. Without the jetties, New Orleans would cease to be a port. Photo by Philip Gould

gers and to river townspeople who had never seen a musical or a play.

Steamboats quickly evolved into flat-bottom craft with powerful engines that could carry heavy cargo yet sail in the shallowest channels. By 1830 there were 350 giant carriers in the Mississippi. Many of them carried both passengers and cargo. They were richly ornamented with gingerbread wood carvings, ornate railings, and colorful flags. They placed the riches of the world on New Orleans' doorstep.

America's first interstate highway system, made up of the Mississippi, Ohio, and Missouri rivers and their various tributaries, had New Orleans as the hub of one-third of the emerging nation's enterprise. One traveler of the time exclaimed:

The wharves were lined for miles with ships, steamers, flatboats, arks—and four deep! . . . The business appearance of this city is not surpassed by that of any other in the wide world; it might be likened to a huge bee-hive, where no drones could find a resting place . . . I stepped on shore, and my first exclamation was: "My God, this is the place for a business man!"

And this tremendous surge in commerce caused the population to grow dramatically. By 1840 New Orleans had become the third largest city in the nation (after New York and Baltimore), with a population surpassing 100,000.

In 1860 the Port of New Orleans surpassed all ports, including New York, in volume of exports. Three thousand five hundred steamboats docked annually, an average of about 10 per day. At any given time, 10,000 cotton bales could be seen marshaled into tidy rows for shipment along the wharves. In 1860 more than 2 million bales of cotton passed through the port.

Just before the Civil War, New Orleans was the nation's greatest export center, with port receipts of $185 million. More than 55 percent of that revenue came from cotton shipped to British and French mills. The city was also the transshipment center for all exports coming down the Mississippi. It gained a virtual monopoly on trade with the vast heartland of the United States.

During the Civil War the Port of New Orleans was occupied by Union troops for three years. Then, for 12 years more, it was given a strong federal army presence as it agonized through Reconstruction. Once second port in the nation, New Orleans declined to 11th before it slowly regained its stature.

Following the Civil War, Captain James Buchanan Eads, an army engineer, was convinced that he could solve a recurrent problem affecting the Mississippi. Over a period of thousands of years, the river built up most of the lower sub-deltas with regular deposits of silt and mud. As a result, water flowing downstream maintained a channel deep enough for navigation except at the river's mouth. There the sediment continually piled up, choking the passes to the Gulf and building shoals. Navigators had such difficulty negotiating the passes that their ships sometimes stalled for months.

Eads believed he could keep the mouth of the Mississippi open permanently. He proposed a system of jetties to scour out a permanent channel. These jetties, or parallel dikes, would constrict the water's passage so it would flow smoothly and swiftly, unclogged. As things stood, the newer, larger cargo ships were constantly subject to blockage by silt and logs. The channel might be 50 feet deep above the bar and then, in late winter and spring, it might be less than 12 feet deep as the bars enlarged.

Captain Eads offered to construct a 600-foot by 28-foot channel in Southwest Pass within two years. After much debate Eads was awarded a federal contract by a special act of Congress. He would be paid one million dollars if he maintained 20 feet in depth. He would receive one million dollars for each additional two feet in depth up to a maximum of 28 feet. And he would bank an additional $500,000 for maintaining the channel for 10 years following completion.

Eads completed his jetties and the channel on July 8, 1879, and proceeded to maintain a depth of 30 feet at the bar. This date marks the beginning of New Orleans as a modern deep-water port.

Once Captain Eads guaranteed a year-round deep-water channel, it became apparent that some sort of coordinating agency was needed to modernize, rebuild, and allocate dock and warehouse space to keep pace with the rapidly expanding requirements of a modern port. In 1896 the Board of Commissioners of the Port of New Orleans (also known as the Dock Board) was created. It was endowed by the Louisiana State Legislature with sweeping powers unprecedented in state and local government.

The Dock Board was given complete authority over all water frontage in Orleans Parish and a considerable amount of river and canal frontage in adjoining parishes. It could "expropriate property, demolish and rebuild structures, operate facilities" as it chose and "lease them at will." Such autonomy was granted for one indisputable reason—the port was New Orleans' and Louisiana's number-one industry. An estimated one-fifth of all the dollars flowing into the state's economy was a direct or indirect result of the port.

Currently the Board of Commissioners of the Port of New Orleans has deep-water jurisdiction extending over more than 25 miles of harbor frontage, on both sides of the Mississippi, including Orleans Parish and parts of Jefferson, St. Bernard, and Plaquemines parishes. The port's authority also embraces both banks of the Industrial Canal (IHNC) and the entire stretch of the tidewater Gulf ship canal to the Gulf of Mexico.

This blue-ribbon Board of Commissioners was the fourth such

It is highly difficult to navigate the constantly changing meanders, sand bars, and barriers of the Mississippi River between the Gulf of Mexico and New Orleans. Well-trained navigators are in demand to handle this difficult task. Photo by Philip Gould

authority created in the United States, preceded only by San Francisco (1863), New York City (1871), and Philadelphia (1885).

In 1901 the Dock Board began demolishing antiquated structures on the waterfront and reconstructing the port according to the demanding standards of a new era and a new century. And within 10 years the Port of New Orleans was completely rebuilt. New cotton warehouses were constructed since cotton represented 40 percent of New Orleans' total product. Also, giant storage warehouses were built along with the largest grain elevator in the world.

The growth of New Orleans as a deep-water port paralleled the development of the Mississippi River Commission, formed in 1879 following Captain Eads' construction of the downriver jetties. The Commission was charged with the "preparation and consideration of plans to improve the river channel, protect its banks, improve navigation, prevent destructive floods, and promote and facilitate commerce." Here was a mandate to finally harness the moody and unpredictable Mississippi. Repeated flooding of the extensive Mississippi Valley overtaxed the uncoordinated resources and the ability of individual states to contain the river. In 1927 the greatest flood in American history left 300,000 homeless in Louisiana alone. Within a year Congress passed the Mississippi Valley Flood Control Act, assigning the U.S. Army Corps of Engineers the job of maintaining federal control of the river valley.

In 1923 a deep-water Inner Harbor (Industrial) Canal was completed below the port, providing access to Lake Pontchartrain. In 1934, on the west bank of the river, a modern system of locks was installed in the

Harvey Canal. Both man-made water systems are today a part of the Gulf Intracoastal Canal. This busy inner channel runs a straight, protected course inside the string of barrier islands that stretches from Apalachee, Florida, to the Rio Grande. New Orleans lies smack in the middle.

For more than a century, a deep-water ship canal had been proposed to bypass the tricky river passes that Captain Eads daringly channelized. Finally, on March 29, 1956, the Rivers and Harbors Act budgeted $100 million in federal funds for excavation of the Mississippi River-Gulf outlet. This seaway canal, deep-water dredged to a depth of 36 feet and 500 feet wide, runs from the Industrial Canal southeasterly into the Gulf. It effectively cuts 40 miles off the meandering route of the lower Mississippi, a 110-mile voyage from New Orleans to the Gulf. The first oceangoing vessel to christen this historic outlet was the *Del Sud* on July 25, 1963. It signaled yet another transition in the nation's second-largest port.

Just as New Orleans rebuilt her port at the turn of the century, the city began to rebuild the port again in the 1960s. The project was designed to cover three decades at a cost of more than $500 million. During this period most of the existing antiquated facilities were torn down. The main functions of the port were moved to the east end of the city or upriver, opening up a new riverfront vista for residential and commercial activity.

The spectacular development of the petrochemical industry along the river between New Orleans and Baton Rouge helped fuel the port's growth and development. It was a boom period for petroleum, which had recently become the financial crux (if not crutch) of the state's government and economy. Later, in the mid-1980s, when oil plunged to $10 a barrel, a sharp recession was felt. The recovery, in light of the circumstances, has been remarkable.

Much of the trade on the Mississippi River is by barge. In the nineteenth century most of New Orleans' shipping was docked near the center of the city. Increasingly complex transportation patterns and greatly enlarged ships mean that many vessels must dock many miles beyond the downtown area. Photo by Philip Gould

CAPTAINS OF THE MARITIME INDUSTRY

New Orleans has produced more than its share of "salty dogs" : entrepreneurs, enterprisers, and captains of the maritime industry who began, in many cases, with one boat, a dream, and the gumption to make the dream come true.

Captain Thomas "Push" Leathers built the first steam packet, *The Natchez,* in 1824 at the mouth of Crayfish Bayou. He then built eight more steamboats, each one bigger and faster. He was "King of the River" until the *Robert E. Lee* beat him in that famous 1874 race.

Captain Tom Harvey took the old Destrehan Ditch on the West Bank and turned it into the Harvey Canal in 1871 (now an integral link between the Mississippi and the Intracoastal Waterway). Though the captain went bankrupt promoting a palatial resort hotel on barren, isolated Grand Isle, he did leave a legacy—the legendary "Harvey Castle" in Harvey, Louisiana.

Joseph Bissot, a Frenchman, ran away from home to go to sea, somehow landed in New Orleans, and dropped the "t" from his name. The 16-year-old Joe Bisso signed on as a tender on the Confederate gunboat *Albatross* and later went into the lumber business. When Old Man River caved in, and the levee washed out his headquarters, he switched to the towboat business. The Bisso family has been a leader in this business since 1890. Joseph's son, "Cap'n Billy," guided the firm through the two world wars and the Depression.

Terence Smith arrived in New Orleans at the age of 13, already an accomplished sailmaker, an immigrant from County Caven, Ireland. In 1886 he organized a stevedoring company. Now the oldest and largest of its breed, its operation has expanded to include Houston, Galveston, and Freeport. Five generations of the Smith family built this firm. Now Cooper/T. Smith, it was the first to develop the revolutionary Smith floating LASH and container loader with three giant derricks mounted on one barge.

Peterson Maritime Services, Inc., was founded in 1960 by a retired sea captain, Dean Peterson, who saw a need and met it. Unskilled work crews unloading barges were unable to clean up cargo areas. Thousands of dollars were being lost. In later years Peterson Maritime Services, Inc., moved from cargo cleaning into the fields of oil pollution, hazardous materials waste, and the operation of high-speed crew boats. The largest hazardous chemical spill of PCP in U.S. history, following a Mississippi River collision, was cleaned up by Peterson.

The tall stacked Mississippi riverboat is synonymous with nineteenth-century romantic American history. Captains, pilots, gamblers, beautiful women, and showboats are all part of America's folklore known to the entire world. Photo by Bob Rowan/ Progressive Image Photography

By 1980 the Port of New Orleans reached its peak, moving almost 170 million tons of waterborne cargo. It was ranked first in the nation. Wharves lined 25 miles of the city's riverside, handling as many as 100 ships at a time. It was tied in with a gigantic shipping-trucking-rail complex involving seven major railroad outlets, the U.S. interstate highway system, the Mississippi River-Gulf outlet, and the Intracoastal Waterway—all this plus 19,000 miles of navigable waterways up and down the Mississippi River's extensive inland system.

The port, nevertheless, found itself facing yet another threat, perhaps the toughest in its long history. Suddenly, smaller ports aggressively entered into competition, armed with a new, revolutionary technology. Cargo freighters, which had evolved over a period of 100 years and dominated ocean trade for most of the twentieth century, had been replaced by ultramodern ships—sophisticated, larger, more maneuverable, and quicker to load and unload. Transfer of cargo no longer was a lengthy, laborious process dependent on sweating gangs of stevedores. Containerization, abetted by the LASH technique of lifting whole barges, made "tote that barge, lift that bale" little more than a quaint line from a faintly remembered song from days gone by. No longer were individual sacks of coffee or flour manually unloaded, one at a time; now they were packed in large containers and transferred from ship to wharf to train (or truck) by gigantic hydraulic cranes and lifts.

High-speed revolver cranes can load a large sea vessel with coal in 28 hours where it once took days. The LASH technique ("lifting aboard ship") unloads a barge simply by lifting the barge itself (complete with contents) aboard a sea vessel. T. Smith & Son developed "floating derricks" carrying as many as three giant cranes mounted on one super barge. Without the ship so much as touching the wharf, the transfer is made in the middle of the river.

The new complexity and speed of modern transshipment forced the port to adapt quickly. Twenty-five miles of wharves jammed against the outerskin of a land-poor, tightly packed island city allowed for no expansion. One by one they became obsolete. New needs had to be met for New Orleans to handle the largest cargo tonnage in the country. New grain elevators were required since the city is the largest grain exporter in the world. Special terminals needed to be built and equipped with modern warehouses, along with refrigeration plants capable of preserving foods and quick-freezing imported meat.

Some innovations have been spectacular. Trains of barges measuring 1,000 feet (longer than three football fields) are effortlessly propelled by tiny towboats commanding the power of 5,600 horses. (On the river "towing" means pushing, not pulling.) These barges move almost anything from molten sulphur at 270 degrees Fahrenheit to refrigerated anhydrous ammonia at 28 degrees below zero. Skilled pilots seated high in the rear cabin of an automated towboat use radio controls to delicately maneuver extended barge trains around the Mississippi's tortuous bends, negotiating its tricky currents and swirls.

With all these new innovations on the waterfront, however, New Orleans' domination of the shipping industry in the Gulf of Mexico, the

Caribbean, and up the Mississippi has been challenged by newcomers in Houston-Galveston, Mobile, Tampa-St. Pete, and even tiny Gulfport, Mississippi.

Over the years the Port of New Orleans altered the river's depth and flow, changed its route where necessary, rechanneled commerce through an elaborate series of man-made waterways, twice rebuilt itself completely, spawned two of the nation's largest sister ports (St. James and Baton Rouge), and was indirectly responsible for the almost continuous line of terminals, wharves, and oil and petrochemical plants extending from below Chalmette to above the state capital. Now the port seems determined to reenergize and relocate. A billion-dollar-plus comprehensive overhaul, which began in 1970 and is scheduled to cover three decades, is under way. This cannot continue on the overcrowded waterfront, however, without seriously disrupting the population. As a consequence, the port is gravitating, more and more, downriver toward the Gulf outlet.

A 53-mile stretch of river between New Orleans and Baton Rouge (a three-parish area) falls under the jurisdiction of the South Louisiana Port Commission. It contains numerous private docks and terminals for grains, petroleum, petrochemicals, and sugar. Similarly, the Plaquemines Port, Harbor and Terminal District oversees Plaquemines Parish terminals for coal, grains, and bulk minerals along the Mississippi River.

When midway through the 1980s the Port of New Orleans discovered that it had run out of space and fallen perilously behind the times, it hired an aggressive modernist, Ron Brinson, as its director. Mayor Ernest "Dutch" Morial issued a governmental imperative: restore the port to its previous standing as one of the three busiest ports in the world. He pointed out that roughly 50 percent of every trade dollar in New Orleans was generated by the port.

In response to the mayor's edict, a new, broad-based team of local business and civic leaders replaced the aging, inbred, and notably conservative former Dock Board. In addition, Brinson introduced a new management team, implemented a new strategic plan, and organized a new staff. And, almost miraculously, the financial picture brightened despite a full-scale depression in the oil industry. In 1987 cargo tonnage jumped 21.5 percent. By 1989 New Orleans again led the nation in total bulk tonnage.

Today cotton represents a mere 4 percent of the port's export cargo, though as late as the 1930s it constituted 50 percent. King Cotton has abdicated in favor of soybeans, rice, chemicals, and petroleum products.

By 1987 steel was the import king. Iron and steel now pour in from 45 countries around the world, principally from Japan. Steel represents close to 40 percent of the total import tonnage. The Mississippi remains unchallenged as the most expeditious means of moving it upstream to Chicago, Detroit, and Pittsburgh. Imports, including a steady flow of Nissans, Toyotas, and Volkswagens, represent more than one billion dollars.

On the export side, Louisiana producers are dependent on the Port of New Orleans and its access to foreign markets. Soybean farmers produce almost exclusively for export. They ship 90 percent of all the soy-

beans sold overseas. In addition 80 percent of Louisiana's rice output is peddled on foreign markets, finding access through the port. Chemicals and petroleum products still account for 40 percent or more of New Orleans' export dollar volume. But it is a give-and-take proposition. Both oil men and sugar planters, hard-pressed to satisfy the gluttonous demands of the American market, must complement their trade by buying extensively on the foreign import market.

The energy business has become the third major pillar of the New Orleans economy (in addition to the port and tourism). The Louisiana Offshore Port (LOOP), the nation's first "Superport," is capable of supplying one million barrels of oil daily to refineries as far away as Buffalo and Chicago. New Orleans has become headquarters for the world's largest supplier of offshore oil. (Ninety percent of all American offshore oil emanates from the Gulf.) New Orleans is also the biggest builder of supply vessels and deck barges in the world.

LOOP, the S700-million offshore oil port, was built by and is operated by a consortium of five major oil companies. Ownership is divided among Maritime Pipeline Company (32.1 percent), Texaco Oil Company (26.6 percent), Shell Oil Company (19.5 percent), Ashland Oil, Inc. (18.6 percent), and Murphy Oil Corporation (3.2 percent). It is specially designed to handle gigantic supertankers that cannot call at land-based ports. LOOP began full-scale operations in January 1982, and within 10 months 86 tankers had docked and delivered 90 million barrels of oil. Today it is linked by pipeline to one-third of the nation's oil-refining capacity.

In addition to claiming the nation's first superport, New Orleans was the second city in America to develop a Foreign Trade Zone (FTZ) or Free Zone, where goods can remain duty-free while awaiting transshipment. The FTZ, located on an 18-acre tract off the Napoleon Avenue wharf complex, has proven so successful that the City of New Orleans and the Dock Board created a second FTZ on a 75-acre tract fronting the Mississippi River-Gulf outlet. Eventually 10 wharves will be accommodated there with a multiuse modern terminal. State of the art, the complex will combine containerized cargo, Ro-Ro (roll-on, roll-off), and heavy lift cargoes featuring huge hydraulic cranes. Designed for the year 2000, the complex will provide maximum speed, efficiency, and rapid water-to-land transfer.

While it is impossible to gauge precisely the total dollar volume of the port's current import/export trade, suffice it to say that it exceeds $2 billion. As Port Director Ron Brinson says: "The message is that the port is now a very new port with ideas and strategy directing a revitalized maritime industry in the New Orleans area."

Fireboats are an essential element at any port. Fortunately they are less often called on to prevent disasters than to test their equipment. Riverfront spectators are often given a spectacular show of waterworks. Photo by Philip Gould

AMERICA'S FIRST
MELTING POT

There are not only the pure bred Indian-American and the Spanish, French, English, Celtic, Italian and African, but nearly all possible breeds of mankind . . . I doubt if there is a city in the world where the resident population has been so intermixed and yet divided in its origin, or where there is such variety of tastes . . . habits and moral codes among its citizens.

Frederick Law Olmsted

Bright flambeaux light the night during the Carnival season. The many ethnic groups that make up New Orleans have all helped to create the city's unique personality. For many people this personality is typified by that most untypical of American festivals—Mardi Gras. Photo by Philip Gould

NEW ORLEANS APPEARS TO BE A CITY OF CONTRAdictions. Though isolated from its mainland neighbors, it has been cosmopolitan in its strong ties with other lands, especially through its port and its open door to immigration. Always ostensibly immersed in its own uniqueness and its devotion to tradition, it has, however, been dependent for survival on newcomers with their new ideas and innovations. As a result, New Orleans has been and still is a "melting pot" city.

The first real flood of immigrants to the city began the moment the Louisiana Purchase was signed in 1803. So many came from so many places that the city published an *Emigrants Directory.*

When Brooklyn was still pastureland and Chicago was just Fort Dearborn, New Orleans, the second-major port of entry during the antebellum period, was already a melting pot. From 1820 to 1860 it opened the gates of freedom to approximately one million immigrants from Europe. Many stayed on to live and die; many survived, intermarried, and prospered.

The Irish came to escape the devastating potato famines of the mid-nineteenth century. They arrived by the tens of thousands and took any jobs available. An estimated 14,000 died digging the New Basin Canal between 1835 and 1838, victims of yellow fever, cholera, and malnutrition.

Immigrants from Germany were more diverse. They mainly fled unsettled political conditions. Carpenters, dairy farmers, brewers, shoemakers, nurserymen, and others arrived during the upheavals of the 1840s, equipped with their skills and crafts. Nearly 70,000 Germans passed through New Orleans' Customs House between 1820 and 1860.

By 1860 New Orleans was the largest city in the Confederacy and sixth-largest in the United States. Almost 40 percent of its citizens were foreign born. There were 25,000 Irish, 20,000 German, and 11,000 French. There were also 24,000 blacks, more than half of them free.

The last great wave of immigration came from Sicily. Barren soil and cruel absentee landowners drove the Sicilians by the hundreds of thousands to America in the period between 1890 and 1910, one of the most massive immigrations in history. New Orleans, with its warm climate and outgoing people, was a primary destination. Many Italians replaced slave labor on Louisiana's sugar plantations. Ten thousand settled upriver near Kenner to operate small, extremely productive truck farms. The majority settled in the French Quarter, which, by then, had been virtually abandoned by the French Creoles. Today there are about 200,000 descendants of those immigrants in New Orleans, making it the most Sicilian city in the United States.

During the period between 1835 and 1910, the city experienced a wave of immigration comparable to that which brought millions to New York City, Boston, Philadelphia, Chicago, and other metropolises in the North. By 1910 the population of New Orleans stood at more than 300,000.

"There is a certain irony," historian Joe Gray Taylor notes, "in the the fact that New Orleans, its older section Spanish in architecture, its popu-

Facing page: The Piazza d'Italia was acclaimed by architects and designers when it was originally built. Located in the heart of downtown New Orleans, it is a monument to the many Italians who settled there beginning in the late nineteenth century and have made a considerable contribution to the community. Photo by Bob Rowan/Progressive Image Photography

lation mainly Black, Irish, Italian and Anglo-American, is mainly thought of as a French city." In a sense, however, it always will be. For the French customs, the French traditions, the French approach to religion, and the French dietary habits remain dominant. The original Creoles no longer are a majority. They have little wealth or power or specific influence, and yet, the city, in assimilating so many ethnic groups, has become thoroughly Creolized.

Today those claiming pure French (or Creole) ancestry comprise about 9 percent of the total population of the New Orleans (SMSA) area.

CREOLES AND CAJUNS

Strictly speaking, a New Orleans Creole is a descendant of an early French or Spanish settler, born in the colony—not in Europe. Most colonials in the eighteenth century were French and dominated New Orleans society for over a century. Most Creoles called themselves "French," and considered themselves the only true natives. The late-coming Anglo-Saxons were considered foreigners and referred to as "Les Americaines."

In Lafcadio Hearn's *Creole Sketches,* written more than 100 years ago, he mentions that some French Creoles residing in the French Quarter wondered why "anyone would care to cross Canal Street." (It was contemptuously known as "The American Side.")

Until the Civil War, the proud Creoles educated their children in France, spoke the French language, centered their lives around their huge families and their cultural nexus, the French Opera. They were, by their own description, the *creme de la creme.*

Creoles were outnumbered and trapped, to some extent, by their historic isolation and hidebound tradition. (Creole men wore coats and ties in the hottest weather and shunned manual labor as uncivilized.) As a result, the ingrown, cultured, pure Creole was submerged by Anglo-Saxon industry and drive.

But one should not despair. The Creole temperament lives on. Creole, as a meaningful term, no longer defines a nationality, race, or breed. Creole defines an attitude toward life—*joie de vivre, laissez-faire, bon apetit!* Their motto is "Dum vivimus vivere" or "While we are living, let us live."

One thing must be understood.

Creoles are not Cajuns, and Cajuns are not Creoles. Both are basically of French descent, dating back for centuries. But there the distinction ends.

While Creoles are cosmopolitan city people, Cajuns, on the other hand, are country people who for two centuries have lived along the bayous and swamps of Southern Louisiana. They are hunters and trappers and fishermen, and, more recently, oil-field workers, breeders of horses, and creators of cuisine.

Their ancestors were cruelly exiled from New Acadia (Nova Scotia) in 1765 and, in one of this nation's largest grand migrations, found a permanent home in Louisiana. The word "Cajun" is a corruption of "Acadian." Until the last two generations, most Cajuns spoke French or a provincial form of the language passed down orally for three centuries since they left their ancestral homes in Brittany, Normandy, and the northern coast of France.

The heart of Acadiana is about a 2.5-hour ride west of New Orleans, centered in Lafayette, Louisiana, the most French of all Louisiana cities. There and throughout most of the Southwest Louisiana bayou and prairie country you can delight to the rhythmic spoken cadences of old Cajun French or, most often, to the distinctive Cajun-accented English of the new, educated generation.

Lacking a written language, isolated by swamp and origin, Cajuns tended to cling together, centering their lives around family and the Church. Derided for years as "bumpkin French," whose flavorful patois and spicy food seemed crude and often comical to outsiders, they resisted assimilation while quietly

assimilating newcomers.

Cajun and Creole food, it is said in Louisiana, eventually makes Frenchmen of all of us. Both cuisines rely on a variety of savory herbs. The Cajuns, in particular, like their food hot and spicy. Paul Prudhomme, raised in a cabin along with 10 other children, has become world famous introducing the glories of crayfish etouffe and blackened redfish to such cities as New York, Washington, D.C., and San Francisco. His Cajun counterpart from Lafayette, John Folse, established the first culinary institute in Moscow in 1988, a kind of gastric glasnost. Folse grew up cooking both Cajun and Creole and insists that there is not that much difference. "Until recently, the major difference, I think, was this," says Folse, "The Creoles ate in the dining room and the Cajuns ate in the kitchen."

The once-scorned Acadian has recently become an object of affection to Americans. The younger generation, once deprived of their cultural pride, is relearning French in Louisiana schools, studying the ancient Cajun culture, and glorying in its unique dance music—Cajun classique and zydeco. All over Acadiana, the fiddle and accordions have come out of the attics, and Cajun musicians, chefs, painters, and poets have come out of the closet.

Old-timers are bemused and philosophical. "Life is a wheel that turns," goes an old Cajun proverb, "What goes round comes round. The wheel, she always come back again."

Like the Creoles, the Cajuns know how to live. Their motto is "Laissez les bon temps rouler" or "Let the good times roll."

However, the only official census ever to attempt a determination of "ancestry" (1980) showed that those of solely or partially French extraction remain the foremost white ethnic group. Roughly 24 percent of the metropolitan area whites, or 263,000 people, were reported to be of French or partially French ancestry.

The second-largest white ethnic group was German or part German, comprising 16.5 percent of the white population or 192,000 people. The Germans were followed by the Irish (166,000), the English (165,000), and the Italians (93,000).

The strong Germanic influence surprises many. However, Germans were among the very first settlers, arriving above the city in 1721 to establish a permanent influence in Des Allemandes ("The German Coast"). German immigrants tended to assimilate more easily than other ethnics, they were generally better educated, more skilled in specific crafts and professions, and, therefore, less likely to be set apart in the group isolation of poverty and illiteracy as were others.

Almost one of every three of the area's 1.2 million residents is black. The 1980 Census reported that Orleans Parish blacks represented 43 percent of the city population.

Since World War II there has been a notable influx of immigrants primarily from Hispanic America and Vietnam. An estimated 12,000 Vietnamese have arrived since the mid-1970s. They have settled mostly in the developing area known as New Orleans East.

The Hispanic population was listed in the 1980 Census as 48,000. This figure is widely disputed by many demographers, including several leading Hispanic sociologists. They feel that it could be as high as 90,000 or more because: 17 percent of the census respondents failed to note ethnic origin; difficulties in understanding English; a reluctance to fill out any more "government" information than required; and the uncertainty, or legality, of their American citizenship.

The majority of Hispanics migrating to New Orleans the past two decades have been of Mexican, Cuban, or Honduran nationality. Many Cubans were either political exiles or middle-class professionals, well educated, who fled their island when Fidel Castro pronounced the Revolution Communist.

New Orleans' link with Honduras dates back 100 years and involves strong ties established by such locally based companies as Standard Fruit and United Fruit. New Orleans traditionally was the nation's leading banana importer. There now may be as many as 10,000 Hondurans living in the area. New Orleans, in fact, is often referred to as the "second-largest Honduran city in the Western hemisphere."

Until recently, the Hispanic community was mainly clustered upriver, along the "Tchopitoulas corridor." Many Hispanics still own small businesses, shops, cafes, and clubs in this riverfront area. "Se habla Espanol" remains a familiar sign in the windows of stores and restaurants throughout New Orleans. The city draws significant numbers of tourists and businessmen from Latin America.

Nearly half the Vietnamese population is concentrated in New Orleans East near Fortier Boulevard and Chef Menteur Highway. Refugee

The various ethnic groups that have moved to New Orleans have brought with them many traditions and festivals. These have been influenced by New Orleans. The Irish have given us St. Patrick's Day, but in New Orleans the activities of that holiday have taken on the air of a mini-Mardi Gras with green beer. Photo by Philip Gould

families began congregating there after the fall of South Vietnam in April 1975. They were attracted by the warm, semitropical climate, reminiscent of their homeland, and, since many previously made their living as fishermen, by the surrounding network of bayous, rivers, lakes, and open gulf waters.

Many Vietnamese, male and female, hold two jobs. The younger generation is strongly motivated to avail themselves of educational opportunities. A recent Abramson High School graduation found Vietnamese students comprising almost half the honor graduates. A second-generation Vietnamese-American, Tulane senior Quan Doc, was one of

Throughout its history, the backbone of the New Orleans working class has been its black population. While job discrimination has decreased, and there is a growing black middle class, many of the old laboring jobs have been eliminated by new technology. Photo by Philip Gould

only 28 Marshall Scholars in the United States chosen in 1990 for postgraduate studies at England's Cambridge University.

One of the city's exotic new attractions is the Vietnamese Open Market on Chef Menteur, where about 50 vendors sell fish, native foods, and products. In addition, several small Vietnamese and/or Southeast Asian restaurants have been established.

Louisiana's tolerance for various minority groups became apparent six years after the founding of New Orleans, when, in 1724, the *Code Noir* or Black Code was instituted. Considered "dangerously liberal" by Southern standards, it established Roman Catholicism as the official religion of La Louisiane, obligated slave owners to provide religious instruction to their slaves, and prohibited the disruption-by-sale of slave families.

Though New Orleans was once the major auction block for slaves and also the place to which slaves were "sent down the river," it was also the only city where *gens de couleur libre* (freed people of color) could live in mixed neighborhoods, own property, enjoy relative freedom of movement, and even own slaves. By 1820 almost 20 percent of the city's population consisted of freed people of color. An estimated 25,000 lived in the city and intermixed with whites before the Civil War.

Black role models in the city's history are not difficult to find. In racially intermixed antebellum New Orleans, John Derham, a freed slave from Philadelphia was the first black physician. He spoke three languages and gamely battled yellow fever. Walter Cohen, a major political figure during Reconstruction, served for years as U.S. Customs chief. The Reverend Alfred Lawless pioneered school reform in the days of "separate but equal." Thomy Lafon, a free man of color, was a wealthy merchant who gave a fortune to establish a Boy's Home and sustain St. Mary's Academy. Oscar Dunn, a music teacher, headed the Freedman's Bureau and later was elected lieutenant governor of Louisiana. Finally, Pinckney Benton Pinchback was, for 30 days, governor of Louisiana.

After the Civil War, Jim Crow segregation was slower in arriving than anywhere else in the South, especially in the world of sports. Black and white baseball teams played baseball together. Black and white jockeys rode against each other. A popular black bantam-weight named George Dixon fought for and won the world championship in 1896.

Full segregation of streetcars was not enforced until 1902. Blacks

New Orleans has always had a large black population which has greatly enriched the city's culture. Without black influence, New Orleans' food and music—jazz in particular— would be far different from what the world knows today. Photo by Philip Gould

The most recent wave of immigrants to New Orleans has been the Vietnamese. Their French and Catholic traditions fit well into New Orleans with its own strong French and Catholic traditions. Photo by Philip Gould

voted by the thousands until the Blessy decision of 1896 established "separate but equal" as the Supreme Court doctrine for 60 years. And, as Dr. Fred Starr writes in *New Orleans Unmasqued*:

Backwardness has certain virtues. New Orleans lagged far behind many cities in introducing zoning laws. Until 1929, in fact, you were free to build anything anywhere, and people did. Fine homes, barrooms, shotgun dwellings for the poor, churches, graveyards, and groceries were all mixed together, often in the same block. So were black and white families.

This racial commingling, dating back to the days of French colonial rule, has produced an amity unusual in today's densely packed central cities. Jazz virtuoso/historian Danny Barker recalls growing up in the French Quarter among Italian immigrants. "I was seven years old before I realized I wasn't Eyetal-ean," Barker says with a twinkle.

The late Dr. Daniel Thompson, the country's leading black sociologist and professor emeritus of sociology at Dillard University before his death in 1989, stated that "for the black community of New Orleans, the present is both the best of times and the worst of times." In measuring the progress achieved by New Orleans' blacks in the previous 30 years, Dr. Thompson concluded:

We see our second black mayor, a black majority on the city council and in the city's legislative delegation, a black superintendent of education, a black chief of police, a black bank president, black judges and a resurgent black middle class with more professionals than ever before in the city's history. But we also see a black underclass whose abundant size remains constant with dim prospects for its members.

Loyola pollster Silas Lee says the black middle class has grown six times since 1960. Today there are more than 300 black lawyers in New Orleans; in 1955 there were only three. Today there are more than 100 black doctors compared with five in 1955. The black middle class comprises 30 percent of the black community compared to 5 percent in 1960.

Monte Piliawsky, professor of political science at Dillard, says the problems of the underclass are not much different from those in most American cities. Piliawsky says: "It has become painfully clear the solutions will not come from government or welfare systems. The city's underclass, bitter about their status, victimized by technological change, feels imprisoned." If there is a key to the situation, it may lie in the growing partnership between the public and private sector.

One of the pioneers in minority training and placement, attorney James Coleman, renovated a derelict three-story building downtown in the late 1960s. Here he developed a highly innovative school designed to train minority women for secretarial work and placement in the offices of major employers such as Shell, Texaco, and city government.

Since 1975 the Gulf South Minority Purchasing Council, based in New Orleans, has effectively matched up purchasing agents for large firms, such as Martin Marietta and Avondale, with qualified minority enterprises.

Three major Small Business Development Centers, under the auspices of the SBA, operate through SUNO, UNO, and Loyola to assist talented students interested in starting up businesses.

Francis Moises of the Chamber/River Region says that 75 percent of all start-up enterprises nationally go out of business within three years. "Despite the common notion that undercapitalization causes this," says Moises, "most small businesses fail because they don't know what to do." To help remedy this situation, the Technical Assistance Center taps the experience and expertise of many local businessmen, networking throughout the city, to actively aid would-be entrepreneurs and small businessmen with free advice and counsel on specific problems.

The Asian presence in New Orleans has been traditionally small and limited to a few shops and restaurants. With the arrival of the Vietnamese beginning in the 1970s, a proliferation of Asian-style businesses across the metropolitan area has been remarkable. This has helped add a new element to the New Orleans melting pot. Photo by Philip Gould

As a result of all this, New Orleans is rapidly developing a new class of black businessmen and businesswomen. Nolan Marshall, president of Nolmar Corporation, runs the largest black-owned janitorial service in the South. He has been in business for 15 years. Preston Edwards started Black College Services on local campuses and now turns out highly sophisticated campus magazines and print material for black and many predominantly white universities across the nation. Bobby Higgingbotham developed Executive Temporaries into the largest minority temporary service in the nation with offices in 16 major cities. Enterprising Bertha C. Pichon's first office was her kitchen. She is now president of a large catering service that offers such specialties as "kosher Creole" food. Dr. Lenny Burns, a successful podiatrist, developed his own travel agency in the 1970s. A longtime member of the Tourist Commission, he has been a leader in the booming hospitality business.

The Code Noir of 1724 referred not only to blacks, but also to Jews. It stipulated that all Jews be banished from the colonies, a peculiar stipulation since, at the time, there were no Jews in the colony to be banished.

It was not until the Americans took over in 1803 that Jews began to arrive in any number. Most of them were merchants or educated Sephardics from the North. The first Jewish congregation was established in 1827. New Orleans historically offered a much more open society, free of the prejudice Jews encountered elsewhere. In fact, there were many "mixed" Creole/Jewish marriages, allowing Jews a higher degree of assimilation and social acceptance. Judah P. Benjamin, Louisiana's first Jewish senator and Jefferson Davis' chief advisor, married a Creole Catholic woman.

Judah P. Touro exhibited that heroic stroke of good conscience that distinguishes people of all faiths, especially when they join forces to combat disaster. In 1847 the wealthy Jewish merchant purchased the second Christ Church building to open the city's first synagogue. Touro became a close friend of the Presbyterian pastor, the dauntless Theodore Clapp. In fact, the Jewish philanthropist temporarily resided in a house on Presbyterian property behind the Reverend Clapp's church.

The Reverend Clapp was a man of overwhelming ecumenical conscience. For 35 years he kept a diary. It is the best record of the virulent yellow fever epidemics during which he and Touro repeatedly risked

Facing page: New Orleans has been historically one of the most integrated cities in the United States. During the nineteenth century, blacks and whites lived in the same neighborhoods and often shared either side of double shotgun houses. Many old racial patterns remain evident in older mixed neighborhoods. Photo by Philip Gould

Above: New Orleans has managed to preserve the nation's oldest streetcar line, which dates back to 1835 and runs along St. Charles Avenue. The newest line in the city is the Riverfront Line, with its distinctive red streetcars, which was established in 1988 and is popular with locals and visitors. Photo by Bob Rowan/Progressive Image Photography

their lives. Eventually, because Touro, a Jew, became the legal owner and landlord of a Presbyterian church (for which he charged no rent), Dr. Clapp was tried for heresy and excommunicated. He then became a Unitarian. Clapp was faced with bankruptcy until Touro stepped forward and paid off the entire church mortgage. He asked for nothing in return. Touro also willed millions of dollars to establish a string of hospitals along the East Coast and up the Mississippi, including New Orleans' Touro Infirmary.

The Jewish community of New Orleans is relatively small but its impact continues to be felt in almost every area, far beyond its numbers. Attorney Donald Mintz, former chairman of the United Way and president of the Dock Board, ran a strong and impressive race for mayor in February 1990. Mintz was the first Jewish mayoral candidate in New Orleans' recent history, and his constituency crossed both racial and religious lines. Mintz is heir to a long and distinguished line of Jewish leaders, merchants, professional men, philanthropists, and advocates of social justice.

Two of the oldest companies in the area, the K & B drugstore chain and WEMCO, manufacturers of nationally known Wembley ties, were built by families who are an integral part of this historically intermixed community. Sidney Besthoff the Third reflects tradition and the family love of fine art in the striking architecture of his home office and the local sculpture and art lining the walls of his building. The Pulitzer family similarly is a pillar of enterprise, employing almost 600 Orleanians.

The death of Edith Rosenwald Stern in September 1980 left a tremendous void in the community. A woman of immense wealth, she used her resources, spiritually and monetarily, primarily to right some of the social injustices she saw. Without her presence, the city today would not have a system of nursery schools, an art museum, a symphony orchestra, a Voters' Registration program, a major black university (Dillard), or the breathtaking Longue Vue Gardens (a major tourist attraction including her home and estate). Once she was asked how she accounted for her lifetime devotion to causes and the family's remarkable philanthropy. Mrs. Stern replied: "I suppose it's a Jewish trait. We were brought up on the philosophy of the Old Testament. Remember? 'One is permitted to glean one's field only once. Thereafter others can partake' . . . one has to give a tithe."

Another group of citizens to find New Orleans more tolerant than other Southern cities was its women. From the earliest colonial days, the city has defied the stereotype of the pampered Southern belle. As early as the 1860s, women worked in all but nine of the 369 professions practiced in the city. Women were business owners, funeral parlor directors, cigar makers, publishers, restauranteurs, and more.

Some of the first cafes in the French Quarter were opened by women who began selling coffee from street carts. Free women of color ran the first guest houses, boardinghouses, and restaurants.

The indomitable Baroness Pontalba personally planned and supervised the building of the historic red brick apartment buildings (1852) that still flank Jackson Square.

Margaret Haughery, widowed as a young woman, sold bread from a donkey cart to survive, bought a bakery and, later, a dairy, and used the proceeds to build the city's first orphan home, St. Theresa's Asylum on Camp Street, in 1840.

The city's first hospitals and educational institutions were founded and staffed by nuns—Ursuline Academy (founded 1727), Dominican College (1860), Hotel Dieu (1858), Depaul Hospital (1861), Charity Hospital (1786), and Sara T. Mayo Children's Hospital (1905).

Two socialite sisters, Kate and Jean Gordon, through sheer determination and dedication, changed the social consciousness of an entire city. Long before suffrage, the Gordon sisters won the fight for modern drainage (1898), established the first hospital for tuberculosis patients (1915), won the right for women to attend Tulane Medical School (1916), established the first day nursery (1910), and pushed through the first child labor bill (1908). Kate Gordon once said: "The reason Jean and I accomplished what we did is because we never cared what people thought when we knew we were right."

The first woman publisher of a daily paper in the United States was Eliza Jane Poitevent, who also wrote poetry under the pen name of Pearl Rivers. She inherited the debt-ridden *Picayune* upon the death of her husband when she was 26. It profited greatly, and she served as publisher until her death 20 years later in 1896.

Sophie Wright, crippled from childhood, opened the first night school for adults in the United States in 1885.

The first American accorded sainthood, Mother Cabrini, pursued her selfless social missionary work with Italian immigrants in New Orleans between 1892 and 1905.

Fast dining at the Camellia Grill has been a New Orleans tradition for about half a century. The staff is just as well dressed, attentive, and sought out by local patrons as those working in the city's most elegant, old-line restaurants. Photo by Bob Rowan/Progressive Image Photography

Such literary luminaries as Grace King, Frances Parkinson Keyes, Kate Chopin, and Shirley Ann Grau wrote in and about New Orleans, and Ann Rice, Sheila Bosworth, and Ellen Gilchrist represent an impressive group of female writers today.

And one of the century's great female sculptors, Angela Gregory, has adorned her city with monumental work, including the statue of the founder, Bienville.

For two centuries, working women in New Orleans have contributed immensely to the city's commerce, social conscience, and culture. Today New Orleans women play a leading role in almost every area of business, political, and community life.

Lindy Boggs was a moving force behind her husband, Hale Boggs, U.S. House majority whip from Louisiana. When he disappeared on a plane trip over Alaska, Mrs. Boggs replaced him in Congress in 1973 and has been elected handily four times. She is leader of the state's Democratic party.

In the mid-1970s Dorothy Mae Taylor, a leading civil rights activist in the turbulent 1960s, became the first black woman in the Louisiana

Restaurants in New Orleans operate in almost any type of building, from warehouses to firehouses. A popular bistro in the French Quarter is now housed in a former laundry on Bourbon Street. Photo by Bob Rowan/Progressive Image Photography

House of Representatives. In 1990 she won reelection to a second term as councilman-at-large in New Orleans.

The first black woman to be elected to the local bench, Joan Armstrong, serves as a New Orleans juvenile judge.

In 1984 Diane Bajoie, another black Orleanian, became the first woman committee chairman in the history of the Louisiana legislature.

Two remarkable women of substantial wealth, the late Edith Rosenwald Stern and Rosa Freeman Keller, actively supported the civil rights movement and helped finance many black institutions. They were vigorously involved in the Urban League, the League of Woman Voters, and activist politics. Along with Martha G. Robinson, they formed the famous "Broomstick Brigade" or Independent Women's Organization in 1945. Small battalions of women volunteers, armed with broomsticks, repeatedly marched on City Hall, vowing "to sweep out the old gang." Eventually they rallied behind Delesseps (Chep) Morrison and turned his underdog candidacy into an electoral triumph in 1948 when he became the first genuine reform mayor in decades. His amazed opponent, the incumbent Robert Maestri, later complained: "Them widow women beat me."

Even as enlightened New Orleans women stepped out of the kitchen, many stepped back in, and in the manner of the famous Madame Begue, wound up running the restaurant. Leah Chase has cooked and managed Dooky Chase's popular black Creole restaurant for decades, but her pivotal role in community service distinguishes her as a leader in black/white cooperative endeavors. Several women in the Brennan family, notably Ella and Adelaide Brennan, have spent their lives in the restaurant business. The family enterprise, Commander's Palace, is internationally prized. Ruth Fertel is one of a growing number of female entrepreneurs who has spread her wings, expanding her initial steak house to include 13 restaurants located across the nation.

Ruth Ann Menutis started with one small boutique on Bourbon Street in 1964 and now operates 13 shops. Menutis was the first woman president of the French Market Association and currently heads the newly organized French Quarter Task Force.

A Dutch emigre, Maria Benton, is the only woman car dealer in New Orleans. In 1977 she opened Classic Imports, which now sells Mazda, Lotus, and Mazzerati automobiles. A champion sports car racer, she also may be the only female in the nation who operates as her own service manager and road tests each of her cars personally. She also flies her own plane.

Two of the most distinctive and creative local businesswomen, Yvonne LeFleur and Mignon Faget, have capitalized ingeniously on New Orleans' unique charms. LeFleur's delicate, ultrafeminine fashions are inspired by the lacy, romantic period dress of the nineteenth century. Faget specializes in dramatically original handmade jewelry crafted from a variety of metals and stones, each piece evocative of this timeless city.

The diversity of New Orleans' people and their various cultures has created something new and very satisfying—a New Orleanian. University of New Orleans history professor Dr. Joseph Logsdon believes New Orleans has a unique personality because of its diversity. In his words: "New Orleans has developed a new ethnicity from old world and new world ingredients. We did not lose our ethnic heritages, we built something new—a breed apart."

Elegant continental dining is often most associated with New Orleans. The typical Orleanian, however, savors something a little more down-to-earth like seafood gumbo, jambalya, and that good old Monday mainstay, enjoyed by nearly every Orleanian, red beans and rice. Photo by Phillip Gould

MIND, BODY, AND SOUL

As we improve our educational system, we improve job opportunities for all citizens, particularly those at the bottom of the ladder . . . We lift our children. We lift the state.

Governor Charles "Buddy" Roemer

Several church structures have been on the site of the St. Louis Cathedral. For Catholics and non-Catholics alike, the church has always been, more so than any other building, the symbolic heart of New Orleans. Most people call it simply "The Cathedral." Photo by Philip Gould

TODAY A VARIETY OF HIGHLY INNOVATIVE COMMITMENTS relating to education are being made in New Orleans; some are models for the nation. They involve new alliances between the public and private sector—partnerships—says Chancellor Gregory O'Brien of the University of New Orleans.

The New Orleans business community has entered actively into creating these partnerships with the area's educational systems. The Business Task Force on Education, Inc., fought to safeguard the $540 million committed to the Louisiana Educational Quality Trust Fund. This political plum resulted from the settlement with the federal government over "windfall oil revenues" based on the Outer Continental Shelf Act.

The New Orleans/River Region Chamber of Commerce conducted vital studies pinpointing two specific educational needs. First, New Orleans-area vo-tech schools have been consistently underfunded for years. Second, education must be matched with vocational needs and the fastest-growing jobs.

Independent oil man Patrick Taylor, a maverick of sorts, has shaken up traditionalists by suggesting that America, the so-called "classless society," now has only two classes: "those that can afford education and those who cannot." He calls it a national disgrace: "Taxing the poor to subsidize the education of the favored few."

In 1988, while speaking to a group of low-achieving, inner-city high school students at Livingston Middle School, 200 of whom were predominately black seventh and eighth graders, Taylor was inspired to make them a deal. If they could complete the required courses to enter LSU or UNO, maintain a "B" average, and stay out of trouble, then he would personally see to it that they went to college. As a result, within a year, 171 of "Taylor's Kids" were still in school and going strong. Twenty-five of the 83 ninth graders were in advanced or honors classes.

Armed with dramatic results, Pat Taylor lobbied the state legislature, stating that "attendance at public colleges and universities must be based on the ability to learn and not the ability to pay." He spoke from gritty experience. Born in the shadow of Spindletop, Texas, the first oil bonanza, he dreamed of being an oil man. But the 16-year-old was on the streets, virtually penniless. Then LSU gave him a loan, and Taylor went on to earn a degree in petroleum engineering. He remained in Louisiana to become one of the nation's top ten independent oil producers.

As a result of Taylor's lobbying efforts, the Taylor Plan has become the basis of a new state law. The State of Louisiana will now pay the tuition for students from low- and moderate-income families to attend state universities and colleges of their choice. Once in college, students must maintain minimum grade standards to continue to have free tuition. More than 1,200 students applied for the fall semester of 1989.

Taylor's crusade did not end there. He and other businessmen and educators were worried about a "brain drain," the loss of the city's best scholars to other states. So he and UNO's Chancellor O'Brien established the Taylor Scholarship program. National Merit and Achievement finalists who choose the University of New Orleans are given full tuition, room and board, a summer of study in Europe, a $2,000 annual stipend, and a personal computer and printer. There are no family-income restrictions. The result of this program is astounding. One hundred twenty-two Taylor scholars, among the best and brightest in New Orleans, now attend UNO, and UNO now ranks 19th among American universities in the number of National Merit scholars (69) on campus.

Educational reforms have also been initiated by the State of Louisiana and Governor Charles "Buddy" Roemer. As the governor has stated:

Louisiana has taken major steps to reform its educational system, with the goal being the best possible teacher in every classroom. We know that a first class education is a necessity for both individual and social progress . . . As we improve our educational system, we improve job opportunities for all citizens, particularly those at the bottom of the ladder . . . We lift our children. We lift the state.

The reforms, called The Children First Act, include the establishment of teacher pay raises, a school incentive program, an education database, regular teacher evaluation, and elimination of lifetime teacher certificates.

In the field of higher education, New Orleans enjoys a remarkable diversity. It is home for 10 major colleges and universities (those with more than 1,000 students) attended by more than 53,000 students from every state in the union and at least 40 foreign countries.

Tulane University, from which many of New Orleans' present-day leaders graduated, is the largest private employer in the city. The university employs 5,300 people and maintains a payroll in excess of $145 million. In addition, about one of every four Tulane graduates lives in

One of the most ivy league universities in the South, Tulane University has been a landmark in Uptown New Orleans since the early 1890s when the first of its many buildings was constructed. It was founded as the University of Louisiana in the Central Business District. Photo by Brad Crooks

the metropolitan area.

The university enjoys a national reputation in many fields, among them public health and science, law and justice, medicine, and the creative arts. It has produced six Rhodes Scholars in seven years and has been a leader in Inter-American research and scholarship, commerce, medicine, and architecture.

This privately endowed school was established in 1891 on land purchased on the current site overlooking gracious, oak-lined St. Charles Avenue. A wealthy merchant named Paul Tulane gave over his valuable real estate holdings for "the encouragement and promotion of education for young men." Its faltering predecessor, the University of Louisiana, was absorbed and moved from its downtown location.

About the same time, Josephine Louise Newcombe, a wealthy widow, founded a woman's college in the Garden District. Its initial endowment was $100,000. In 1918 Sophie Newcombe Memorial College, named in honor of Josephine Newcombe's deceased daughter, joined the main Tulane campus under the administrative structure of Tulane. Newcombe College was the first coordinate college for women within a larger university in the United States.

Today Tulane is a major resource for research, talent, and new ideas in New Orleans. The Boggs Center for Energy and Biotechnology has become a seeding ground for industry. The A.B. Freeman School of Business is a major training ground for commerce. The highly respected School of Architecture is actively involved in the city's ongoing planning projects, mindful of the delicate balance between preservation and innovation.

Tulane's international outreach extends into many areas. The School of Public Health and Tropical Medicine has been long established as expert in its field. The Center for Latin American Studies works with Central American specialists.

The university's Howard-Tilton Library is the largest such facility in the city. Special collections include materials on jazz, Latin American culture and history, and architecture. One of the most important archives on black history in America, the Amistad Collection, is also housed on the campus.

Located next to Tulane on a compact, 19-acre campus is another of New Orleans' excellent universities—Loyola University of the South. The campus is a fascinating collection of impressive Tudor Gothic buildings and extremely modern architecture.

The Orleans Parish School System was founded in 1841, and ever since then the city's officials have been committed to public education. Photo by Bob Rowan/Progressive Image Photography

Founded by the Society of Jesuit in 1912, Loyola typifies the 450-year-old Jesuit teaching tradition grounded in a commitment to excellence and social justice. Its Institute of Human Relations, inspired by Father Frances Twomey, was in the forefront of the struggle to break down century-old segregation barriers. The Loyola Law School has prepared many of the city's most notable public leaders, including Maurice "Moon" Landrieu. Landrieu, twice mayor of New Orleans, desegregated municipal government and broadened the political arena. He later headed the U.S. Department of Housing and Urban Development.

The university's 5,000 students find the small classes and personal relationships stimulating, especially since one-quarter reside permanently elsewhere. This cosmopolitan mix includes 45 states and 49 foreign countries. Yet 70 percent of Loyola's graduates work, teach, and live in New Orleans. Many have children and grandchildren enrolled in the university. Father James C. Carter, S.J., the university's president, takes pride in the fact that "Loyola grads comprise the largest number of alumni in our community."

In the Jesuit tradition, Loyola operates a law clinic for the poor and indigent requiring legal assistance. And the university has the only law school in America requiring a course in poverty law.

In the fine arts, Loyola's music school has fostered the talents of a great many outstanding singers, including the late Norman Treigle, lead bass-baritone of the New York City Center Opera, and Charles Anthony, tenor for the Metropolitan Opera House.

Loyola's state-of-the-art communications school ranks among the nation's best. It provides hands-on training with modern equipment. Working professionals augment a faculty expert in both theory and practice. Internships at local and regional radio and television stations have

Loyola University, which embodies the Jesuit elements of faith and education, is next door to Tulane University on St. Charles Avenue. Standing opposite Audubon Park, the two schools form one of the most attractive, as well as important, assets in New Orleans. Photo by Bob Rowan/Progressive Image Photography

provided entre for dozens of Loyola grads.

In addition to Loyola, another New Orleans Catholic institution of higher learning is Xavier University. Archbishop James Blenk, who organized the Catholic school system and became its first superintendent in 1907, was the prime mover in the establishment of Xavier in 1915. The Archbishop induced the Sisters of the Blessed Sacrament to come to New Orleans that year "to establish a college of higher learning for Negroes and Indians," and they have operated the school ever since.

Xavier, which began as a teacher's college and later evolved into a small but select university, was the nation's only black Catholic university when it was founded and it remains so today. A significant cross section of today's black leadership has been educated at Xavier and/or its sister school, Xavier Prep. The university's president, Dr. Norman Francis, is one of the community's most respected educator/activists.

Xavier, with a student body of 2,000, is a private, liberal arts school that includes a graduate division and schools of pharmacy and music. The Xavier Opera is nationally renowned. As the first major black opera company in the South, it was the inspiration for the nationally renowned Opera South in Jackson, Mississippi, and the training ground for many professional artists.

Another liberal arts college in the New Orleans area, predominantly black Dillard University, is a prime example of the rich diversity of higher education in America's international city. Located on a 46-acre campus in the Gentilly area, Dillard is an undergraduate college with an enrollment of 1,320 students from 28 states and more than 40 foreign countries.

Dillard's educational ancestry dates back to Straight College (1869), which was founded by Congregational Church missionaries to offer freed slaves an opportunity for learning, and Union Normal (1869), fostered by the Methodist Church.

The Dillard campus is distinguished by its spacious greensward and the impressive white-columned Southern Colonial buildings that house its classrooms and offices. Lawless Chapel and the University Library are community landmarks, and the school maintains one of the finest repositories of documents and source material on Afro-American history.

Among Dillard's most notable alumni and faculty are Dr. Barbara Guillory Thompson and her late husband, Daniel Thompson. A Dillard graduate, Barbara Thompson was the first black to integrate Tulane and is currently working on a comprehensive study of the black family. Dillard professor Dr. Daniel Thompson was considered the leading black sociologist in America. He also played a significant role in the development of an enlightened black political leadership in New Orleans.

In the field of public education the University of New Orleans is a phenomenon. Created in 1956 as a commuter college by an act of the legislature, its first classes were held in rickety, abandoned barracks left over by the former landlord, the U.S. Naval Air Station. Located on 195 acres of reclaimed lakefront land, Louisiana State University in New Orleans was, for a while, a kind of appendix to the mother school in Baton Rouge.

Under the determined stewardship of its founding chancellor, Dr. Homer Hitt (a former associate dean at LSU in Baton Rouge), the school opened to about 1,500 students and grew into a major university with its own identity (UNO) and an enrollment of 17,000 students.

UNO has subsequently developed a core curriculum that includes colleges of business administration, liberal arts and sciences, education, engineering, and urban and public affairs.

One hundred more acres have been added, forming an East Campus with a 12,000-seat arena, home of the school's nationally ranked basketball team. The arena is multipurpose and serves as the venue for a variety of public concerts, sports events, and other entertainments.

The university has made great progress in interacting with a city where public education traditionally was either ignored or scorned. Its professors are highly visible in community affairs, frequently "published," and activists in major projects, especially urban and public affairs.

The university's Metropolitan College, established in 1980, has developed a downtown subsidiary on the premise that "if you can't come to the campus, we'll bring the campus to you." The division of Continuing Education furthers the university's outreach to all citizens, regardless of age.

For the first time in history, new leaders—UNO alumni with strong roots in public education—are filtering into the community. And to further strengthen the ties, the city's magnet school for its top scholars, Ben Franklin, has been relocated to the university campus.

The campus of the University of New Orleans is modern: none of its buildings predate the 1960s, and the Student Union is symbolic of this new look. UNO was originally called LSUNO, but today it proudly boasts its own identity, as well as a winning basketball team. Photo by Brad Crooks

UNO's expansion has primarily involved preparing young Orleanians for jobs in local areas where its economic strength lies. For example, since 1986 UNO has been one of only four schools in the nation to offer a degree in naval architecture. Since then 82 graduates have entered the shipbuilding industry, 40 of them in the New Orleans area. This is appropriate since shipbuilding and waterborne commerce represent 30 percent of the city's economy.

The port and tourism are the city's economic mainstays, and UNO's School of Tourism and Hotel Management recently was rated 20th in a survey of more than 150 such specialized schools.

Additionally, Chancellor Gregory O'Brien has proposed a Research Office Park, a partnership between the public and private sector, which would involve an International Hotel Conference Center. The center would offer onsite training for students, a vitally needed Center for

Ochsner Foundation Hospital in suburban River Ridge is among the world's most respected hospitals. Its unexcelled services are often sought out by internationally famous celebrities and dignitaries. Photos by Bob Rowan/Progressive Image Photography

Research in Ocean and Space Sciences, and an Advanced Technology Center designed to teach and advance image and information delivery. "The idea," says O'Brien, "is to develop a coalition of public and private resources that build on the city's strengths—tourism, aerospace, energy, and marine industries."

Among New Orleans' other institutions of higher learning are Southern University of New Orleans (SUNO), Our Lady of Holy Cross College, and Delgado Community College. SUNO is a predominantly black, state-supported member of the Southern University system. It offers a full range of four-year undergraduate programs to its 3,300 students. In addition, its graduate program in social studies is noteworthy. Our Lady of Holy Cross College, a coeducational liberal arts college, offers both day and evening courses leading to a variety of master's degrees. Located on the growing West Bank, the college has embarked on a $5-million development program aimed at better serving its area. Delgado Community College, which began as a trade school for boys in 1912, has been transformed into a huge community junior college with strong vocational and technical orientation. Its 7,315 students are involved in career-oriented courses in everything from auto mechanics to computer technology. The multilingual faculty and student body relates well to the aspirations of the students, many first-generation emigres trying hard to bridge the cultural and language barriers, necessary to earn a living. In a sense, Delgado is the ultimate equal opportunity school in America's first melting pot city.

New Orleans also offers theological study at two major institutions, the Roman Catholic Notre Dame Seminary and the New Orleans Baptist Theological Seminary. In addition, St. Joseph's Seminary in St. Tammany Parish is operated by the Catholic order of the Benedictines.

Five outstanding teaching hospitals, two major medical schools, a school of nursing, and Louisiana's only schools of allied health professions and dentistry make New Orleans a major provider of well educated and excellently trained health care practitioners for the region and the nation.

The New Orleans metropolitan area today offers the finest, most technologically advanced health care and medical facilities in the Gulf South. The three-parish area of Jefferson, Orleans, and St. Bernard contains 31 hospitals (26 with cardiac care units and 22 with established OB-GYN units and birthing rooms) with a total of 7,930 beds. All but four of these hospitals operate 24-hour emergency rooms with corresponding intensive care. In addition there are 48 nursing home facilities with 6,000 beds total. The health care industry accounts for more than 37,000 jobs in direct employment, including 3,590 physicians and 700 dentists.

Within a 30-minute radius of the Central Business District is located a wealth of excellent medical facilities and emergency services.

Depaul Hospital is the pioneer facility in mental health treatment. Dating back to 1861, it was the first mental hospital in the South. Today it incorporates special units devoted to Adolescent Discovery and alcohol/drug addiction (The New Life Center).

The Counterpoint Center of Coliseum Medical Center offers a modern 52-bed facility staffed with 11 doctors and counselors. It has enjoyed success rehabilitating drug and alcohol abusers and those people with eating disorders.

Southern Baptist Hospital, dating back to 1926, is one of the most comprehensive medical complexes in the city. It is a recognized leader in sports medicine with an advanced professional rehabilitation unit (The Human Performance Center) specializing in cardiac rehabilitation. The 360-bed hospital offers advanced cardiac technology and is noted for its development of angioplasty and other non-surgical vascular procedures.

Touro Infirmary, founded in the 1840s through the largess of Jewish philanthropist Judah P. Touro, is the oldest private hospital in the city. This long-established institution pioneered the first clinics, other than

Although the first building of Southern Baptist Hospital was opened on Napoleon Avenue in 1926, over the years it has expanded to become a major complex covering several square blocks and serving a wide area. Photo by Bob Rowan/Progressive Image Photography

The Veteran's Administration Hospital is one component of the Health Education Authority of Louisiana, and is located in the heart of New Orleans' Central Business District. Photo by Bob Rowan/Progressive Image Photography

Charity Hospital, for both black and white patients. Its psychiatric and obstetrics units are excellent. It is the fourth-largest general hospital in the metropolitan area (with the exception of "Big Charity"), ranking in size behind Ochsner Foundation, East Jefferson, and West Jefferson.

Mercy Hospital, founded by the Sisters of Mercy in 1924, occupies the old Saulet plantation grounds. The original main building was erected about 1816. It opened the first free clinic in New Orleans. A postwar building program expanded it to 225 beds with improved cardiac and catheterization facilities and a rehabilitation program.

Pendleton Memorial Methodist is among the newer private hospitals and one of the largest (318 beds). It services the growing New Orleans East area. Its modern psychiatric wing employs 16 doctors and counselors involved in dual diagnosis of adults and adolescents in alcohol and drug abuse treatment.

Among the medium-sized and specialized hospitals are the Eye and Ear Institute, Humana Women's Hospital in East New Orleans, Montelepre Memorial, New Orleans General, St. Charles General, and the United Medical Center.

Other modern specialized facilities are the Lakeside Hospital in Jefferson Parish, which is noted for women's health care, and Children's Hospital, the only full-time pediatric hospital between Birmingham and Houston devoted solely to the care of children.

For a long time New Orleans has enjoyed a reputation as an international medical center with especially strong ties to Latin America. The first school of medicine was founded on January 5, 1835, by seven young New Orleans physicians. It later became the Tulane University Medical School, the first medical school in the Deep South. Today it is the heart of a downtown consortium that embraces the famed School of Public Health and Tropical Medicine, a 300-bed hospital and outpatient clinic, plus numerous research facilities working on various projects from developing an AIDS vaccine to controlling African parasitic disease.

Another local major medical facility, the LSU Medical School, was, ironically, born out of political wrath more than necessity. In 1930 Senator Huey P. Long, resentful of the Tulane Board of Administrators' opposition to his manipulation of state-operated Charity Hospital, established a competing medical school. Funded through LSU, the school was located in downtown New Orleans. Long is said to have been infuriated that Tulane refused his request for an honorary law degree. (In 1914 the Kingfish had breezed through an eight-month Tulane law course, passed the bar, and leaped into politics, sans degree, headed for glory.)

Since its founding in 1931, LSU Medical Center has grown rapidly to include six professional schools, a university hospital in Shreveport, and the Pennington Biomedical Research Center in Baton Rouge. The LSU system has educated about 70 percent of all the physicians now practicing in Louisiana. Its researchers receive almost half the federal grant money awarded to the statewide LSU system.

Any friction that may have existed between the Tulane School of Medicine and LSU's School of Medicine, however, eventually gave way to a cooperative modern downtown medical center. Through a long-standing agreement, LSU Med Center and the Tulane Medical School faculty and residents provide the majority of patient care at the state-operated Charity Hospital with its 1,800-patient load. Long before the government began providing comprehensive health care for the poor and indigent, Charity offered free services to the dispossessed of New Orleans. Created in 1736 by the will of a bachelor shipbuilder, Jean Louis, Charity Hospital is one of the oldest hospitals in continuous operation in North America. The number of doctors who opt for postgraduate training at Charity has always been impressive, perhaps because it offers physicians a great opportunity for first-hand study of the wide-ranging ills found in an international, racially mixed city.

One of the finest and most diverse health complexes in the country is located in the heart of New Orleans' Central Business District. The Health Education Authority of Louisiana (HEAL) is comprised of the LSU Medical Center, the Tulane Medical School and Hospital, Charity Hospital, the Veterans' Administration Hospital, and Hotel Dieu. HEAL is a state executive agency established in 1968 to develop this mega-medical center. It ranks among the largest health complexes in the world. Tulane Medical Center has become the area's fourth-largest employer with approximately 3,500 full-time employees and an annual payroll of nearly $80 million. Accep-

With its oldest building dating to the 1890s, Touro Infirmary and its associated medical services form a landmark complex in Uptown New Orleans. With the exception of huge New Orleans Charity Hospital, Touro is the biggest hospital in the city proper. Photo by Bob Rowan/Progressive Image Photography

tance into its medical school is so prized that only 148 applicants out of an average of 3,000 are chosen each year.

Hotel Dieu, founded in 1852 at Canal Street and Claiborne Avenue in a house (Maison de Sante) owned by Dr. Warren Stone, is New Orleans' oldest private hospital in continuous operation.

The internationally renowned Ochsner Medical Institutions, including the Ochsner Clinic and Ochsner Foundation Hospital, are often referred to as "The Mayo of the Mississippi." Many of its patients over the past three decades have come from South and Central America. Ochsner physicians developed heart and liver transplantation in the Gulf South. The Pediatrics Department is one of three centers in the world pioneering extra-corporeal oxygenation, a highly advanced procedure that has given new life to babies with rare lung disorders. Ochsner is famous for its Cancer Institute, interconnected by a special information network with the nation's leading hospitals, clinics, and research centers.

The fastest-growing sector in local medicine is biomedical technology. LSU's and Tulane's medical schools have provided the impetus in this field, while Ochsner has also moved steadily to the forefront.

Ochsner is one of eight medical centers in the United States testing the so-called "smart probe," which sends out a sound signal when contact is made with a cancer cell during surgery, and Ochsner cardiologists have devised a new technique that sends laser beams, unshielded, through artery walls to vaporize artery-clogging plaque in blood vessels.

Dr. Gerald Berenson at the LSU Medical Center has gained world renown for his "Bogalusa Heart Study." This ongoing $17-million project, which began 18 years ago, has followed the lives and habits of 8,000 children and adults in a small South Louisiana community. Already, the study has yielded the largest collection of data on childhood cardiovascular risk factors in the world. Additionally, LSU researcher Dr. Jack Strong was the first to document that smoking causes progressive atherosclerosis (hardening of the arteries), and LSU's Eye Center is using lasers without heat to eliminate vision problems and the need for corrective lenses. The Eye Center also is testing a drug for AIDS-related blindness.

Tulane's School of Tropical Medicine is participating in a special project in Cameroon, Africa, involving control of parasitic disease, while the university's Delta Primate Center has taken on a new five-year, $7-million grant to develop a vaccine for AIDS. New Orleans is one of 19 national medical complexes studying the safety of drugs such as AZT to combat the AIDS virus.

While, according to Dr. Merrill O. Hines (former president of the Ochsner Foundation), "research doesn't bring in money," he also acknowledges that "you can't have a great medical center without it." Dr. Russell Kline, director of continuing medical education at the LSU Medical School adds: "For some time, New Orleans was a world and national leader in medical research. The city has not slacked off—but other heavily funded research complexes (Boston, Chicago, New York) have expanded."

New Orleans' world of medical research is also expanding. The new Tulane F. Edward Hebert Research Center conducts revolutionary work

Stained-glass windows in New Orleans churches are history unto themselves. Many date to the first half of the nineteenth century and are memorials to some of the most historically important families and individuals in the city. Photo by Bob Rowan/ Progressive Image Photography

in neuroendocrinology under Dr. Akira Arimura. It is located on a 509-acre site outside the city near the New Orleans International Airport. It has been dubbed the Japanese-American Center because of extensive seed money from corporations such as Nissan and Hitachi. Both nations envision it as the possible hub of a futuristic international research village, a core laboratory for scientists all over the world.

While every metropolitan area must be attentive to the health and educational needs of its residents, the spiritual well-being of its people must not be overlooked. For many newcomers to New Orleans, the city is a spiritual paradox. It is a city mythically regarded as preoccupied with pleasures of the flesh, and yet it is essentially a close-knit family town. Its activities are still strongly oriented to its distinctive neighborhoods and their houses of worship.

There are more than 850 places of worship in this city described by one nineteenth-century visitor as "tasting of both heaven and hell, while thoroughly enjoying the flirtation between the here-and-now and the hereafter." Forty percent of the citizens are Roman Catholic. About 70 other Christian denominations are represented. The faithful worship in high-arched brick splendor and ornamental Greek Orthodox and Roman Catholic cathedrals, as well as in plain frame one-room structures covered with brick-patterned tar paper.

There are congregations devoted to Islam, Buddhism, Bahai, Judaism, and various unification groups, and 15 New Orleans churches are more than 100 years old and qualify as historical and architectural treasures.

The influence of the Roman Catholic Church is deeply ingrained in New Orleans history, its culture, and its psyche. The first religious services were conducted by Jesuit missionaries accompanying Bienville, the city's founder, up the Mississippi "for the purpose of establishing a Catholic church and converting the Indians."

Dating back to the city's founding, the St. Louis Cathedral houses the oldest parish in New Orleans. Few churches anywhere embody the strong religious traditions that have gone to make up the personality of New Orleans. Photo by Philip Gould

Bienville's raw frontier outpost gained its first respectability when a group of 12 Ursuline nuns and two novices arrived in 1727. They administered the first hospital and orphanage, and they schooled poor, black, and Indian girls. The Ursuline Academy, now located at 2635 State, is the oldest girls' preparatory school in the nation. The old Ursuline convent building, on Charles Street, is the sole surviving structure from the French Colonial era in the Mississippi Valley.

The French Roman Catholic pioneers of New Orleans first worshipped in a small wooden dwelling in 1721. Today the majestic St. Louis Cathedral, with its twin spires, muralled ceiling, and distinctive tinkling bell, occupies the site, the oldest basilica in America. (It was rebuilt in 1798.)

For more than 100 years New Orleans was essentially a French Catholic city. Then the Louisiana Purchase brought a flood of Anglo Protestants from the North. Today it is still one of the most Catholic cities in North America, although the percentage of Catholics has decreased to around 50 percent. Because of the historical influence, New Orleans neighborhoods generally correspond to Catholic parish lines. The Church was the central unifying force, the focal point for education and recreation as well as for worship. Catholic priests kept careful records long before accurate census taking was undertaken. Even today, in various neighborhoods, church spires rise up above this table-flat, vertically constructed city, punctuating miles of one- and two-story housing, ecclesiastical exclamation points.

Religion, as practiced by the Creole Catholics, reflected a most tolerant and relaxed way of life. Protestant Anglo-Saxons were taken aback. One noted that "They celebrate Sundays here the way we do the Fourth of July." Historian "Pie" Dufour commented:

To these austere Yankees, New Orleans appeared to be a city of godlessness and depravity. Eventually the relaxed attitude of the Creoles . . . exercised an important influence on the spirit of tolerance for which New Orleans became noted.

The first organized Protestant service in New Orleans was held on July 15, 1805, in a private home on Royal Street. It was Episcopalian, and Philander Chase was installed as rector. In 1816 Christ Church was built. The present Christ Church Cathedral, located at 2919 St. Charles, is an historic landmark. The legendary "Fighting Bishop," Leonidas Polk, is interred under the choir floor. Polk, who was a West Point graduate and Confederate general, died in battle during the Civil War.

The First Presbyterian Church figured in the Confederate cause. Its pastor, the Reverend Benjamin M. Palmer, presided for more than 40 years. The Reverend Palmer's ringing two-hour oration glorifying the cause of secession is widely believed to have influenced a divided city to close ranks.

The first Baptists met as a group in 1812 at a private home. It was not until 1843, however, that the First Baptist Church was organized. The current church at St. Charles and General Pershing is one of the largest

THE CONJURE RELIGION— VOODOO

Voodoo arrived early in New Orleans, an import from the Caribbean Islands, in particular from St. Dominique (Haiti). By 1809, 9,000 Dominguens, mostly free people of color, poured into New Orleans as they fled bloody slave uprisings on their island.

The first legal record of voodoo being used in New Orleans was the "gris-gris" (gree-gree) case of 1793 in which three blacks were charged with conspiracy to poison a brutal overseer with a gris-gris made up of alligator innards and herbs.

Voodoo, the "conjure religion," was a fearful thing as practiced in the tropical jungles of the islands. It was invested with miraculous powers by the outnumbered whites whose cruelties left them superstitiously paranoic over the strange incantations, potions, and spells. Transmigrated to an urban atmosphere, however, it took on a more benign character, reflecting the sophistication of the interracial cosmopolis of New Orleans.

The leading practitioners of voodoo in the city were Dr. John (Montaigner) and Marie Laveau. Shrewd psychologists, they tailored voodoo to the time and clime, developing both a black and white clientele.

Dr. John, a towering "descendant of Singhalese princes," left the jungle rituals to minor priestesses. He concentrated on potions and faith healing, branching out into the sale of patent medicines. He specialized in hexes and was able to cast a spell or lift one. Dr. John made a fortune practicing voodoo, and he kept it buried in his backyard.

His protege, Marie Laveau, was a Roman Catholic quadroon who married once, bore 15 children, and operated out of a cottage on St. Ann Street in the French Quarter. Not far from there she presided over the weekly slave dances in Congo (Armstrong) Square. People came from all over the world to see these exotic performances involving members of at least 17 differ-ent African tribes. At Congo Square slave musicians introduced such hand-made instruments as the Congo drum ensemble, the marimba bret, and the first banjo.

Marie achieved a special eminence in a city that, at one point, supported 60 voodoo priestesses, 6 of them white women. She staged elaborate voodoo rituals for audiences approaching 1,000 at her "Wishing Spot" on the banks of Bayou St. John. Live chickens were sacrificed, and virtually nude dancers gyrated in a frenzied ritual choreographed by the "Voodoo Queen." Marie closed each well-orchestrated show by dancing with her great snake, Zombie, described vari-ously as from 5 to 15 feet long. Local newspapers covered the orgiastic ritu-als in detail, and a special spectator section was staked out for politicians and reporters.

Marie Laveau learned how to gather information and retail it at a proper price by working as a hairdress-er in the homes of the rich and privi-leged. Prominent politicians sought

Marie Laveau, shown with her daughter, is New Orleans' most leg-endary voodoo queen. She was very powerful among her followers and was famous for her good and evil charms called gris-gris. Courtesy, The Historic New Orleans Collection

consultations with her. One judge paid $500 for a reading behind closed doors. Her network of spies—black servants, valets, cooks, and porters—supplied her with inside infor-mation lest they be permanently hexed. So Marie hoodwinked her way to remarkable power.

In her declining years, the Voodoo Queen "renounced Satan and all his pomps" and embraced Catholicism. She spent much of her time consoling prisoners on death row and built them a chapel at Parish Prison. Her death was front-page news, and Marie was given a Catholic burial with full rites. The woman once scorned as the "Last Great American Witch" was mourned as a modern Magdalene.

congregations in the South. Its dynamic pastor for more than 30 years, the Reverend J.D. Grey, was a driving force in developing the New Orleans Federation of Churches, and, later, in forging a new ecumenical understanding with the Catholic community.

While it is significant to note that Corpus Christi Parish in New Orleans is the largest black Catholic parish in America, and Xavier University is the largest black Catholic University, several hundred of the metropolitan area's Baptist churches (which account for almost half the churches in the area) are comprised of black congregations, many dating back to the missionary activity among freed slaves following the Civil War.

Historian Joe Gray Taylor says that:

The most important religious movement in Louisiana during the past century was the withdrawal of black members from existing protestant churches to form churches of their own. While most blacks became Baptists, Methodism also flourished.

Although blacks throughout the South are predominantly Protestant, in New Orleans a large percentage are Roman Catholic. This stems from the city's strong French past when everybody spoke French and was Roman Catholic, regardless of race. Photo by Philip Gould

Many of the black churches are the social-economic-political core of black communities in the New Orleans metropolitan area. Historian Taylor maintains that it is no accident that "black leadership in Louisiana and the nation has tended to come from the churches . . . because there the leadership has the opportunity to develop on its own."

In New Orleans the man who led the first organized demonstrations and sit-ins during the civil rights crisis was the Reverend C. Avery Alexander; and one of Martin Luther King's young adjutants, Andrew Young, the twice-elected mayor of Atlanta, was born and raised in New Orleans, the son of a black minister.

Religious traditions are very strong in New Orleans. Ash Wednesday, All Saints Day, the reenactment of the Ways of the Cross on Good Friday, and other religious observances are still an important part of life for many Orleanians. Photo by Philip Gould

It would be a mistake to assume that native Orleanians, for all their reputation for celebration, are not really at heart (and soul) a concerned group of people. They make up a city of extremely close-knit families with strong attachments to its parish churches and old school ties. According to black sociologist Dan Thompson:

It is a city of three centuries of mutual sharing, both triumphs and disasters. Nowhere else were the races so intermixed. New Orleans was integrated even when it was segregated; black and white families lived, for generations, side by side.

Surviving together, New Orleans' people learned to live together. In a rather broad, meaningful sense, New Orleans was America's first racially open city—mind, body, and soul.

Outside of the Central Business District, New Orleans is a relatively low-level city with few tall buildings. All over town, the skyline is punctuated by tall church belfries and steeples that attest to New Orleans' strong ties to religious faith. Photo by Bob Rowan/Progressive Image Photography

PLAYTIME IN THE BIG EASY

New Orleans worships leisure time with a religious fervor.

Angus Lind

If anything symbolizes the spirit of The Big Easy, it is music. Whether it is a top-40 entertainer at the annual Jazz and Heritage Festival, or a swaying, gyrating high school marching band in a Mardi Gras parade, music is a vibrant part of the New Orleans mystique. Photo by Philip Gould

THE PEOPLE OF SOUTH LOUISIANA HAVE ALWAYS LIVED close to nature in all its variety and splendor—giant live oaks festooned with Spanish moss; the evergreen foliage renewing itself endlessly; the seasonal explosions of color; giant magnolia blossoms, azaleas, and camellias—all make South Louisianians feel at one with nature.

The nation's third-largest municipal park, lush, verdant City Park, has been a family gathering place for 130 years. It covers 1,500 acres within the city limits, its historic oaks shading miles of languid bayous. Though the park showed serious signs of neglect a decade ago, an energetic citizen movement, The Friends of City Park, has rejuvenated this giant tract, once site of the Allard sugar plantation.

City Park encompasses four 18-hole public golf courses, a double-decker driving range, 39 tennis courts, and 18 baseball/softball diamonds. Family picnicking under gnarled 800-year-old oaks is a popular pastime. Pedal boats and bicycles can be rented for leisurely cruising along the winding roads and bayou streams. Bass fishing is popular as is horseback riding. Riding lessons for all abilities in English and Western are available at City Park stables as well as lessons in dressage and horse care.

City Park also contains Storyland, a charming theme park with an antique carousel, miniature trains, hayrides, and puppet shows. The

Part of City Park was once a plantation, but it was left to the city in the 1850s. Since then, the park has grown by many times and has become one of the lushest and most beautiful urban breathing spaces in the United States. Photo by Brad Crooks

Botanical Gardens cover seven acres and feature rose gardens, sculptures, and fountains. The New Orleans Museum of Art commands the park entrance approaching the Beauregard statue at the end of Elysian Fields.

Audubon Park, a storied 385-acre retreat, is a shady bower of serenity, snugly fit within the trim and tidy University and Uptown neighborhoods, overlooking the Mississippi River. The park is named for the great painter and naturalist, John J. Audubon, who began his historic folio *Birds of America* in New Orleans. A statue of the man who revolutionized ornithology stands beneath a canopy of live oaks.

Audubon Park, which began as the site of the World's Industrial and Cotton Exposition in 1884, is now divided into three sections. The front section, facing St. Charles Avenue, is a deep-shaded grove of live oaks and winding paths offering tranquillity to walkers, joggers, golfers, picnickers, and fishermen. It con-

tains a tropical plant conservatory. The second section includes the 55-acre Audubon Zoo, a riding stable, swimming pool, tennis courts, and a miniature railway. The third area, between the zoo and the river, contains soccer and baseball fields and a spectacular walkway along the Mississippi River.

The original Audubon Park Zoo was built by the WPA. A cramped cluster of cages, the zoo was totally dependent on government funding. Over the years, as funding dwindled, it deteriorated badly, flooding often, until it became so disgraceful that it was called by one local critic "the slum ghetto of American zoos." Today a completely new, self-sufficient zoological garden has risen from the wreckage to become one of the five finest natural habitat zoos in the nation. It is a tribute to the determination of literally thousands of people, donors and volunteers, who banded together to demand a better vision of the natural world for their children. Three times in the 1970s the Friends of Audubon inspired the city's voters to approve bond monies vitally needed to transform the "jumbled jungle" into a position among the country's "Zoo's Who."

It is a textbook example of community action, involving strong volunteer work, staunch support by local business, and an overflowing of civic pride. A series of benefits at the park, whimsically called "Zoo to-Dos," raised large sums of seed money. Today a modern, naturalistic series of exhibits recreating the native jungle, savanna, or rocky habitats of the liberated (once-caged animals) has replaced the run-down, antiquated operation.

While the old zoo once drew fewer than 200,000 people a year, the

Audubon Park was laid out in its present form between 1902 and 1920. Today it is one of the most popular recreation areas in New Orleans, and its superb zoo draws visitors and applause from all over the world. Photo by Bob Rowan/Progressive Image Photography

new zoo hosts one million or more, the highest per capita visitation rate of any zoo in a major American city. According to a recent study by UNO researchers, the all-new zoo has become "the major family attraction in the Gulf South."

The Audubon Zoo is also self-sufficient, generating $33 million in annual income while consistently winning national awards.

Among the rare or endangered species to be seen at the zoo are the exotic white tiger, twin orangutans, white rhinos, clouded leopards, bald eagles, Asian elephants, and red wolves. The most popular zoo exhibit recreates the primordial swamplands of South Louisiana, teeming with life rarely seen elsewhere in America. Among the critters populating the Louisiana Marsh exhibit are alligators, armadillos, black bears, and the extremely rare white gator. Cajun food and music complete the authentic rustic bayou atmosphere.

On November 4, 1986, the people of New Orleans voted a $25-million property tax increase to finance a world-class aquarium and riverfront park. An umbrella agency, the Audubon Institute, was created in 1989 to coordinate the project. Soon 12 acres of Vieux Carre riverfront land, once filled with large, empty, unsightly metal warehouses, were transformed into a beautiful open greenspace landscaped with more than 400 trees and thousands of plants and annual flowers, including native cypress, live oak, red maple, and crepe myrtle.

The park's crown jewel is the new Aquarium of the Americas. While traditional aquariums have been a series of glass cages, modern technology has made possible the recreation of total habitats without barriers. The Aquarium of the Americas is the first aquarium to do this on a large scale. Four of the five major exhibit areas are walk-through replicas of natural habitats, including a Caribbean reef, the Amazon River basin, the Mississippi River delta, and the Gulf of Mexico. A transparent tunnel leads the spectator through each "world," allowing him to see sharks face to face, travel beneath tropical waterfalls, and cross suspension bridges. Some 7,000 fish, reptiles, amphibians, and birds representing 395 species are featured at the aquarium.

Not all of New Orleans' and South Louisiana's wildlife are to be found in the zoo and the aquarium. Louisiana abounds with more different species of animal, fish, and birdlife than any other state in the nation. Alligator, bear, duck, geese, prairie chicken, deer, even such "originals" as the choupique (a fish-eating aquatic bird) and the razor-toothed gar, the largest freshwater fish in the contiguous states. The variety of wildlife is endless. Scores of hunting grounds and fishing spots lie within an hour or two of the metropolitan area.

Some years ago, when descriptive slogans were in vogue on license plates, Louisiana had no difficulty coming up with one: "Sportsman's Paradise." The title stuck. South Louisiana's mild, semitropical climate, its bountiful wildlife, and plentiful fishing grounds offer year-round outdoor pleasure for sportsmen.

Fishermen did not begin to appreciate the bounty of South Louisiana until the first offshore oil drilling platform was completed off Grand Isle in 1947. The platform provided an artificial reef offering shelter and food

(such as barnacles, plants, and other vegetation) around its deep-driven steel pilings. It became an irresistible attraction for fish.

Today there are more than 5,000 platforms providing artificial reefs where, initially, hosts of small fish congregate. They touch off a food chain. The small fish attract larger fish and so on. Deep-sea anglers soon discovered that every time a new rig went up, another fishing bonanza was created. Saltwater fish convene in great numbers and variety. Speckled trout, redfish, red snapper, flounder, bluefish, mullet, croakers, drum, king mackeral, bonita, tarpon, alligator gar, and barracuda. Black bass and small saltwater fish alternate in abundance with changing tides and weather conditions in the bayous and lagoons.

New Orleans is one of the few major cities where you can fish in the heart of town (City Park), and Chef Menteur and nearby tide races afford the highest quality sport—large sheepshead, redfish, jackfish, and tarpon. The fishing is best from April to October.

Freshwater fish abound: perch, sunfish, bass, pike, garfish, trout, catfish, and the tasty little denizen of the bayou and the ditch, the crayfish. Pronounced "craw-fish" and known locally as "craw-dads" or "mudbugs," these exotic morsels resemble miniature lobsters. In fact, they form the basis, along with freshwater catfish, of two modern industries, commercially stocked in "ponds" and "farmed."

The Gulf and its estuarine waterways also constitute a vast incubator for crab, shrimp, and oysters, major industries in themselves.

Whether it's fresh or saltwater fishing or deep-sea angling, fishing is virtually a year-round sport. So are crabbing, shrimping, and crayfishing. Complete hunting and fishing regulations, season dates, and license requirements can be obtained from the Louisiana Wildlife and Fisheries Department.

For those who hanker for spectator sports, New Orleans offers an abundance of choices based on a rich sporting heritage.

Horse racing is strongly rooted in South Louisiana. As early as the 1830s, New Orleans was the established thoroughbred horse racing capi-

The Fairgrounds Racetrack has been a tradition in New Orleans for nearly 120 years. During the spring for two weekends it hosts the annual Jazz and Heritage Festival, which can draw a total attendance in excess of 300,000. Photo by Bob Rowan/Progressive Image Photography

tal of America. In 1854 the two finest thoroughbreds of their time, Lexington and LeCompte, met in an epic match race at the old Metairie course before 10,000 avid fans. Some of the finest jockeys and trainers in the nation started out on quarter-mile strips in Cajun country, and early plantation owners raised their own thoroughbreds. The Fairgrounds, opened in 1872, continues to operate. The third-oldest thoroughbred track in America, it is predated only by Saratoga and Pimlico. In 1924 Black Gold won the Louisiana Derby there and then went on to glory by capturing the Kentucky Derby. The gallant, jet black steed,

Above and right: Orleanians live for the Saints. They have supported their beloved team through thick and thin. Who'dats, or Saints fans, continue to talk about and cheer on the team year after year, from training through the fall football season. Photos by Tim Alexander

purchased with oil money by the Hoots family, ran his last race at the Fairgrounds. He is buried in the track's infield. In addition to the Fairgrounds' traditional meetings, Jefferson Downs dovetails consecutive schedules to provide year-round thoroughbred-racing entertainment.

The first world heavyweight boxing championship fought with gloves, under modern Marquis of Queensbury rules, was held at the old Olympic Club in 1892. "Gentleman Jim" Corbett dethroned John L. Sullivan in 21 rounds. The Olympic was boxing's mecca in the Gay Nineties. At one point, three world championship bouts were held on three con-

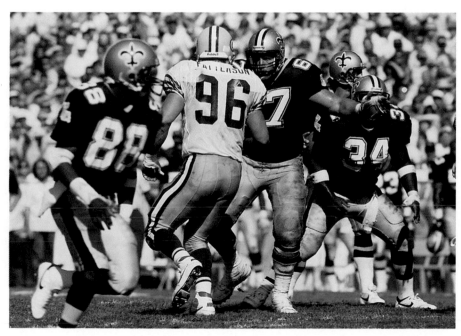

secutive nights. The biggest boxing event of the twentieth century saw Muhammed Ali regain his heavyweight crown from Leon Spinks at the Superdome in 1978 before 63,000 spectators.

The first fencing academies were introduced in New Orleans, a necessity for young hot bloods subject at any moment to a challenge to duel.

The country's oldest tennis club, the New Orleans Lawn Tennis Club, was founded in 1876. National champions like Hamilton Richardson and Linda Tuero carried the tradition into the twentieth century.

The Southern Yacht Club is the second-oldest of its type next to the New York Yacht Club. Skippers Gilbert Gray and "Buddy" Friedrichs from the SYC have won two Olympic gold medals, Gray in 1932 and Friedrichs in 1968.

The Sugar Bowl football classic, the dream of New Orleans sports editor Fred Digby, was founded in 1934 by a small group of civic-minded businessmen. Twenty-two thousand fans filled Tulane Stadium to watch Tulane storm past Temple, 20-14. Both the bowl game and the stadium grew appreciably. Aided by Sugar Bowl receipts, Tulane Stadium expanded to 80,000 seats—the largest all-steel constructed stadium in the country before the Superdome replaced it as the Sugar Bowl's new home. Some of football's greatest names have added luster to the nearly 60 games played each New Year's Day; among them are Davey O'Brien, Sammy Baugh, Jarrin' John Kimbrough, Archie Manning, Bobby Layne, Tony Dorsett, Herschell Walker, Dan Marino, "Bear" Bryant, Bud Wilkinson, Joe Paterno, Vince Dooley, and Ara Parseghian.

Today the city has only one professional sports franchise, the adored New Orleans Saints of the NFL, but its cosmopolitan reputation as a

The Louisiana State University Stadium is host to countless New Orleans football fans who attended LSU. The LSU-Tulane rivalry resurfaces in earnest every football season. Photo by Philip Gould

CARNIVAL AND MARDI GRAS

It is doubtful that New Orleans could exist without Mardi Gras. Even if it could, it wouldn't really be New Orleans.

Carnival, from the Latin *carnevale*, means, literally, "farewell to flesh." It describes the season, opening Twelfth Night (January 6) and climaxing on Mardi Gras (literally Fat Tuesday), the final day, the final fling before Ash Wednesday and the austerity of Lent. Carnival has been celebrated in one form or another in New Orleans since the mid-1700s, when royalist French and Spanish colonists staged fancy *bals masque*.

Following the Louisiana Purchase, Les Americaines arrived, overcame their initial shock, and joined in the festivities. A reporter from the *Picayune* called the event "outlandish and grotesque."

Undaunted, New Orleans celebrated nevertheless, if only to rejoice in its survival between epidemics of cholera and yellow fever. Carnival persevered even when the great financial Panic of 1837 closed 14 banks. A *Picayune* reporter enthused over the first Mardi Gras float, "A giant fighting cock waving and nodding its head while drawn by a team of horses." The *Picayune* described the event as "a beautiful, joyous cavalcade . . . The whole town doubled up in laughter."

"Maskers" soon were pitching out the first Carnival "throws" —little sweetmeats—to their sweethearts. Today a single krewe will throw a million doubloons and uncountable numbers of beads and trinkets to the shrieking crowds. The most prized "catch," doubloons (in memory of the local heritage of piracy), are medallions about the size of a half dollar, generally aluminum anodized coins. They were first thrown by Rex in 1960.

Carnival almost came unglued in the 1850s as bands of thugs roamed the streets, pelting people with sacks of flour. In 1856 the bilingual newspaper *L'Abeille* or *The Bee* declared: "We hope we've seen the last of Mardi Gras."

Within a year, however, a spirited group of young men crowded into a small room above the old Gem Saloon

on Royal Street and guaranteed Carnival's life (far beyond their own modest expectations). They formed the Mystick Krewe of Comus (from the Greek "komus" meaning "revelers"). On Mardi Gras night, 1857, they burst forth with the city's first torchlight parade. It consisted of only two floats, sassily irreverent but highly symbolic of a city once described as "tasting of both heaven and hell." Comus, the Olympian god of the never-empty wine cup, wielded a silver chalice instead of a scepter, riding the lead float. Behind him rode Satan brandishing a pitchfork. Following them were 80 costumed devils dancing about the street.

The four oldest marching organizations are Comus, Proteus, Rex, and Momus, all possessing social pedigrees dating back a century and a quarter or more.

The Civil War, three years of Federal occupation, and 12 years of Reconstruction detained Carnival but did not derail it. In 1872 the first Mardi Gras day parade took place. It was an impromptu affair whipped up by a number of civic-minded leaders ostensibly to honor the visiting Grand Duke Alexis Romonoff of Russia, a notorious international playboy. Since Louis Salamon raised the most money, he got to wear the crown (borrowed) and wield the scepter (loaned). And so it was that Rex ("king") became the once and future king of all Carnival, riding horseback and wearing a rented king suit from a traveling

Shakespearean drama troupe.

Momus, a separate krewe, was formed in 1872. Named for the god of ridicule, Momus appeared in that year's celebration, flaunting the Latin motto: *Dum Vivimus Vivere* ("While we are living, let us live"). It set the tone for all future celebrations.

In 1909 a group of black working-men formed the krewe of Zulu and satirized the white man's Mardi Gras. His majesty wore a lard can for a crown, toasted his queen at an under-taking parlor, and delegated business through his captain, "The Big Shot."

Gradually Carnival Americanized, though old-line groups tended to stick with themes from Greek, Roman, and Egyptian mythologies and rigid ball formats that resembled Royalist court functions from the eighteenth century.

In the later days of the Depression two new krewes—Hermes and Baby-lon—saw business and professional men group together, thus broadening the social base. The first women's orga-nization, Iris, was formed, and the first neighborhood krewe, Carrollton, orga-nized. On the West Bank, the krewes of Alla and Grela rolled on.

It was not until the turbulent 1960s that the democratization of Car-nival was achieved. In 1967 Bacchus (Sunday) broke down the barriers with a Sunday night parade that had as its king, not a local socialite, but, rather, the first of a long line of super celebrities—Danny Kaye. Instead of the traditional tableau ball, Bacchus circled its giant, illuminated floats inside the Rivergate at parade's end and threw a party.

Soon Endymion's (Saturday) young members followed suit and assembled the largest krewe in history, 1,250 maskers. To top it off, big-name entertainers joined in a post-parade party at the Superdome.

The Endymion and Bacchus pa-rades gave a giant boost to tourism, creating a full weekend of pageantry leading up to traditional Fat Tuesday

revelry.

Today at least 60 separate krewes parade the last two and one-half weeks of Carnival within the metropolitan area. It has become the largest audi-ence participation show on earth.

Mardi Gras day, in a sense, resem-bles a gigantic "Peoples' Circus" with a million maskers in the streets and people dressed like apes and clowns and de-mon monsters. Anything your heart de-sires (and your inhibitions may have de-nied you) can be yours on Mardi Gras.

Below and facing page: Although the Carnival season has both its private, social side and its public, street party side, the most familiar to everyone is the latter. For two and a half weeks, life in the metropolitan area is punc-tuated with parades, parties, and general fun. It is capped by the cos-tumed, good-humored mayhem of Mardi Gras itself—Fat Tuesday. Pho-tos by Philip Gould

good-time "sportin' town" continues to make it an ideal neutral ground for big-time national events and championships. The Superdome, with its 80,000 seats and all-purpose, all-weather, climate-controlled atmosphere, serves as a magnet. The world's largest indoor arena is adaptable to just about any sporting enterprise from football and basketball to motocross racing and tractor pulls.

The Superdome is home today for both the Saints and Tulane collegiate football. The Saints expansion franchise, beginning in 1967, suffered through 19 consecutive seasons before producing a winner. Saints fans, undaunted, supported their team with a fervor seldom seen and with a sense of humor. When the team floundered to a 1 and 15 season, the fans donned bags with eye slits over their heads labeled "Aints" instead of Saints. New ownership, led by local auto dealer Tom Benson, and a youthful, inspiring coach, Jim Mora, has transformed the losers into consistent contenders.

Tulane traces its athletic tradition back to 1893. A privately endowed university of 10,000 students, it once was a Southeastern Conference power. Unable to compete with the large land-grant universities in the SEC after World War II, it has since gone independent with some successes, including trips to the Liberty, Bluebonnet, and Independence bowls. The Tulane and UNO baseball teams are consistently ranked nationally, perennial Sun Belt powers.

Louisiana State University (LSU) technically is not a local school, but it might as well be. Though the university in Baton Rouge is 90 miles away, thousands of students hail from New Orleans, and local Tiger alumni meetings are banner affairs. New Orleans is definitely "Fighting Tiger" territory. The LSU athletic program is ranked number four in all-sports competition in the United States with championship programs in football, baseball, basketball, track, golf, tennis, volleyball, and swimming.

New Orleans hosted one of the first full-time professional baseball teams in the 1870s. Under pacesetter Abner Powell, the original Pelicans helped form the old Southern League. Powell is credited with the invention of the rain check, Ladies Day, and the use of tarpaulins during rain delays. Diehard Pelican fans still refer to the hotel stands at South Carroll-

New Orleans is a street-oriented city, and that is part of the charm of The Big Easy. Jackson Square-strollers can spend many happy hours watching the many street entertainers, such as jugglers, clowns, magicians, balloon artists, musicians, and so on. Photo by Philip Gould

ton and Tulane as "The Stadium." For 42 years it was the home base for eight Southern Association champions, home of feisty Earl Weaver, future manager of the Orioles, and home for "Shoeless Joe" Jackson in his prime.

Although New Orleans currently has no professional baseball team, a local group is lobbying for the next major league expansion team, while eyeing possible franchise shifts. The Superdome annually hosts at least three major league exhibitions and the Busch Challenge, pairing UNO, LSU, and Tulane against three teams from California, Florida, or Texas in a weekend tournament. And the city's NORD and prep school programs have produced a number of major league luminaries, most recently Will Clark with the San Francisco Giants. He follows in the footsteps of such other big-league standouts as Rusty Staub, Mel Parnell, Zeke Bonura, Connie Ryan, Howard Pollet, and Hall of Famer Mel Ott.

Tulane offers intercollegiate football, baseball, and men's and women's basketball. UNO has developed highly competitive baseball and men's and women's basketball. Southern University (SUNO), Xavier, and Dillard also offer men's and women's basketball. Delgado fields junior college-level baseball and basketball teams.

In general, it is difficult to be bored in the city where the Creoles declared boredom a sin. New Orleans' love for sports, says columnist Angus Lind, fits right in with "its love of food and drink, partying, music and good times."

Mardi Gras is not the only time New Orleans puts on parades. Holidays like St. Patrick's and St. Joseph's days are marked by several parades. These are complete with beads and doubloons thrown to the crowd—an expected part of every New Orleans parade. At the St. Patrick's parades cabbages and potatoes are also given to the crowd. Photo by Philip Gould

Numerous fairs and festivals hosted by the region attract hundreds of thousands to New Orleans every year. In addition to the gargantuan Mardi Gras and the ever-growing Jazz and Heritage Festival, there are at least 75 other festivals, fairs, celebrations, and fetes each year.

La Fete, the July Fourth French Quarter celebration, joins with the Jackson Brewery to offer a lavish fireworks spectacle, climaxing a day of French Quarter revelry. The *New Year's Eve Countdown* at Jackson Square has become a national event, as hundreds of thousands of visitors join in welcoming in the New Year with fireworks as the giant countdown ball inches closer to the tip of the Jackson Brewery turrets. There is an annual *French Quarter Fiesta* with costumed vendors, street singers, and entertainers. Each May, the *New Orleans Spring Fiesta* offers guided tours of French Quarter homes and patios and Garden District mansions. *A Night in Old New Orleans* features a costume parade in antebellum fashion and a lavish outdoor soiree in Jackson Square with music, dancing, and buffet delicacies prepared by the finest chefs in New Orleans. The *Food Fest* is a kind of culinary Superbowl. Staged in the Rivergate, it offers a showcase for the extraordinary talents of chefs de

grand cuisine.

During *Mardi Gras* New Orleans is the only city in the nation that makes a virtue out of abandon, while encouraging both anonymity and insanity. In its own peculiar born-free, hang-loose way, the spirit of tomfoolery during Mardi Gras seems to embrace 2 million strangers in a giant bearhug of brotherly nonsense.

Outsiders marvel at the huge crowd's self-governing ability. Over the centuries a sort of mystic accord seems to have enveloped the

masqueraders. It is indeed "The People's Day," and they intend to keep it that way. Mardi Gras is for everyone.

It costs an estimated $50 million to produce Mardi Gras' 60 street parades and balls, galas, and rendezvous. Four mammoth krewes (up to 1,250 members) spend more than one million dollars on one 24-hour extravaganza. None of the parades or parties is sponsored by the city or

In New Orleans masks have become big business, especially at Mardi Gras. Some people have their faces painted, while others don glorious artistic creations. No matter what the mask, New Orleans allows its citizens and guests to indulge that human desire to sometimes be something different. Photos by Philip Gould

We must eat to survive, but in New Orleans, eating has become a fabulous indulgence. Every conversation in New Orleans sooner or later turns to the city's favorite topics—food and restaurants. Photo by Philip Gould

businesses. The krewe members pay. It is the ultimate in selfless, self-centered entertainment. The people do it because they want to do it, because it is traditional to do it, but mostly because it's fun.

This unique industry involves thousands of specialists—artists and artisans, designers and builders, costumers and mask makers, dressmakers and gownmakers, simulated-crown jewelers, and coin (doubloon) experts (not to mention a legion of caterers and cooks and musicians and tractor drivers, bakers, vintners, etc.). The float-building business is year-round. It employs a professional cadre of expert painters and woodworkers, artists in the field of papier-mache and sculpture, sound and animation engineers, and lighting and crowd control technicians.

Some cynics say that Mardi Gras practically paralyzes local business for a month and temporarily drains the economy, yet the Tourist Commission estimates that it brings in $40 million from tourists during the last five days alone. A city-commissioned survey reveals that the money generated by the event within the metropolitan area approximates $250 million. Mardi Gras 1989 attracted more than 900,000 people to Orleans Parish alone with a total economic impact of $309 million.

The New Orleans Jazz and Heritage Festival, which drew a record 312,000 people in 1989, is 10 days of nonstop music, a genuine New Orleans jambalaya of musical styles and performers. Festivalgoers are treated to everything from funky and ultramodern jazz to rhythm and blues, rock, Cajun classique, zydeco, gospel, vintage blues, ragtime, bluegrass, Latin, country western, and Afro-Caribbean.

This monster musical mash featuring more than 3,000 musicians entertaining over 300,000 spectators has as its principal staging area the huge infield of the mile-around Fairgrounds racetrack. Modern legends such as Tina Turner and Pete Seeger turn out to raise their voices along with an incredible variety of local performers.

The Heritage Fair is jammed daily with people strolling and sampling food and music from five special food tents, 10 large sound stages, and a circus-size gospel tent. In the food tent there is a dazzling variety of cuisine, distinctively Creole or Cajun, Afro-American and Italian, and plain, nourishing soul food. Such exotic dishes as barbecued goat and hot boudin are guaranteed to make your palate resonate.

The festival and fair also include one of the largest crafts fairs in America. Resident Choctaw Indian tribes display pineneedle and cane basketry, and you can see the last great artists at decoy carving and basketmaking. Elders from Cajun country demonstrate the century-old arts of quilting, palmetto weaving, and pirogue carving. Black members of local Mardi Gras Indian tribes show off their breathtaking, handmade costumes, resplendent with more than 100,000 hand-sewn beads. The giant headdresses are masterpieces in themselves with each feather individually plucked, colored, and mounted.

The New Orleans Jazz Festival is not just an event, it is an experience involving all the senses. It has been largely responsible for the rediscovery of New Orleans as the birthplace of jazz.

The 32nd annual Grammy Awards ceremony in February of 1990 offered stunning evidence of the continuing vibrancy of what musicians call the New Orleans Sound. Local performers captured four awards—Aaron Neville, Harry Connick, Jr., Dr. John (Mac Rabenack), and the Neville Brothers. In addition, two Grammy nominations went to six-time winner Wynton Marsalis, and for the first time, two Cajun ensembles, "Beausoleil" and "Cajun Tradition," received nominations in folk music.

Obviously, when it is playtime in The Big Easy there is no room for boredom, no lack of something to do, somewhere to go, something new to hear or see. New Orleans is a city that dearly loves a "party" and clearly knows how to celebrate an "occasion" even if it is obliged to invent one.

As for food, television journalist Linda Ellerbee summed it up in one word. Asked to name her favorite American restaurant, she replied: "New Orleans!"

Umbrellas are used for more than just rain in New Orleans. "Second liners" follow and dance with open umbrellas behind a jazz funeral. For many people the second line umbrella has become a symbol of party time in New Orleans. Open umbrellas not only now appear at some jazz brunches, but at the welcoming of some dignitaries at the airport. Photo by Philip Gould

THE LIVELY
ARTS

A sensuous city, alive with new sounds and sights and sensations . . . resonant with music and redolent with a mixture of tantalizing aromas . . . alive with possibilities and a feeling of adventure. A banquet for all the senses.

Sherwood **A**nderson

Orleanians like to be entertained, and entertainment is an important aspect of life in the Crescent City. In any given week there is a choice of anything from jazz, to little theater, to Broadway musicals, to the symphony—something to please any appetite. Photo by Philip Gould

N EW ORLEANS' FIRST SETTLERS EXCELLED IN THE
joie de vivre or "joy of living," and this spirit of celebration
inspired its unique culture—its performing arts, visual arts,
and literature.

Grand opera was performed regularly in New Orleans when Chicago
was still a frontier outpost and cows grazed in Brooklyn. The first performance, Gretry's *Silvain,* was staged in 1796. The first opera house was
opened in 1806 next door to the first plush gambling casino and one-half
block from the St. Louis Cathedral.

Entrepreneur John Davis used his gambling profits to subsidize
America's first permanent opera company and later sent the troupe touring the Atlantic Coast. Thus, New Orleans not only pioneered grand
opera in America, it also introduced opera to Baltimore, Philadelphia,
Boston, and New York City.

The imposing French Opera House at Bourbon and Toulouse was
completed in 1859, and for more than a half century it was the center of
the Creole universe, constantly aglow with opera, debutante and Carnival balls, ballet, and orchestral concerts.

**Music has become a part
of the street life in the
French Quarter. Bands can
be heard playing traditional jazz, ragtime, rock and
roll, country, and so on for
the enjoyment of passers-
by. Photo by Philip Gould**

When the Opera House was struggling financially, the legendary prodigy, 18-year-old Adelina Patti, was engaged to sing four concerts. She grew enamored with New Orleans and ended up singing 40 performances of eight different operas, assuring grand opera a permanent place among the city's enduring traditions.

When the old French Opera House was gutted by fire in 1919, it symbolized the end of Creole dominance in the French Quarter. The opera tradition, buttressed by tens of thousands of Italian immigrants, managed to survive however. It continues today with a regular season each year under the auspices of the New Orleans Opera House Association.

Distinguished American composer Carlisle Floyd staged the world premiere of his opera, *Markheim,* in New Orleans. It was written specifically for the talents of the great local bass-baritone Norman Treigle.

Such artists as Treigle, Charles Anthony, Audrey Schuh, Rosemary Rotolo, and Arthur Cosenza (now general director of the New Orleans Opera House) began their North American careers on stage in New Orleans. Opera is yet another indication of the city's abiding love of music.

The New Orleans Philharmonic Symphony Orchestra, which staggered, debt-ridden, through the economic recession of the mid-1980s, has experienced a dramatic revitalization. Renewed support from the private sector and the dynamic leadership of Ron Jones (president of Louisiana Coca-Cola) has put the orchestra back on a sound, paying basis. The symphony, which was organized in 1935, is currently under the direction of Maxim Shostakovich, son of the illustrious Soviet composer. In addition to its regular performance seasons (it performs split seasons to accommodate Mardi Gras), it provides the music for all grand opera productions, conducts special school concerts, and tours the southern and eastern United States.

The 1980s also saw the orchestra finally ensconced in its own permanent home, the renovated Orpheum theater, and its 1982 tour of Europe attracted packed houses and enthusiastic reviews.

From earliest times, New Orleans was a city of many voices and many rhythms, alive with both grand opera and street music. The city was populated by a unique legion of street vendors called *marchandes.* They peddled their wares house to house, filling the streets with their peddler's chants, the original singing commercials.

Music in New Orleans was everywhere, an essential part of daily living. "Jass" (as jazz was first spelled) evolved from many sources, including brass bands that paraded for any and all occasions; black churches

The Mardi Gras Indians, blacks dressed in ornate feathered costumes, have become a part of the New Orleans mystique. Whether the costumes are seen on parade on Mardi Gras, or in performance at the Jazz and Heritage Festival, the feathered finery of the Indians has rapidly become one of the most recognizable things that says New Orleans to the world. Photo by Philip Gould

with great gospel choirs; the old Milneburg dance pavilions; Storyville front parlors where Jelly Roll Morton and Sonny Jackson pounded the uprights; African answering chants, first heard in Congo Square; and white plantation music.

The word "jass" is supposedly a corruption of an African word meaning "speed it up." For black and white, jass (or jazz) was, above all, a shared experience reflecting the mood and atmosphere of a racially intermixed city.

Jazz was made for dancing, and how Orleanians loved to dance. As many as 80 public dance halls flourished in the city during the middle 1800s. Even slaves were allowed Sunday afternoons to dance to tribal rhythms in old Congo Square (now Louis Armstrong Park). Visitors came from all over the Western world to observe and write about them.

The New Orleans jazz funeral, where the jazz band accompanies the hearse to the cemetery, "slow-draggin' along," playing dirges, then jazzes up the beat returning, dates back to the grim days of yellow fever, when as many as 250 people were buried in a week. These frequent epidemic burials created an unbearable atmosphere of doom, accompanied by the almost constant clanging of funereal bells across the city. The church fathers, at one point, ordered the bells muffled, even stilled. "To break the unrelieved gloom," one observer noted, "the bands began to strike a gay and lightsome air as they returned from the grave."

There may be more great musicians playing today in New Orleans, some of them unable to read a note, than there are musicians playing any kind of music anywhere else. The list of New Orleans-born musicians who transformed jazz into their own sounds includes such notables as Jelly Roll Morton, Buddy Bolden, King Oliver, Papa Celestin, Nick La Rocca, and present-day virtuosos Pete Fountain, Al Hirt, Fats Domino, Wynton Marsalis, and Allen Toussaint. Of New Orleans and jazz Pete Fountain says, "My roots are here. If I'm away too long—on a tour, for example, I get itchy. I get miserable. I just don't play as well anywhere else."

The city that birthed jazz and cradled it vibrates constantly to its insistent beat. The infectious rhythm has been transposed in the twentieth century into a multiplicity of new sounds: the big "swing" bands of the 1930s and 1940s, the modern jazz of the 1950s, the revolution in rhythm and blues, and rock and roll. All had their roots in New Orleans.

New Orleans' ability to constantly reinvent its rhythms remains the heartbeat of jazz, and, unknown to many, has inspired much popular music. Forty years ago the tiny recording studio of Cosimo Matassa at Rampart and Dumaine started turning out epochal records, creating what became known as rhythm and blues and rock and roll. It was located across from old Congo Square. The first rock and roll record using the term in the title was recorded at Matassa's studio in 1947. It was called "Good Rockin' Tonight," and Roy Brown's pounding, preaching vocal inspired Elvis, Buddy Holly, and the Beatles.

In 1949 Fats Domino broke the sound barrier. His producer/writer/leader Dave Bartholomew calls his first big record, "The Fat Man," the "cornerstone of rock."

THE BEAT GOES ON

Nightclubbing in New Orleans can encompass anything from an informal combo playing funky jazz from a small platform in a smoky neighborhood bar to a slick big band performing on a formal stage in some posh establishment. There's actually not a moment, day or night or morning (in the Quarter), when you're out of range of music, whether it be a lonesome street saxophonist playing a solo on Royal Street, street dancers stomping for quarters near the Square, or the distant moan and growl of off-hours jazz men, jamming it up 'til dawn.

The music is eclectic, and each club has its own special charm. Dixieland traditionalists delight in tapping their feet to the pure funky beat at Preservation Hall, located at 726 St. Peter. After 30 years featuring jazz pioneers like the late George Lewis and Sweet Emma the Bell Girl, this modest, unadorned room is close to being a jazz shrine. Some of the players are in their eighties. This is the place for vintage jazz, songs such as "St. James Infirmary," "Bill Bailey," "Milneburg Joys," and "Basin Street Blues." The audience sits, enraptured, on hard benches and claps time, hearing the music how it originally was meant to be played and still is.

Snug Harbor, at 626 Frenchmen, just a few steps from the French Quarter, is probably the city's foremost modern jazz emporium. It features both local and national performers.

Uptown, Tipitina's, at 501 Napoleon, is a yuppy landmark for devotees of regional blues, R&B, Cajun, and local "root rock" bands.

Orleanians are addicted to live music, and dancing remains a passion. A recent newspaper "entertainment" section listed 190 clubs, bistros, and cafes where live bands and performers can be heard nightly. This includes 25 dance spots.

The Famous Door, at 339 Bourbon Street, is a Dixieland institution. Large signs on the doors read like a roster from the jazz hall of fame, listing those who have played there in the last 50 years.

Storyville Lounge, at 1104 Decatur, is a carousel of entertainments, a huge place with two bars and continuous music that starts early with traditional jazz and Cajun music and finishes late with rhythm and blues and rock and roll.

Lulu White's Mahogany Hall, located at 309 Bourbon, is home for the Dukes of Dixieland, who begin wailing every afternoon at 3:30 p.m. and, with the aid of the Mahogany Hall Stompers, pack in the tourists seven days a week.

It's a mixed bag of blues and reggae at Benny's Bar at 938 Valence, a neighborhood watering spot for Up-towners for as long as most folks can remember. In fact, it is virtually impossible to run out of new, distinctive musical sensations in this town, where, as Jelly Roll Morton put it, "the real music of America was invented."

Two of the classiest nightclubs on almost every visitor's "must-see" list feature the virtuoso talents of Pete Fountain and Chris Owens. Fountain holds forth nightly in his own large room in the Hilton Hotel. It is usually packed, and Fountain's seemingly effortless artistry never disappoints.

Chris Owens is a phenomenon, a gorgeous dancer-entrepreneur who delivers an energetic, sultry song and dance revue twice nightly in her spacious club at 502 Bourbon Street. A small-town Texas gal, she boasts she is the only woman on Bourbon Street who doesn't have to take off her clothes to warm up an audience.

Music critic Rick Coleman states that "there isn't a night you can't hear it—and feel it—in one form or another in the town where music is like air, impossible to live without, breathing in, breathing out."

Ernie K. Doe, a local musical legend, says ingenuously (but with soulful persuasion): "I'm not sure, but I'm almost positive, that all music came from New Orleans."

Music in the streets—that's New Orleans. Jackson Square and Bourbon and Royal streets are alive every day with any variety of tunes. During the annual spring French Quarter Festival there is music on every corner. Photo by Bob Rowan/Progressive Image Photography

Today the reigning queen of New Orleans soul is the incomparable Irma Thomas. Like the Neville Brothers, the current kings, her sound transcends category. The Nevilles have remixed all those many ethnic strains, adding distinctively Afro-Caribbean themes. Aaron Neville's number-one soul classic, "Tell It Like It Is," (1966) is their best-known tune. Second-generation Nevilles include Aaron's son, Ivan, and the talented Charmaine.

New Orleans, the city of Carnival, has never lacked for entertainments or stages on which to mount them. Band concerts, neighborhood playlets, street mimes, and strolling troubadours have kept the town constantly throbbing.

New Orleans is a city of musical sounds, especially in the French Quarter. In the old city a pedestrian can on many corners find a musician plying his talents with his open instrument case nearby, sometimes littered with dollar bills. Photo by Bob Rowan/Progressive Image Photography

Today's permanent venues include the Municipal Auditorium, a multipurpose stage for plays, operas, circuses, ice shows, concerts, and Carnival tableau balls. The Auditorium, opened in 1930, can be partitioned into two theaters. The combined seating capacity is 9,000.

The ultramodern Cultural Center includes the Theater of Performing Arts. Completed in 1973 at a cost of $8 million, it offers 10,000 square feet of stage area and more than 2,300 seats. All the scenery battens are hydraulically operated to accommodate the most lavish Broadway productions.

The Saenger Performing Arts Theater is a $10-million renovation of one of America's most lavish silent movie palaces. It is in constant use for both rock and pop concert attractions, touring Broadway musicals and dramas, and a variety of other live productions.

The University of New Orleans Lakeside Arena can seat 10,000 and is home base for UNO's basketball team. It, too, is convertible and equipped with state-of-the-art sound and lighting. A wide variety of special presentations and concerts fill up its calendar.

Le Petit Theatre du Vieux Carre (The Little Theater) at 616 St. Peter Street in the heart of the French Quarter is of special note. It is the oldest continuing amateur theater company in America. Organized in 1916, it presents an annual subscription season while operating a Children's Theater Workshop.

For centuries the French Quarter has captivated painters, engravers, watercolorists, and photographers. Few urban landscapes offer such snug, time-defying vistas as the Vieux Carre. There is something about the cool courtyard hideaways, the Parisian-style skylights, the lantern-

shaped streetlights, and the crooked banquettes that remind visitors of old Europe. The wall-to-wall intimacy of two-story brick buildings constructed more than a century ago are reminders of the Creole style of living (family shop below, family residence above). Ornate "iron lace" grillwork adorns the many galleries and gateways.

Dozens of painters hang their French Quarter scenes on the wrought-iron fences that surround the venerable Place d'Armes, now Jackson Square. Artists set up their easels on the sidewalk and render instant portraits of passing tourists in crayon or charcoal or peddle romantic watercolors and oils depicting misty bayous and old plantations bathed in moonlight.

During the antebellum period (1820-1860) New Orleans became known as the "Mecca of American artists." Samuel F.B. Morse, inventor of the telegraph, first gained fame as a painter working in New Orleans from 1816 to 1820. George Inman, John Wesley Jarvis, and Jean Joseph Vaudechamp were among the men who found their Muse in the "Paris of the Americas." At that time, French was the first language of the city.

In 1872 French master impressionist Edgar Degas visited relatives in New Orleans and lived on Esplanade. While there, he painted a portrait of his cousin, Estelle Musson, that now hangs in the New Orleans Museum of Art. Another Degas work, "The Cotton Office in New Orleans," is considered one of the most significant paintings ever produced by a foreign artist in America.

The Newcombe Art School, an outgrowth of the women's division of Tulane, developed a unique process of clay molding with a glaze and tints so distinctive that it is recognized today as "Newcombe Pottery," now a collector's item.

Above, top and bottom: The Saenger Theater, which was designed to look like a Roman villa, opened in 1927 and was New Orleans' most ornate movie palace. Almost abandoned, it was converted into a live theater, and now instead of showing Academy Award-winning movies, it shows Tony Award-winning stage productions, as well as other popular live shows. Photos by Bob Rowan/Progressive Image Photography

The absence of jaded attitudes and worldly pressures in New Orleans has helped produce artists of national stature. Among the most celebrated is septagenarian Angela Gregory, still active in her Uptown studio. The first woman to sculpt in heavy metals, she studied under the renowned Parisian master, Bourdelle. Ms. Gregory has left a lasting imprint on the New Orleans cityscape with such monuments as her statue of Bienville (facing the Union Passenger Terminal downtown).

In 1976 Rolland Golden became the first American artist accorded a one-man show inside the Soviet Union. The late Charles Reineke left a legacy of brilliant watercolors, oils, and murals capturing the charm of his city and the unspoiled beauty of the nearby bayous. Ida Kohlmeyer, George Dureaud, and sculptress Lyn Emery are among the numerous active New Orleans artists who have won national recognition.

The collections of the New Orleans Museum of Art include holdings from Western civilization (pre-Christian era to the present), the arts of Africa, the Far East, and pre-Columbian America. Reflecting the city's rich historic and cultural heritage, the museum has formed a comprehensive survey of French art as well.

The Contemporary Arts Center offers a broad-based look at modern, innovative artistic techniques, and, through its theater wing, has introduced a number of new playwrights and plays.

Part of the street activity in the French Quarter is people browsing around the abundance of paintings displayed on the fences around Jackson Square. While few of the works may be considered great art, many have come to adorn the walls of locals and visitors alike. Photo by Bob Rowan/Progressive Image Photography

Tennessee Williams called New Orleans a "magnificent city of ironies and paradoxes." This creative atmosphere has provided and still provides a continuing source of inspiration for musicians, artists, novelists, journalists, and poets.

In his autobiography Tennessee Williams wrote: "In New Orleans I found the kind of freedom I had always needed." His first play, "Vieux Carre," takes place at his first local address, a boardinghouse at 722 Toulouse. For 42 years, long after his masterpiece, "A Streetcar Named Desire," placed him in the first rank of all twentieth-century American playwrights, Williams kept an apartment in the Vieux Carre.

In the 1920s the French Quarter became a little bohemia, a rendezvous for those whose creative energies found there a personality and unhurried pace. One poet called it a "branch office for Paris' Left Bank."

William Faulkner wrote his first novel, *Soldier's Pay,* while living in the Vieux Carre. Sherwood Anderson found inspiration for his ground-breaking work on Negro spirituality, *Dark Laughter.* Truman Capote

Left: New Orleans has one of the most lively and important art communities and markets in the United States. Many of the city's artists, like George Dureau, shown here working in his New Orleans studio, are widely known, and their works are sold far beyond the state lines of Louisiana. Photo by Philip Gould

Below: Art in New Orleans is alive and well and makes the city even more exciting than it already is. Here, artist Rain Webb poses in front of one of his outdoor creations. Photo by Bob Rowan/Progressive Image Photography

STATE OF THE ARTS

There's a fresh wind blowing in culture-rich New Orleans, involving an infusion of new ideas, new capital, and the growing involvement of the private sector in community affairs.

One of the great success stories of the 1980s was the near-impossible recovery of the New Orleans Symphony. For years it was kept alive mainly through the heroic efforts of Adelaide Benjamin, who poured her energy and personal resources into the fiscally moribund operation. After almost 14 months of payroll crises and management problems, the symphony reopened in March 1989 with new management leadership, a sold-out season, and a healthy financial outlook. Many outstanding musicians, members of the orchestra for years, suffered the ordeal, they said, because "when you play in New Orleans, music surrounds you."

Two new local projects underscore the attention the arts are receiving. In March 1989 a $10-million Metropolitan Arts Fund was announced. It pumps at least one million dollars a year into New Orleans arts organizations. The money comes from local businesses, and it is distributed to the New Orleans Symphony, the New Orleans Opera Association, the New Orleans City Ballet, and the Arts Council of New Orleans, among other groups. In the "birthplace of jazz" the University of New Orleans has joined hands with The Chamber/River Region in the development of a New Orleans Music and Entertainment Center. Local officials view it as a kind of "musical incubator." The Center will create a revolving credit loan pool to help finance musical ventures and a resource center to provide educational programs and technical advice. Another example of public-private sector ingenuity, the Center aims at promoting regional music and Louisiana as a site to shoot motion pictures and television programs.

In recent years colorful Louisiana and picturesque New Orleans have become "media darlings." More than 40 films were shot in the state between 1986 and 1990. Among them were *Steel Magnolias*, *The Big Easy*, *Blaze*, *Tightrope*, *Everybody's All-American*, *Angel Heart*, and the television series, *Frank's Place*.

During the same period, 96 television programs and other projects were filmed in New Orleans, including 15 music videos.

The very active Louisiana Film Commission estimates that in 1988 alone, film and video activities in the state had an economic impact of $120 million.

Museums exist in abundance in New Orleans. This is to be expected in a city so rich in history and art. From small historic houses and specialty collections to large, nationally noted institutions, a person will never have a difficult time finding ways to delve into the city's past and arts. Photo by Bob Rowan/Progressive Image Photography

worked on his atmospheric short stories as well as his heralded roman a clef, *Other Voices, Other Rooms,* while living there.

The traffic in new talent was so intense that it inspired one of the great "little magazines" that marked the American literary scene in the 1920s— "The Double Dealer." This publication introduced works by Ernest Hemingway, Erskine Caldwell, John Dos Passos, and John Steinbeck.

Within the last 20 years there has been a conspicuous renaissance of high-quality literature emanating from the New Orleans area or from New Orleans residents. Walker Percy, who resided in nearby Covington, won an international reputation with such locally inspired works as *The Moviegoer* and *The Last Gentleman.* New Orleans-born Ann Rice catapulted to the top of the bestseller list with *Interview with a Vampire* and subsequent novels rooted in the city's fascination for the myster-

Many famous writers and artists have been inspired by what they see and feel in New Orleans. Such inspiration helps to enrich the lives of less-noted New Orleans artists as well. Photo by Bob Rowan/Progressive Image Photography

ies of the occult and the legendary. Shirley Ann Grau's *Keepers of the House* won the author a Pulitzer Prize as did *A Confederacy of Dunces* by John Kennedy Toole. The latter novel deals with the eccentricities of New Orleans life. The city's major historians include the late John Churchill Chase, whose *Frenchmen, Desire, Good Children* is now a classic, and Charles "Pie" Dufour, author of a dozen regional works including *The Night the War Was Lost* and *Ten Flags in the Wind.*

University of New Orleans history professor Steven Ambrose has

emerged as a major biographer with his critically acclaimed two-volume series on Dwight Eisenhower and Richard Nixon.

New Orleans is more street pageant than history preserved. Bravura performers are commonplace, whether striding the grand opera stage or strutting down Canal Street dressed as apes. Everyone, it seems, is a born performer, if only on Mardi Gras. No other city views its arts and architecture, its music, literature, and fun and games in such an intimate way—as life essentials, extensions of the city's persona, not merely separate adornments.

If, as has been said, "Music is the food of gods," then well-nourished New Orleans cries: "play on!"

INTERNATIONAL
ACCOLADES

This area has great health care facilities, a good team of state leadership committed to carrying out a sound international policy. Lastly, the business environment is competitive with advantageous tax incentives readily available.

Didier **D**estremau
French Consul General to Louisiana

New Orleans has become a convention and meeting center of the first rank. Many organizations can boast that the reputation and hospitality of New Orleans have helped make their conventions here the best ever. Photo by Brad Crooks

Tourism is now the most important industry in New Orleans. Towering downtown hotels and riverboat tours are just two signs of this important part of the economic life in New Orleans. Photo by Philip Gould

WEBSTER'S NEW COLLEGIATE DICTIONARY DEFINES the word "international" as "an organized group that transcends national limits." With little or no effort, that description can, quite aptly, be correctly applied to the city of New Orleans, a historical melting pot of cultures and nationalities, a veritable gumbo of guarded values and staunch traditions, and a proving ground for new international ideas and groundbreaking initiatives.

Some of the most ardent admirers of New Orleans and its way of life are the French. Says Didier Destremau, France's Consul General to Louisiana:

To the French, New Orleans and Louisiana have a marvelous sound. Why? Because what France was before is what New Orleans is today. No Frenchman would be indifferent to coming to New Orleans. In fact, most are very eager to come here.

Travel statistics showing that over 100,000 French citizens visited New Orleans during 1989 bear out Destremau's contention. Even then, the British and German citizens showed a surprising resolve for visiting the Crescent City.

Destremau continues:

New Orleans is a very strange city within America—much, much different from other cities in America. Speaking for myself, I don't feel completely in the United States here in New Orleans. Instead, I feel maybe as if I were half in the United States, the other quarter in France and still another in Latin America. It is a very mixed city, still geographically in the United States, but thinking, working, and acting like a city somewhere in the middle of several countries. In a word, it is unique in that respect.

Fellow colleague Fernando Fontoura of Brazil, who is Consul General for Brazil and also serves as Dean of the Consular Corps, agrees with Destremau and adds:

The image of New Orleans abroad is very good! When my family and I moved to the city, we were astonished by the wonderful atmosphere and the marvelous hospitality of the people here.

Noting New Orleans' international reputation for great food, Fontoura takes the distinction one step further saying:

I believe that there are more good restaurants in New Orleans than in New York City. New York may have more sophisticated restaurants but they are much more artificial. Here, in New Orleans, the feeling is very real and that helps alot.

Even Japan's Consul General, Mitsuru Eguchi, notes the quality of life, saying:

The people of New Orleans are open to different experiences and ways of doing things. There never seems to be any hard feelings toward anyone in this city. People always seem to be enjoying themselves and there's no tension.

Eguchi goes even further when describing the similarities between the Japanese and the people of New Orleans by saying:

Japanese people love jazz music and they associate jazz with New Orleans. They also love festivals. Every small town in Japan has at least one festival every year where they celebrate their character and heritage. Here in New Orleans there are long-standing traditions such as the Mardi Gras, St. Patrick's Day celebration and the Jazz and Heritage Festival.

Eguchi also points to a striking similarity between Japanese business etiquette and that of New Orleans businesspeople: Japanese businesspeople always put personal relationships first in any business deal. And, like New Orleans, many business deals are struck at a local dining establishment or bar. Nardo Oliveti, Consul General for Italy, describes himself as "the luckiest man in Italy to have landed the plum assignment to New Orleans." He, too, lists the attributes of the city as:

Having the world language of Jazz, and the Mississippi River, images of Mark Twain and the Civil War. During my tenure here I have found a vision of the happy South, no problems and no conflicts between the races.

Oliveti describes New Orleans as a very European city:

New Orleans is built like many European cities, on a human scale. Where people walk in the streets, meet people, see friends. And, like most southern cities in the world, like Athens, Naples, Rome, there's a

There is no cuisine in America quite like that found in New Orleans. The presentation of food in the Crescent City can range from the elegant to down-to-earth. Photo by Philip Gould

*way of life, an openness, easy-going, an eagerness to make friends that
seems to permeate life in New Orleans.*

Still, while members of the local Consular Corps have solid, positive
views on the city of New Orleans and the state of Louisiana, not enough
of their fellow countrymen were getting the message to visit Louisiana.
In fact, the latest figures on international tourism indicate that out of the
estimated 34 million foreign visitors to the United States, only 487,000
visited New Orleans. And that is precisely why Louisiana Tax Free Shopping (the first of its kind in the country) was instituted by the World
Trade Center (WTC) in 1985. The WTC and its International Business
Committee worked for more than three years in developing the tax-free
shopping concept to the point of approaching the Louisiana Legislature
for consideration. Senator Francis E. Lauricella introduced the bill and
was instrumental in its passage.

On July 8, 1988, Governor Buddy Roemer signed into law Act 535,
authorizing the tax-free program and establishing a five-member
commission to oversee its implementation and operation. Following a
statewide bidding process, The Chamber/New Orleans and the River
Region was selected in May 1989 as the refund agent to operate the tax-
free shopping program throughout the state. The Refund Center at the
New Orleans International Airport opened on November 1, 1989.

With the opening of the Refund Center, Louisiana became the first
state in the United States to implement a program to refund sales tax to
international visitors on purchases made in the state. All revenues, after
operating expenses, are used to promote international tourism in
Louisiana. The goals of the program are simple: to increase Louisiana's
market share of international visitors to the United States; to increase
spending by international visitors; and to encourage the international visitor to see the entire state.

The program is patterned after the highly successful European
Tax Free Shopping program. Retailers in Louisiana become members
of Tax Free Shopping by paying an annual fee of just $100. In return
they receive store identification as a tax-free shopping location, a listing in the Louisiana Tax Free Shopping Directory, a book of vouchers
for use in providing refund checks to international visitors, and training for their sales clerks. Merchants routinely collect sales tax from all
purchases of merchandise made by international visitors. But, after
checking the visitor's passport, the sales clerk then fills out a voucher
form. He gives the form to the visitor for redemption upon leaving
Louisiana.

The program is equally simple for the international visitor. The visitor
who is entitled to a tax refund pays the full sales price, including tax, for
his or her purchase. At the same time, he receives a voucher for the
amount of the sales tax, which may include both state and local tax.
When the visitor leaves Louisiana, he or she again shows a passport
along with his or her international travel ticket to the refund agent to
cash in the vouchers, less a nominal handling fee.

Besides increasing the number of international visitors to New

Orleans and the state of Louisiana, there are added benefits to the program, namely incredible amounts of marketing information. Says Ann Bourne, the first director of the program:

Based upon the information we're gathering, we can determine which nationalities visit Louisiana, where they're most likely to visit, how long they'll stay, how much they're likely to spend and what they like to buy. This will afford us a great opportunity in the future so that we can directly market New Orleans to specific areas of the world in the correct way.

The Tax Free Refund Center is located near Concourse C at the New Orleans International Airport, the primary artery for incoming and outgoing international visitors. In addition to working directly with The Chamber in order to construct the tax-free shopping facility, the airport has begun an intensive capital facilities program.

The New Orleans International Airport is a vital element in the New Orleans metropolitan area economy and is clearly the gateway to the New Orleans tourist industry. Airport activities directly generate 5,317 jobs and $205 million in revenue annually, according to a recent economic impact study conducted by the University of New Orleans. Indirectly the airport generates an additional 4,000 jobs and $240 million in secondary spending. In addition, it provides the primary source of transportation for 1.6 million tourists annually.

Currently New Orleans International Airport capital improvements are funded through a combination of federal funds, lease rates, and fees paid by airport tenants and users of the airport such as the airlines. In addition, the recently approved Transportation Trust Fund gives the airport some $100 million in improvement monies. All totaled, the infrastructure improvements will move the New Orleans International Airport into the forefront of state-of-the-art airports in the country.

Following a U.S. Department of Transportation's (DOT) decision to make it easier for international carriers to enter under-served domestic markets, New Orleans Aviation Board and Convention Center officials began a concerted pitch to attract international flights to the Crescent City. The major advantage of this ruling is that it allows new international service without lengthy and complex bilateral negotiations. Officials with the DOT predict that the new rules will improve international service and will help cities realize the economic benefits of improved air transportation.

Increased international direct flights are important to the city because of its convention center business. Major conventions such as the American Heart Association and the American Newspaper Publishers Association routinely attract 10 to 20 percent of their attendance from the international marketplace. The available figures do not include spouses or other unregistered guests.

As New Orleans' share of the convention business grows, officials are beginning to work with the airport, recognizing that boosting business at the New Orleans Convention Center depends in large part on the city's ability to fly thousands of delegates in and out of the airport in one day. At the same time, increasing service to the airport depends in large part on demand generated by conventions.

In sheer numbers, Louisiana enjoys relative success in attracting foreign investment. Currently, Louisiana ranks fifth among states in terms of foreign investment. Only Texas, California, New York, and Alaska have greater investments. There are more than 500 foreign corporate locations in Louisiana representing over one billion dollars worth of investment. This figure represents the gross book value of property, plants, and equipment held in the United States by U.S. affiliates of foreign countries and fixed assets of the companies valued at historical cost, before depreciation.

Arnold Lincove, Louisiana's Secretary of Economic Development, says:

Since 1989, we've seen a dramatic increase in international interest in our state. Our reverse investment and trade development offices have been strengthened. Our international office has increased its staff from three to 14 professionals, with a budget increase from $500,000 to $1.5 million. We've opened new offices in Taipei and Tokyo. We're also planning a major presence in Europe. We've increased the number of trade missions abroad, in particular to the Far East, Europe and Central America.

Lincove warns that successful international trade missions don't bring results overnight, but he emphasizes that there is a noticeable difference in the way Louisiana delegations are received around the world. Lincove concludes: "Louisiana is being recognized as a state that welcomes business. Investors understand that we have a pro-business attitude now and that awareness is beginning to pay big dividends."

Again, Nardo Oleveti of the Italian Consulate says:

Antiques and high fashion can be found in New Orleans. The city abounds with shops of all kinds catering to the whims and pocket books of every shopper. Photo by Bob Rowan/Progressive Image Photography

A joint venture is much like a marriage in that both arrangements are deeply personal commitments. Both parties should know each other and what they want in great detail. A Consul General can help sponsor trade missions but it all depends on the willingness and readiness of the parties and the surrounding fiscal environment as to whether or not the relationship will last.

Consul General Didier Destremau of France thinks that the assets of Louisiana and, specifically, New Orleans cannot be dismissed easily. Says Destremau:

There are so many advantages such as the low cost of labor, the competitiveness of real estate. The infrastructure is sound with great mass transit capabilities, the Mississippi River and good roads and bridges. In addition, this area has great health care facilities, a good support network of universities, a good team of state leadership committed to carrying out a sound international policy. Lastly, the business environment is competitive with advantageous tax incentives readily available.

Ships from all over the world regularly visit the Port of New Orleans. This adds not only to the city's enviable trade record, but further enhances its already exotic character. Photo by Brad Crooks

Besides joint ventures, Louisiana is working hard to implement the financing and facilitating of import and export of goods and services. During the late 1980s Louisiana produced more than $6 billion in sales of export-related manufactures annually. Many top users of ports alongside the Mississippi River have publicly stated that they would increase operations if greater international financing was made available. To that end, the business community, in tandem with local and state officials, is working to put the finishing touches on an international trade finance program through the Louisiana Imports and Exports Trust Authority (LIETA). What follows is a brief description of how the LIETA loan program will be designed utilizing federal government programs in conjunction with a LIETA loan pool.

In recognition of the importance of small- and medium-sized firms in job creation and in response to the criticism of the inadequacies of existing federal programs, federal program managers have made special efforts to meet the export financing needs of small and medium firms. For example the Eximbank's City/State Program is designed specifically to improve the bank's level of support to small and medium-sized exporters. The program utilizes state and city export finance agencies to recruit qualified applicants and assist them with the application process.

The U.S. Small Business Administration (SBA) operates a loan-guarantee program called the Export Revolving Line of Credit. Through a co-guarantee program with Eximbank, the SBA can guarantee up to 85 percent on loans to one million dollars.

An effective LIETA program will leverage these initiatives into tangible economic benefits for Louisiana firms and workers.

Eximbank is a federally funded bank that provides financial services to facilitate U.S. exports. Programs include direct loans for periods of one year or more, loan guarantees, and export credit insurance through its agent, FCIA.

The Eximbank Working Capital Guarantee is designed to provide eligible exporters with improved access to working capital loans from commercial lenders. Under the proposed LIETA structure, the authority could use this facility for guarantees in excess of its own limits or as the primary guarantee facility. Eximbank would issue preliminary commitments that an exporter can then "shop" with commercial lenders.

In addition to using existing federal programs, officials are urging that LIETA set up its own loan-guarantee program. The loan-guarantee program developed by LIETA will, indeed, be a separate program under which LIETA guaranteed loans will facilitate export or import transactions that do not fit the criteria of "partner" federal programs. This type of loan guarantee program is the heart of some very successful trade finance programs in the United States.

Another incentive, outside the financing aspects, is the availability of foreign trade zone status throughout the River Region. New Orleans Foreign Trade Zone No. 2 is the second oldest in the United States. Foreign goods may be brought into the zone without formal customs entry and the payment of duty and taxes until and unless they leave the zone for a U.S. destination. No duties are paid on merchandise exported from the zone. While in the zone, the goods may be consolidated, processed, reassembled, repackaged, comingled with domestic goods, used in manufacturing, repaired, or simply stored until such time as they are needed. The number of foreign trade services available in New Orleans is substantial, ranging from barge lines to testing laboratories to dry and cold storage facilities.

New Orleans is "America's International City" and that's because New Orleans is a city where the world comes together—geographically, culturally, and socially. New Orleans transcends its national limitations and rises above a host of other American cities because of its contrasts and unique international appeal. New Orleans stands apart as an international destination, whether for tourism or trade. Long known as the "Gateway to America," New Orleans once again strives to regain that moniker. For nearly 300 years New Orleans has anchored the South with an indisputable link to the Old World and its ways and customs. Layers of formal tradition give a romantic allure to a city preparing for its fourth century with a will forged from confidence and experience.

New Orleans truly is "America's International City."

AN ECONOMY
REBORN

No problem is too tough for us. Historically, we have sought and found better ways to get tough jobs done. And one better.

Mayor Sidney Barthelemy

Economies must change in order to successfully compete and survive. One of Louisiana's oldest industries, and a real success story, is the sugar industry. Photo by Philip Gould

FOR THOSE FAMILIAR WITH THE NEW ORLEANS ECONOMY, the changes and retooling have been nothing short of cataclysmic. Fundamental changes have taken root and are now beginning to show promise. The residents, businesspeople, and politicians of New Orleans have learned well the lessons of recession and economic decline brought on by an overdependence on the area's natural resources.

Today utilizing the oil and gas industry as a major piece of its economic recovery plan, New Orleans and the River Region seem poised on the precipice of a promising future.

Old ways of doing business die hard in a city steeped in tradition. But new, innovative management techniques and dynamic leadership from the statehouse to local government have pushed New Orleans into a new twenty-first century reality fiercely protecting its vaunted, valued past while preparing for the increasingly competitive world economy that is fast approaching at breakneck speed.

As world markets continue to develop and discriminating developers closely examine potential areas for expansion or relocation, the assets of low taxation, sound infrastructure, solid educational opportunities, an available, trainable work force, proper geographic location, and state-of-the-art transportation networks become necessary ingredients in the scramble for economic diversification and progress.

The citizens of New Orleans and the River Region have recognized these trends and have taken on the task of rebuilding a robust, healthy economy based on a variety of businesses and business interaction. A regional approach to problems has greatly helped this process. Coordination and cooperation have been described as an unnatural act committed by unwilling adults, but in New Orleans and the River Region, coordination and cooperation are the bywords of success. The City of New Orleans serves as the hub of business activity and the base of a burgeoning tourist industry, while the surrounding suburbs, themselves alive with development and planning activity, serve as an umbrella of varied business locations and housing opportunities.

Earlier this year, Mayor Sidney Barthelemy was reelected by the voters of New Orleans to another four-year term. In addition to sending a signal to the rest of the world that business and government were united in the city, it also reaffirmed the notion concerning New Orleans' strengths. Barthelemy ran a campaign based on the accomplishments of his administration during

Below and facing page: Still among the greatest sugar-producing areas in the world, Louisiana's sugar processing is an example of changing with the times to stay alive and viable. The American Sugar Refinery in suburban Arabi, for example, is still one of the largest sugar plants in the world, and puts sugar on the tables of many Americans. Photos by Philip Gould

tough economic times. During the campaign he lifted the spirits of the community by identifying a vast array of historical accomplishments, stating, "No problem is too tough for us. Historically, we have sought and found better ways to get tough jobs done. And done better."

In the area of oil and gas, Barthelemy pointed to the offshore industry, calling attention to the fact that the sophisticated technology driving this multinational, multibillion-dollar industry was born and perfected in New Orleans. He referenced the design and manufacture of the marvel called LOOP, the world's only offshore oil port, and the LASH vessel, a whale of a ship that carries barges in its belly. Other accomplishments included the first skyscrapers built on pylons, the world's longest bridge, and the discovery of the process for granulating sugar.

During his victory speech, Barthelemy proclaimed:

We are standing on the threshold of greatness. We have the potential of making New Orleans the greatest city, not in the State of Louisiana, not in the South, but the greatest city in the world.

Louisiana has experienced an economic turnaround. Staggered by double digit unemployment resulting from the downturn in the petrochemical industry during the 1980s, the area's work force has stablized considerably and job opportunities in nearly every sector are predicted over the next business cycle. A major contributing factor in this resurgence can be attributed to the residents of Louisiana voting for the so-called Highway Trust Fund, which dedicates a portion of the gasoline tax to infrastructure improvements to roads, bridges, the ports along the Mississippi River and New Orleans International Airport. The multibillion-dollar package was enacted at the beginning of the 1990s and is expected to benefit the people of Louisiana for generations to come.

One of the areas especially helped by the implementation of the Highway Trust Fund was the Port of New Orleans. Because of the additional revenues available to the port through the state, a modernized,

The vast trade carried by the Mississippi River in South Louisiana goes far beyond the limits of New Orleans. All of the ports and industries between the Crescent City and Baton Rouge form one great network that has built southeast Louisiana's economy. Photo by Philip Gould

computerized water transportation network has been established, thus providing a more attractive and highly competitive port of entry or exit in relation to other Gulf ports.

When Louisiana voters overwhelmingly passed the Highway Trust Fund they did so with the confidence that the port would receive $100 million of the earmarked funds. Additionally, the port's board of commissioners pledged another $87 million for improvements along both the Mississippi River and the Industrial Canal. The capital improvements program has since been renovating and expanding the upriver wharves into three distinct terminals: the Napolean-Nashville Multi-Purpose Complex, the Louisiana Avenue Multi-Purpose Terminal, and the Harmony-First Street No-Bulk Center. The multipurpose facilities are now handling general cargo, including heavy equipment and cargo that moves in railcar-type containers.

As planned in the late 1980s, the neo-bulk terminal is now a dedicated steel-handling facility. The need for such a terminal became clear in recent years as the Port of New Orleans became the largest steel-importing port in the United States. Imported steel now represents 70 percent of all breakbulk cargo handled in the area.

Just upriver from the Port of New Orleans is the Port of South Louisiana, which is the top port in the United States in terms of total tonnage, imports and exports and combined. The Port of South Louisiana serves the parishes of St. Charles, St. James, and St. John the Baptist. A total of more than $1.5 billion is now being invested in the area by such heavyweight companies as: Chevron, Shell Oil, Union Carbide, Colonial Sugars, and many, many others. The biggest export commodity in terms of tonnage coming out of the Port of South Louisiana remains unmilled corn, with nearly 8 million short tons of the grain being exported annually. This amount represents nearly 78 percent of the commodity exported from Louisiana and over 50 percent of the total shipped from the United States. The biggest import commodity continues to be crude petroleum. Crude oil imported through the Port of South Louisiana accounts for almost 30 percent of that imported into Louisiana. Other major import commodities are aluminum ore, fertilizers, minerals, and other petroleum products.

In short, the ports of New Orleans, South Louisiana, and the entire state of Louisiana are showing substantial improvements over recent years according to a survey released by the Port of South Louisiana. The survey shows a strong turnaround in Louisiana's industrial growth due to worldwide economic conditions and the efforts of state and local economic development officials.

The oil and natural gas industry remains a major piece of the local economy. Although extensive inland reserves exist, the region's principal resources of oil and natural gas are found offshore in the Gulf of Mexico. New Orleans functions as the hub for the exploration and production of these vast resources. Louisiana's offshore industry leads the world in wells drilled, number of producing oil and gas wells, and prospects for future production. Seventy-five percent of the total U.S. offshore production of crude oil and 78 percent of the total U.S. production of offshore natural gas comes from Louisiana waters. The Central Gulf region off the Louisiana coast is rated by both the oil industry and the U.S. Geological Survey as having the highest resource potential of all outer continental shelf areas.

In the New Orleans area, oil exploration and production has stabilized considerably and prices have risen to a level commensurate with profit and risk taking. While it looks as if the natural gas market, almost single-handedly cornered by Louisiana, will be one of the hottest areas of venture during the coming decade, the number of rigs working in the Gulf is up some 15 percent from the 1980s. A work force numbering in the tens of thousands and acknowledged by industry experts as a veritable vanguard of innovation in oil field technology remains intact for the challenges that lie ahead.

An explosion of activity is predicted for the area's third largest economic sector, tourism. Since the Louisiana World Exposition was held in New Orleans in 1984, demonstrating the true potential for this sleeping mecca for tourist and conventioneers alike, the awareness of tourism has grown exponentially. Currently, New Orleans enjoys a tourism rate of approximately 7 million visitors annually. Over the next few years that figure is expected to increase dramatically. Aided by developments such as the New Orleans Convention Center, the Aquarium of the Americas, and the multi-uses of the Louisiana Superdome, the hotel/motel infrastructure has grown to more than 25,000 first-class rooms in the metro area with high occupancy rates year-round. Another boom in the construction of hotels is expected during the 1990s. Hotel/motel employment remains as the largest in any sector of the economy.

Special events such as the NFL Super Bowl, the NCAA Final Four, Mardi Gras, and the Republican National Convention have pushed New Orleans to the forefront of worldwide recognition and acceptance as a city ideal for the mega-challenge. Logistics, traffic flow, ambience, and the human scale on which the city is built all contribute to a flavor and feel that is distinctly New Orleans. In addition, the New Orleans Convention Center, which is currently upgrading to some 700,000 square feet, will soon add phase three, making it the largest convention center on one level in North America. Since opening in 1985, the convention center has proved to be an economic bonanza for the community, contributing $2.5 billion in terms of economic impact, not to mention the nearly one million delegates who have utilized the facility.

A surge of new building construction during the early 1980s has resulted in more than 23 million square feet of office space conveniently located in the Central Business District, with highly competitive rates compared to other cities. Major manufacturing facilities such as Martin Marietta's Manned Space Flight Center in eastern New Orleans, which fabricates the external tank for the space shuttle, and Avondale Shipyards on the West Bank of the metro area, have shown considerable gains in obtaining additional government contracts and increasing employment.

To serve the financial needs of this growing commerce and industry, New Orleans has a well-established banking community. The larger banks have international departments experienced in the complex financial transactions involved in international trade, while numerous savings and loan institutions (which emerged relatively unscathed from the problems affecting the national S & L scene) provide the capital for home construction.

New Orleans was recently cited as a leader in the health-care industry. In fact, health services has been one of the area's strongest and most consistently growing sectors over the past 10 years. Currently the area is served by more than 34 hospitals with approximately 10,000 beds. Bolstered by such health-care heavyweights as Tulane Medical Center, Ochsner, Southern Baptist Hospital, and LSU Medical, each of which has achieved national and international recognition, the New Orleans market is well served by both research and development in the medical community as well as hands-on physician care.

New Orleans and the River Region provide a public system of

elementary and secondary schools and a well-developed system of private and parochial schools. Curriculum and instructional methods are designed to accommodate various achievement levels in order to maximize opportunities for students to realize their learning potential.

Programs are also specialized for students preparing for entrance to college or university programs as well as students advancing to the vocational-technical schools or the arts. Competitive examinations are used as the basis for selective placements of students in a variety of advanced or specialized instructional programs. Higher education is provided by four public and five private colleges and universities. In addition, there are two major medical schools located in the downtown Central Business District of New Orleans. Programs of instruction are also offered by two public community junior colleges and eight vocational-technical schools in the region. These schools provide training in many vocational skill areas including electronics, computers, and other high-tech subjects.

As New Orleans continues to diversify its economy, it finds itself turning its unique heritage into a thriving, growing, national business. The music that made New Orleans famous is now making the city legendary. The hottest and coolest jazz musicians in the world, including Harry Connick, Jr., Wynton Marsalis, Dr. John, and Aaron Neville, born and bred New Orleanians, are now attracting major recording studios and fellow artists to the city. Film crews have become an everyday presence on the streets of New Orleans with feature film production up 500 percent from five years ago. The film industry, seeking relief from astronomical budgets and extraordinary delays in New York and Los Angeles, now knows that in New Orleans it can get more of a film for less money in less time. Recent Hollywood productions have raved about the range of architectural locations that spans centuries and about the climate that translates into more back-to-back shooting days.

Creole and Cajun food, once regional delights, have become a national and international addiction, spawning offshoot industries ranging from fast-food franchises to seafood exports and the manufacture of special spices for nouveau New Orleanians.

Because of its prime geographic location served by the Mississippi River, New Orleans and the surrounding region is being designated as a center for distribution centers. The recently opened Pic-N-Save distribution center in eastern New Orleans is a prime example of this new activity. With a permanent employment of nearly 400 new jobs operating in a massive facility of some one million square feet, additional distribution facilities will be the focus of future forays into the economic development marketplace.

Adjacent to Pic-N-Save is the recently constructed Rhino Modular Structures, Inc., which manufactures plastic containers and employs some 150 permanent employees. All of this activity is concentrated in an area of eastern New Orleans known as the Almonaster-Industrial District (A-MID). A-MID is an economic development zone served by a board of commissioners responsible for providing economic incentives and marketing necessary to attract and serve its clientele. In addition, A-MID offers reasonably priced industrial property, an extensive transportation

Above, and far left: In 1988, New Orleans hosted the Republican National Convention, which provided the city with incalculable international publicity. It is likely that New Orleans will always be considered as one of the front-runners every four years for one, or both, of the lucrative national political conventions. This is an excellent example of how New Orleans' "Big Easy" reputation can be turned into real profits. Photos by Philip Gould

infrastructure, and plentiful energy resources. Located only minutes from the French Quarter, A-MID is a 7,000-acre Louisiana Enterprise Zone composed of private and publicly owned tracts of land ranging from one to 1,000 acres. A-MID also encompasses a 92-acre Foreign Trade Zone that provides additional savings on duty fees. A-MID is zoned for heavy and light industrial use with a federally approved environmental impact statement.

Economic conditions in the river parishes of St. John, St. James, and St. Charles have improved over recent years. The construction of the Aristech Chemical Corp's phenol/cumene plant, which began production this year, has created nearly 200 permanent jobs. Additionally, the phased construction of the Formosa Plastics Corp.'s new manufacturing complex has created more than 7,500 construction jobs and 2,000 permanent jobs to the area. The expansion and possible "satellite plant" developments planned for several existing petrochemical industries in the region could greatly augment not only construction jobs but also create an expansion phase for this sector's permanent job base into the next century.

The Energy Center in downtown New Orleans is typical of the new look in the area. A proliferation of skyscrapers and shopping centers in the Central Business District has altered many traditional patterns, but has also provided an exciting new aspect to the life of Orleanians. Photo by Brad Crooks

New Orleans and Louisiana have taken aggressive steps to attract new business to all sectors of the economy. A variety of tax incentives is available to enhance investment and job creation. The city works closely with the state and the local business community in designing vocational, technical, and job training programs. Furthermore, Louisiana is a "right-to-work" state, where workers are free to join labor unions but cannot be forced to do so as a condition of employment.

An important factor in strengthening an area's viability as a desirable location for business is the development of an available, trainable work force. The labor pool in the New Orleans region is 603,600 strong, of which 59 percent is male and 41 percent is female. The general composition of the work force by occupation and skill groups includes a majority of professional/technical/management-related workers as well as skilled and semi-skilled craftsmen.

The New Orleans unemployment rate has dropped significantly over the past few years and currently hovers near the national average. A new source of labor, some 51,000 students are enrolled in area universities with another 14,000 enrolled in the regional vocational-technical schools.

Over the past few years New Orleans has worked very hard to develop an expanded inventory of business incentives in order to attract business from outside the state and encourage expansion from local businesses. Among the more attractive incentives include programs involving tax reduction and exemption, bonds and financing programs, and government-sponsored programs.

Under the tax reduction/exemption heading probably the most successful incentive has been the development of several enterprise zones throughout the region. These enterprise zones offer firms locating and/or expanding in these areas two distinct tax incentives: a sales tax exemption on the purchase of machinery, tools, and equipment as well as materials used in construction and a $2,500 tax credit per new employee. Additionally, there is no property tax in Louisiana, though a local property tax is levied at a uniform assessment ratio established by the Louisiana State Constitution. However, the Louisiana Board of Commerce and Industry is authorized to grant 10-year tax exemptions to new and expanding manufacturers covering building, machinery, tools, and equipment. Further, instead of accepting the 10-year property tax exemption, employers can opt for a one-time credit of $100 for each new job created against any tax liability otherwise due the state. An additional incentive provides that all goods and commodities in public or private storage in Louisiana are exempt from property taxes while moving in interstate commerce through the state to a final destination outside the state.

Under bonds and financing programs, 100 percent financing may be provided by industrial revenue bonds with no referendum required with the approval of the State Bond Commission and the Secretary of Commerce and Industry. Qualified projects usually include manufacturing facilities, site and site improvements, buildings, machinery, and tools. Enhanced by the combined resources of the area banks through interstate and branch banking, which was enacted by the Louisiana Legislature in 1983, New Orleans financial institutions are now providing ample resources and money for new and expanding industries.

Governmental support is provided by industrial training programs. These programs include all phases of training to start-up operations as well as existing plant expansion. Depending on company needs, funds are made available to conduct labor availability surveys, to recruit and screen potential employees, implement preemployment training programs, and provide on-the-job training. More than 250 companies have utilized this particular program over the past four to five years, which demonstrates the flexibility and ease of the program's implementation.

No discussion about an area's business climate would be complete without attention being paid to the tax system. The corporate income tax is levied upon the net income of domestic and foreign corporations derived from Louisiana sources at a rate of 4 percent of the first $25,000 of net income and rising to 8 percent of net income in excess of $200,000. Unlike most states that have a state corporate income tax, Louisiana law permits the deduction of federal income tax prior to the calculation of the state tax, which actually reduces the Louisiana tax rate by approximately one-third. The corporate franchise tax is levied annually at the rate of $1.50 per $1,000 of the first $300,000 and $3 per $1,000 for the remainder of the capital employed in Louisiana. The minimum tax is $10 per year. Individual income tax is levied at the rate of 2 percent on the first $10,000 of taxable income, 4 percent of the next $40,000, and 6 percent in excess of $50,000. As mentioned earlier, federal income tax payments are deductible. Property is assessed on a uniform basis at the following percentage of fair market value: land—10 percent and building, machinery, tools, equipment, and inventories—15 percent. The River Region's tax rates range from $3.90 to $13.23 per $100 of assessed value. A controversial subject in the Louisiana tax code involves the homestead exemption, whereby a principal residence automatically receives an exemption on the first $75,000 of market value. Finally, the Louisiana state sales and use tax is 4 percent and local sales taxes in the New Orleans metropolitan area range from a low of 3 percent to a high of 5 percent.

An area that has greatly benefited from its recently forged public/private partnership can be found in the parish adjacent to Orleans-Jefferson Parish. In 1988 parish officials created the Jefferson Parish Economic Development Commission (JEDCO). JEDCO represents the embodiment of the partnership that has developed between the parish government and the business sector of the parish with both parties recognizing that they would each be much more powerful and effective by working together than working at cross-purposes. JEDCO is funded through a dedication of a portion of the occupational license tax, which was expanded to include professionals such as attorneys, physicians, and architects.

From its inception, JEDCO has consistently proposed and implemented an array of innovative projects including the federal government bid center, a small business incubator, and a local enterprise zone program that promotes business development through tax and hiring incentives.

New Orleans offers a wide range of housing styles and living environments to suit any personal preference. Costs are relatively low in comparison to other metropolitan areas of the United States. The average cost for the purchase of a single family home is between $42-48 per square foot of living area (including the land). The average cost for monthly rental units is between 34 and 46 cents per square feet.

International executives looking to New Orleans for business opportunities invariably ask about the quality of life. Few cities can match the excitement and variety of amenities offered by New Orleans. With its temperate climate and rich culture, New Orleans and its surrounding region offers year-round entertainment and recreational opportunities.

Louisiana is known as the sportsman's paradise because of its abundant lakes and rivers. Not only is Southeast Louisiana a thriving commercial fishery, but it is a very popular recreational fishing and hunting area as well. The fertile coastal zone creates a proliferation of fish, waterfowl, and other wild animals. The waterways are also popular with boating enthusiasts for sailing, motorboating, and waterskiing.

The New Orleans region offers parks for other outdoor sports including tennis, golf, softball, biking, skating, and archery.

Probably the most unique aspect of the River Region's offerings is its rich history, with one of the largest collections of historic buildings of any U.S. city. In addition to its historic infrastructure, and given the previous French and Spanish stewardship of the city, New Orleans takes on a decidedly international flavor, making it one of the most cosmopolitan areas in the country. Some of the fruits of this rich cultural tradition are several remarkable cuisines, including Cajun and Creole, and several innovative music forms, the best known of which is jazz.

New Orleans offers year-round cultural activities including an opera company, symphony, a ballet company, touring Broadway shows, and numerous professional and amateur theater groups. There are numerous historical museums and art galleries as well as the New Orleans Museum of Art.

The New Orleans River Region offers residents shopping facilities comparable with the largest U.S. cities, with stores ranging from big names such as Saks Fifth Avenue, Macy's, Lord and Taylor, to numerous specialty stores like Banana Republic and Gucci. Seven new malls have been built in the region over the last decade, the newest of which is the New Orleans Centre, which opened in 1988.

Throughout its long and colorful history, New Orleans has gained an enviable reputation for its Southern hospitality and service. New Orleanians are proud of their city and insist that every visitor immediately feel like they're a part of the community. With so many nationalities and ethnic groups represented for so long in this truly international city, New Orleans welcomes the opportunity to prove itself in every aspect of social, economic, and political life in the United States.

A rare combination of environmental elements makes New Orleans an unusually easy and comfortable place to do business. When it comes to urban dynamics, New Orleans is the exception to the norm in every way. New Orleans has a thriving Downtown teeming with life and offering an extraordinarily eclectic variety of consumer and business goods and services. The service industry, in fact, is one that the Massachusetts Institute of Technology has described as New Orleans' special forte. Even getting to work is easy with expanding freeway systems, modern spans across the Mississippi River, and a state-of-the-art public transportation system citywide. The business districts are relatively concentrated, making shorter travel times during the work day. And even the pace of New Orleans is less stressful, which means healthier, longer, and more profitable business lives.

New Orleans is a city on the move, and the members of its business community, civic groups, and government organizations are poised to meet the challenges of tomorrow.

HOST TO THE
FUTURE

The positive thinking of our business and civic leadership is looking to the future . . . In fact, as our ever-growing tourist industry attracts business and new residents, New Orleans in the '90s may well become 'America's Host to the Future.'

Mayor Sidney Barthelemy

A battalion of modern skyscrapers now rise from what was once a swamp. Photo by Bob Rowan/Progressive Image Photography

AS THE 1980S GAVE WAY TO THE FINAL DECADE OF A century of sometimes turbulent growth, New Orleans was poised and ready, it seemed, to play a major role in America's future.

In December 1989 three banner headline stories made news all across the nation, harbingers of things to come: "Billion Dollar Rig Planned for the Gulf" ; "Tulane: AIDS Vaccine a Major Step Closer" ; and "Expansive Riverfront Development Plan Unveiled."

First New Orleans-based Shell Offshore Inc. revealed it will set a world record in the Gulf of Mexico by installing a $1.1-billion platform in almost 3,000 feet of water. Analysts were quick to proclaim "a new wave of optimism in offshore drilling." Cliff Haigler (an analyst for the locally based brokerage house of Howard, Weil, Labouisse & Friederichs) called it a "milestone for the offshore industry . . . and a sign of things to come." Economist Timothy Ryan foresaw a "shot in the arm for a lot of other companies in fabrication and marine construction."

One day later, on December 8, 1989, Tulane University researchers revealed the development of a potential AIDS vaccine that one national authority called "the most heartening event yet in the worldwide search."

The vaccine's success in protecting eight monkeys at the university's famed Delta Primate Center excited the world medical community. "It offers unambiguous proof that an effective vaccine for an AIDS virus is possible," said Dr. Michael Murphy-Cobb, the leader of Tulane's research team.

Dr. Wayne Koff, chief of AIDS vaccine research at the National Institutes of Health stated:

This is a giant leap . . . The most significant advance in the vaccine field since the program started . . . The development has dispelled any doubts about our ever being able to create a vaccine against HIV.

Yet to come was another announcement, this one of particular significance to New Orleans itself. City and state officials unveiled plans for a $268-million development—Riverfront 2000. They include a second expansion of the Woldenberg Riverfront Park and the Aquarium of the Americas and a complex of family-oriented museums, including a $40-million natural history museum, a $10-million species survival park, and a $10-million plant conservatory.

Economist Timothy Ryan estimates the plan's various projects will create 18,000 to 23,000 jobs, generate up to $950 million, and help entice from 900,000 to 1.4 million new visitors. But not all the good things

Facing page: Old and new have been successfully combined in New Orleans. The 1890s Jackson Brewery in the French Quarter is now a thriving shopping center, and old time streetcars follow the city's newest transportation route. Photo by Philip Gould

Above: The Moonwalk, along the French Quarter riverfront, was once a no-man's-land of wharves and warehouses. The Moonwalk, which dates to the 1970s, was among the first projects to open up the river to people. Photo by Bob Rowan/Progressive Image Photography

about New Orleans await the future. New Orleans always has been a city of enterprise and civic rejuvenation.

With the opening of the Superdome in August 1975, the Poydras Street Corridor, once a smorgasbord of rundown buildings, barrooms, and luncheonettes, was transformed into a major commercial artery. Within five years eight new high-rise office buildings were completed or under construction, averaging 27 stories in height with a total investment of $193 million.

The Hilton Riverfront anchored the river end and the Superdome stood at the opposite end. Midway between them the tallest building in New Orleans, Number One Shell Square, nudged the city's skyline ever higher. Since 1970 a battalion of modern skyscrapers has emerged from the swamp, an engineering impossibility 30 years ago.

Soon Poydras was a modern canyon of commerce, impelled by the growth of offshore oil. Amoco, Louisiana Land and Exploration (LL & E), and Freeport-McMoran each constructed distinctively different tall towers. The Lykes Center, a 22-story building, became headquarters for the Lykes Brothers Steamship Company.

The Energy Building commands the intersection of Loyola and Poydras kitty-corner to the city hall and council chambers. New Orleans City Hall, an $8-million, 11-story building, is part of one of the most modern civic centers in the United States. The complex includes an eight-story, $4-million state office building, a three-story, $2-million state supreme court building, a four-story, $2.5-million civil courts building, and a four-

Nothing is as evocative of New Orleans as the sound of jazz being played along the banks of the Mississippi River. Jazz and the mighty river go together comfortably, but they are only parts of the gumbo that makes up the charm of the grand old Southern city. Photo by Bob Rowan/Progressive Image Photography

story, $2.5-million main public library. This complex covers an area of 11 acres in the Central Business District.

The ultramodern Hyatt-Regency Hotel with its huge atrium lobby and Poydras Plaza shopping mall is connected to the Superdome by a 60-foot-wide elevated concourse. Between the Dome and the Hyatt, the de Bartolo Company has opened another shopping mall—New Orleans Centre.

At the river end of Poydras, the Rouse Company approaches its fifth anniversary with the half-mile-long Riverwalk, billed as a "festival marketplace" with more than 140 shops and restaurants overlooking the Mississippi. The Riverwalk has a stage in Spanish Plaza, directly behind the World Trade Center, where you can listen to native musicians playing jazz. And all along the downtown riverfront are docked paddle wheelers. One of them, the *Natchez*, features a giant calliope that can be heard five miles away on a good day. These boats offer a variety of delightful cruises.

Downstream the Aquarium of the Americas and the 10-acre Woldenberg Park overlook the Mississippi. Upstream the New Orleans Convention and Tourist Center has nearly doubled its capacity to rank among the largest, most versatile facilities of its kind. The Warehouse District, running uptown behind the converted wharf frontage, has seen dozens of historic buildings, long vacant and obsolete, converted into office buildings and apartments. Lester Kabacoff, who sparked the revitalization of the current riverfront in the mid-1970s, predicts that by the year 2000, the Warehouse District will be transformed into a viable community of apartments, condominiums, shops, small businesses, and professional offices.

New Orleans residents are in the process of rediscovering the river. Many who fled in the 1960s and 1970s are moving back. Within a period of fewer than 20 years, billions of dollars have been invested in the Central Business District. More than 25 new high-rise office buildings and hotels, all within easy walking distance of the French Quarter, have completely altered New Orleans' Downtown skyline. Lester Kabacoff envisions a new faubourg on the Uptown side of Canal (within minutes of the CBD) that will be an extension of the Central Business District with a potential 10,000 inhabitants.

Jerry Moomau, director of the Downtown Development District, says:

New Orleans City Hall has over the years become responsible for many of the incentive and training programs needed to help the city's private economy. Today, government and the private sector realize that they must work together to maintain a healthy economy. Photo by Brad Crooks

I think we have built one of the finest downtown areas in the country . . . I say this because, through a successful public/private-sector partnership, we were able to systematically plan the growth of the downtown area since 1975.

This development boom provided the city with more than 23 million square feet of office space, up dramatically from 5 million in the 1960s.

Dr. Gordon Saussy, a University of New Orleans professor of economics, says:

We now have considerable office space and hotel accommodations. Our transit system is the second or third most effective in the nation, in terms of use. Our location, on what is now called the Sunbelt Buckle, puts us at the gateway of the nation's mightiest energy source—the Mississippi . . . The river drains 2/3 of the subcontinent, giving us the economic advantage of moving (by container) all kinds of items over water. The area is virtually untapped for the development of manufacturing plants and new businesses based on such resources as fish and shellfish.

As the 1990s begin, employment in New Orleans is up. Military spending is keeping Avondale Shipyards

Bed and breakfast hotels are an exciting new travel phenomenon that are becoming popular all over the world. New Orleans is a natural city for these accommodations because of the city's many fine old homes which would normally be unavailable for visitors. Photo by Bob Rowan/Progressive Image Photography

busy. There is a strong federal commitment to space contracts, fueling new activity at the NASA facility in Michoud. And, according to UNO professor of finance, Dr. Ivan Miestchovich, Jr.:

New Orleans is definitely moving in the right direction . . . We're beginning to vigorously promote tourism (with a new $6-million war chest). Boat fabrication is viable. Oil-related small industry is bouncing back. Oil and gas prices are stable.

In addition, the Port of New Orleans is growing, enjoying a remarkable rebound to once again lead the nation in total tonnage. A $187-million construction program approved by voters in 1989 will enable the port to transform the Uptown wharf areas into the main focus of operations.

Donald Walls, noted McGraw-Hill economic forecaster, foresees a steady employment growth for New Orleans during the next decade and beyond. Walls says the port gives the city an important advantage over most Southern cities as the chief catalyst for job growth through the year 2000. The port's strength, Walls states, lies in its being a magnet for national and international trade. Futurist Walls predicts that, stimulated by a low dollar, the port will experience a boom through the 1990s. He also sees Latin America as a major trading partner of the future with strong benefits to New Orleans.

Meanwhile, at the beginning of the 1990s, the city's cost of living index remains the lowest of all major cities including Atlanta, Dallas, Miami, San Diego, Houston, and Charlotte across the broad, coast-to-coast southern stretch known as the Sun Belt.

New Orleans also maintains the lowest cost of housing, transportation, groceries, and miscellaneous services. Though its health-care costs rank second, its health-care facilities are among the nation's best.

Furthermore, the average home price for a single-family, three-bedroom house in an upscale neighborhood is the lowest in the Southeast.

To reiterate Mayor Sidney Barthelemy's rallying cry as he ushered in the new decade of the 1990s, "New Orleans in the '90s may well become 'America's Host to the Future.'"

A popular address for many Orleanians is Uptown, the area upriver from the Central Business District. One of Uptown's great gathering places is Audubon Park where there are ancient oak trees, Spanish moss, pathways, and lagoons beckoning people from all over the city. Photo by Philip Gould

PART TWO

. . .

NEW ORLEANS' ENTERPRISES

THE
MARKETPLACE

New Orleans' location, culture, and favorable business climate make the Big Easy a great city to visit or call home.

Photo by Brad Crooks

THE LOUISIANA SUPERDOME

THE LOUISIANA SUPERDOME dominates the New Orleans skyline with its breathtaking immensity and space-age design. No other facility in the downtown area has generated the economic impact, worldwide recognition, or impetus for development like the Superdome has.

Construction began on the Dome in 1971. The building opened on August 3, 1975, and today still stands unique among the public assembly facilities in the world. Time has attested that Louisiana's bold venture into the twenty-first century was a wise one, and the Superdome is now paying handsome dividends to the citizens and taxpayers of the state.

The Superdome's success story relates directly to the future; it paints an even brighter picture. The flexibility of the Superdome has enabled it to become a home for the nation's biggest sports and entertainment spectacles, while maintaining a schedule of day-to-day entertainment staples.

The Superdome was the first large

New Orleans and the Superdome are two NFL favorites.

stadium to host both a Final Four and a major political convention. The NCAA gambled in March 1982, leaving the small arena atmosphere for the spectacular surroundings of the Superdome to hold its Division I basketball championships. The results proved to be a howling success, with a world-record crowd of 61,612 people enjoying every minute of the Final Four. The Final Four returned in 1987, establishing still another record with 64,959 fans in attendance.

The Super Bowl takes on a special flavor because of the unique atmosphere of the Superdome and the city of New Orleans. Other Super Bowl games are constantly compared to ones in New Orleans. In fact, by hosting the Super Bowl in 1990, New Orleans became the NFL's most preferred Super Bowl city, having hosted the affair seven times, once more than its closest rival, Miami.

Other significant milestones for the Superdome include hosting Pope John Paul II, who addressed more than 88,000 schoolchildren in 1987, and holding the Republican National Convention in 1988.

In addition, the Superdome is the proud home of the NFL's New Orleans Saints; Tulane University football; the Bayou Classic, which features Southern University and Grambling in an annual rivalry; the Busch Challenge College Baseball Series; and the Superdome Classic, Louisiana's high school football championship.

The Superdome has scores of attendance records to its credit, including the biggest indoor concert crowd in history (87,500 for the Rolling Stones in 1981), charitable events (12,000-plus patrons playing bingo for the Lion's Eye and Ear Hospital Fund), and dozens of convention and trade show attendance marks.

Events such as the Sugar Bowl, the Super Bowl, and the NCAA Final Four Tournament infuse millions of dollars into the local economy. Another major plus is the wealth of free publicity generated in international media coverage of Superdome events. That exposure greatly enhances tourism, New

Above: The Rolling Stones played the Louisiana Superdome in 1981 and drew 87,500 fans, setting an indoor rock concert attendance record.

Left: Night falls, bringing on the evening's events at the Lousiana Superdome.

Orleans' third-largest industry.

The Greater New Orleans Tourist and Convention Commission (GNOTCC), which is housed in the Superdome, aggressively pursues and successfully sells the New Orleans area as a destination city for tourists and conventioneers alike. Formed in 1960, the GNOTCC became an independent selling arm of the city, with its own charter and bylaws. During the first year of operation, the GNOTCC had a staff of three employees and less than 100 members.

A turning point in the tourism industry occurred in 1975 with the opening of the Louisiana Superdome. As a result of the sales efforts led by the GNOTCC, working in tandem with officials at the Superdome, New Orleans grew in the number of conventions hosted. Today the city has the capacity to house 1.6 million delegates and accommodate more than 26,000 overnight visitors. The GNOTCC has expanded its operations to serve the growing demands

of the fastest-growing industry in the New Orleans area.

In order to help in attracting convention business to the Superdome, a huge curtain was ordered for the interior in 1986. The curtain, used to quarter off the Superdome for more intimate areas, is comprised of 27, 90-foot drapes made of a synthetic, non-flammable fiber. Each drape weighs about 200 pounds and is raised using a motorized truss system permanently affixed to the Superdome's ceiling. Utilizing an efficient Velcro-fastening method, the entire drape configuration can be raised in less than two hours.

Management officials at the Louisiana Superdome believe that the $400,000 purchase price for the curtain system has already been justified. After all, the curtain was one of the primary reasons that New Orleans was selected to host the 1988 Republican National Convention. The curtain also plays a major role in the Superdome's concert business, scaling the building into a venue of 11,500 to 27,000 seats.

"Without the curtain," says Bob Johnson, general manager, "the Superdome wouldn't have the flexibility that it does now. We can now satis-

factorily host the smaller groups who want to use our facilities."

But for trade shows, sometimes bigger is better. For example, the International Association of Fire Chiefs held their annual trade show in the Superdome. Because of the ceiling height at the Superdome, the fire-truck ladders were able to be fully extended and displayed.

An added benefit is the fact that most television networks relish the thought of covering Superdome events. "No doubt, the Superdome is the best facility we have ever worked with," says Steve Israel, unit manager for ABC Sports. "The building and the people are the most accessible in the country. Everything and everybody we need is there. It's made for television."

The Superdome is not just a location for sporting events, family entertainment, trade shows, and conventions. The building is also one of the top sight-seeing attractions in the South, with an annual attendance of more than 75,000 people.

Officials at the Superdome also support and provide housing for the recently created New Orleans Sports Foundation (NOSF), a nonprofit, nonpolitical organization. The NOSF's goal is to contribute to the economy of greater New Orleans and Louisiana by bringing not only huge events such as the Super Bowl and Final Four, but also small- to medium-size sporting events to the metropolitan area.

The sports industry has grown to

become a $50-billion industry nationwide. The Sports Foundation was formed to capitalize on that growth by giving the metro area an organization dedicated to increasing the quantity and quality of sporting events, help relocate national offices of sports governing bodies, help establish a sports manufacturing base, and help work with local sports organizations and promoters.

The economics of sports for the New Orleans area is well documented. The 1986 NFL Super Bowl brought an estimated $226 million to the area economy. And other large national sporting events have also made a major impact—$45 million from the 1986 Sugar Bowl and $65 million from the NCAA's Final Four Basketball Tournament.

But other sporting events can also generate tourism dollars. Leaders with the NOSF contend that New Orleans

Right: Flashing lights and carnival rides create fun and excitement for young and old alike at the Indoor Super Fair, held annually at the Superdome. Photo by Troy Gomez

Below: The 1982 NCAA Final Four basketball tournament took place at the Louisiana Superdome, with the University of North Carolina winning the championship.

should be the first choice for hosting events such as tennis championships, bowling tournaments, exhibition games, and national and international amateur championships. A recent study concluded that hosting only 5 percent of the nation's amateur sports events would equal an impact of $50-million gross revenue and $2.7 million in direct tax revenue.

Says Mike Millay, NOSF's executive director, "The people who come to New Orleans to participate in these events will be staying in hotels, eating in restaurants, and shopping in local malls and stores, enjoying something that most of us here take for granted—the uniqueness of the city of New Orleans."

Perhaps the happiest chapter in the history of the Superdome and its related activities is the positive effect

it has had on the surrounding area. Once laced with rusty railroad tracks and abandoned warehouses, the western end of Poydras Street corridor is now one of the most prosperous areas of downtown New Orleans, leading the recent construction boom with magnificent towers of steel and glass, with the Superdome as its centerpiece.

The immediate neighborhood—within a three-block radius—has seen the development of more than 3 million square feet of office space, which translates to an estimated 30,000 people at work.

Success has not come easily. Snarls of political entanglement had the Superdome mired in controversy in the early days.

On July 1, 1977, the management and operational responsibilities of the Superdome were turned over to private management. Facility Management of Louisiana, a Spectacor Management Group company, took the challenge.

The management agreement called for an overall savings of $30 million in the first 10 years. FML saved the state $60 million.

Despite the fact that the Superdome is still an investment—costs of annual operation, maintenance, and bond indebtedness still exceed total revenues—the architectural wonder is

Large-scale, national conventions, such as this National Education Association Convention (left) and the 1988 Republican National Convention (above), are held at the Superdome—the ideal convention facility. Photos by Troy Gomez

already paying dividends. A study by professors at the University of New Orleans revealed an economic impact of $2.68 billion in the State of Louisiana in the Superdome's first 10 years of operation. That represents a return of $96.40 for each dollar spent.

It has taken a lot of work, but today the Greater New Orleans Tourist and Convention Commission and the New Orleans Sports Foundation, led by the world-famous Louisiana Superdome, are major success stories for New Orleans, the river region, and Louisiana.

BLAINE KERN ARTISTS, INC.

BLAINE KERN, ALSO KNOWN AS "Mr. Mardi Gras," founded Blaine Kern Artists, Inc., in 1947. As founder and president of this unique enterprise, Kern has traveled to more than 65 countries, where he has become friends with various artists and directors of some of the most famous parades in the world. The ideas that he has gathered have helped him build Mardi Gras in New Orleans into a world-renowned celebration.

Blaine Kern Artists, Inc., "Builders of the Famous Mardi Gras Parades," pioneered the introduction of large, animated floats and other modern innovations while also bringing back traditions that were almost lost during the 200-year history of the New Orleans Mardi Gras. Today designers, artists, sculptors, carpenters, electricians, and an experienced staff repre-

A Blaine Kern float takes part in the Bastille Day parade in Cannes, France.

senting a cumulative 750 years in the trade produce what are considered to be the most beautiful floats and figures in America.

As the largest float-building firm in the world and famous for numerous Mardi Gras parades, Kern's business is also responsible for various celebrations worldwide. The Dallas Cot-

ton Bowl parade, Macy's Atlanta Christmas parade, and the Bastille Day parade in Cannes, France, are only a few of the events the company has produced. A vast selection of beautiful props and figures is available to enhance any celebration—large or small.

In addition to building floats and producing parades, Blaine Kern Artists, Inc., really knows how to throw a party. Only in New Orleans at Mardi Gras World, a unique facility comprised of a series of four warehouses or dens located directly across the Mississippi River from the city, can groups be accommodated in one of the most spectacular settings in America. The 60,000-square-foot covered area includes a gift shop, a movie theater, a prop fabrication shop, the administrative offices, and many of the world-famous Mardi

Blaine Kern, Sr. (left), and Barry Kern, dwarfed by some of the sculptures created by Blaine Kern Artists, Inc.

Sculpting the god Neptune for the World's Fair.

Gras floats.

Kern's staff can transform these dens into a brightly lit visual treat, day or night, for a seafood boil meal for 3,000 people or an intimate formal dinner for six. Crawfish boils, wine and cheese receptions, fish frys, cocktail parties, Dixieland Jazz buffets, King Cake parties, or elegant dinners are just some of the possibilities. Guests can sip champagne with a symphony orchestra or dance the two-step at a Cajun Fais-Do-Do (pronounced fay-doe-doe), surrounded by colorful floats completely outlined in twinkling lights, all under the gaze of an 18-foot Frankenstein or a favorite cartoon character or the gigantic residents of Camelot. Party planners only

have to name their theme because anything goes at Mardi Gras World, where fact and fiction come together.

In a city known for conventions, Blaine Kern Artists can set the stage anywhere. The staff decorates and enhances convention displays with beautiful papier-mache and fiberglass figures. They set the mood and carry out any theme for special banquets and bring parades right to the guests, dazzling them with colorful floats, lively marching bands, and elegant costumes.

Kern also provides specialties aimed at promoting businesses or organizations to their employees or members in a unique fashion. Blaine Kern Specialties has an extensive se-

lection of coins, medallions, plaques, charms, and speciality items made of bronze, silver, and gold as well as the traditional aluminum doubloons used in the Mardi Gras parades. Currently, Kern Specialties mints more than 30 million of these doubloons each year. The company can use logos or special designs to create any quantity to · be used as gifts, souvenirs, or promotions of any kind.

Mardi Gras World provides carnival time year-round. Professional tour guides escort individuals or groups through the carnival dens. Guests are able to view the artists and sculptors creating the floats and magical figures. The theater is filled with elaborate costumes worn by the royalty of Mardi Gras. Mardi Gras World is open daily to the public from 9:30 a.m. to 4 p.m. by admission, with group tours available by appointment.

One of the fastest-growing sectors of the Kern family's business is the special designing/building of three-dimensional figures in fiberglass, papermache, and synthetic forms of bronze and marble.

Their clientele includes amusement and theme parks such as Disney, water parks, public areas, museums, zoos, hotels, shopping centers, and countless displays and promotions. After more than 40 years of producing specially designed pieces for their floats and displays, the Kern artists and sculptors are considered the best in the business. Their ideas and techniques are state of the art, dramatically changing and upgrading the art form and copied by the rest of the industry.

Barry Kern, the company's general manager, who has studied extensively at home and abroad, now specializes in this field and is regarded as one of the most knowledgeable in the industry. He has helped the company move into the market nationally as well as internationally and is the main catalyst of its recent growth in this field. The company maintains studios both locally and abroad specifically for this specialized field.

Blaine Kern Artists, Inc., created the entrance gate for the 1984 World's Fair held in New Orleans. The elaborate structure included a four-story-tall river god and goddess and seven 100-foot-long alligators.

NEW ORLEANS CONVENTION CENTER

THERE ARE NOT MANY STORIES that can match the success of the New Orleans Convention Center. Opened in January 1985, the center is already undergoing an expansion that will more than double its present size. Construction of the expansion will provide the center with more than 700,000 square feet. When the project is completed in 1991, it will offer an additional 35,000-square-foot ballroom (complementing the existing one of 30,000 square feet) and a total of 83 meeting rooms.

In addition to offering increased space for diversity of activities, the expansion will translate into even greater flexibility in accommodating multiple events. The 118,000-square-foot lobby will provide easy access to all exhibit areas.

Just as important as this increased physical capacity is the commitment, by those who book and manage the New Orleans Convention Center, to maintain the same world-class service for which the center has become recognized. From the nuts and bolts of state-of-the-art electrical, telecommunications, and technical equipment to the excitement of their gourmet foods, the staff at the convention center is dedicated to ensuring that every

More than 1.5 million delegates attended 180 major conventions and trade shows at the center during the late 1980s.

The New Orleans Convention Center will be more than doubled in size when its current expansion project is completed in 1991.

event is a memorable experience—equally for the absence of managerial problems as for the positive response from both delegates and exhibitors alike.

The center is continuing to enhance New Orleans' long-established reputation as the ideal meeting site in a unique city with its bounty of visitor attractions—the irresistible cuisine,

the stimulating music, the fascinating historic sites, and the new riverfront development. The city offers more than 20,000 first-class hotel rooms in the French Quarter/central business district area, most within easy walking distance of the center's front entrance.

With the abundance of assets surrounding the new, expanded world-class facility, convention center officials are more confident than ever that conventioneers will share the conviction that New Orleans ranks as the number-one meeting site in the nation.

Statistics from the economic impact of the New Orleans Convention Center further demonstrate that confidence. In its first five years of operation, the center had a $3.4-billion postive impact on the surrounding community. More than 1.5 million delegates attended 180 major conventions and trade shows during the latter part of the 1980s, further expanding New Orleans' burgeoning tourist industry.

In fact, the center has been so successful that discussions by convention and tourism officials are now involving a proposed third expansion. The New Orleans Convention Center continues to grow by leaps and bounds and a few hundred thousand square feet here and there.

THE NEW ORLEANS HILTON RIVERSIDE AND TOWERS

THE NEW ORLEANS HILTON Riverside and Towers has it all under one roof. Guests can meet, dine, play, and, of course, sleep under one grand roof at the 1,602-room New Orleans Hilton. This grand hotel features four restaurants, six lounges, two swimming pools, a highly sophisticated Business Center, one of the top 50 racquet and health clubs in the country, and an enviable riverfront location, with Rouse's Riverwalk Festival Marketplace at its front door.

One of the newest facilities under the New Orleans Hilton's roof is the 22,000-square-foot Exhibition Center, which can handle 135, 8-by-10-foot exhibition booths. The center is accessed by a ramp and two loading bays. Exhibitors can either ride the elevator or take the escalator to their display area. With the Exhibition Center, the hotel has the ability to

Above: Guests at The New Orleans Hilton Riverside and Towers are offered all the amenities for a comfortable stay within the hotel and Rouse's Riverwalk Festival Marketplace at its front door.

Left: One of the 12 suites in the Hilton's Towers, which is elegantly appointed to satisfy the most discriminating taste.

handle a total of 300 exhibits in house, making it the largest hotel facility in the city.

Hand in hand with the Exhibition Center go other facilities in the second floor of the main complex. There the meeting executive will find eight all-purpose meeting rooms, ranging from 25 to 713 square feet.

Located at street level, in the main complex, is the Grand Ballroom of 26,894 square feet, and its close rela-

tive, the multipurpose Grand Salon with comfortable space of 24,179 square feet.

On the third floor of the hotel, there are 17 rooms ranging from 304 to 8,796 square feet. Three of these rooms look out on a landscaped pool and deck area. All told, the New Orleans Hilton offers 127,000 square feet of meeting space.

The sophisticated, multifaceted Business Center has one of the most

comprehensive presentations of software and state-of-the-art data-processing equipment operations found anywhere. The Business Center provides services such as graphics design/slide production, secretarial and word-processing services, and desktop publishing.

In addition, the Business Center features six Dictaphone Connexions systems, each with full telephonic and dictation/transcription capabilities and a software package integrating the units with computers for added services. The center provides 24-hour remote dictation from each guest room via Dictaphone's MVP system, a different cassette-based system that permits simultaneous use by two authors, or transcriptionists.

For the guest who desires the per-

Above: The Grand Ballroom provides more than 26,000 square feet for meetings or social events.

Left: The Hilton is a particular favorite with guests who are attracted to its enviable riverfront location.

sonal services of a small luxury hotel, he or she can find such service in the elegant Towers. In fact, today's discerning traveler will find that the Hilton has made its Towers development a highly desirable retreat.

The Towers concept first came into being at New York's internationally renowned Waldorf-Astoria (also a Hilton Hotel). The Towers in the New Orleans Hilton is patterned after this famous hotel.

The New Orleans Towers has 132 guest rooms and 12 suites. Six high-speed elevators whisk guests up and down. In 1987 the Towers received a million-dollar face lift. Designers researched local history and came up with specific themes that were used to bring a touch of local color and ambience to the rooms. Guests at the Towers now experience the feeling of warmth and hospitality of New Orleans, known around the world as "the Paris of the Americas."

The mood and feeling of each room reflect directly upon a name and that name's specific place in local history. Many of the suites bear the historic names of people connected directly with the emergence of Louisiana as a state.

For example, there's the Bonaparte Suite (the story says that Napoleon was to join Josephine in New Orleans, but Elba got him instead) done in highly stylized Empire. And, while making an eighteenth-century statement with its accoutrements, it is comfortable and has a modern look and feel.

Within the past 24 months all 1,200 guest rooms in the main building have been refurbished. The $15-million renovation included all new wall coverings, draperies, carpet, and furnishings. Included in this was a servibar in each room, complete with beverages, cocktails, and dry snacks.

Paul D. Buckley, general manager of the New Orleans Hilton, says, "The fabrics we've used in our new design are smart, yet practical, durable, and easily maintained while, at the same time, surround the guest in luxury."

The Hilton also has its own jazz lounge. Pete Fountain, the master of the clarinet and the New Orleans bon mot, moved his musical roots from Bourbon Street right into the heart of the Hilton in 1977, where he re-created his French Quarter club on the hotel's third floor.

After staying at the New Orleans Hilton Riverside and Towers, guests truly understand the meaning behind Fountain's soulful ballad, "Do You Know What it Means to Miss New Orleans?"

NEW ORLEANS MARRIOTT

WITH NEW ORLEANS' famous French Quarter surrounding it and America's widest shopping avenue, Canal Street, at its front door, the 1,300-room New Orleans Marriott offers guests a great location for both sight-seeing and shopping when they come to "The City That Care Forgot." Convention visitors will appreciate that convenience as well as the fact that the Marriott also offers a perfect location with approximately equal distance to the New Orleans Convention Center and the Louisiana Superdome. In addition, the Marriott is situated just across the street from the Rivergate Exhibition Hall.

Early in the history of New Orleans, the median of Canal Street was called the "neutral ground," as that stretch of land was all that separated the French colony of the Vieux Carre (French Quarter) from the American sector. These two factions were not the best of friends at that time and represented two entirely different cultures. Today the phrase "neutral ground" has become part of everyday conversation in New Orleans, and the Marriott now sits strategically between the remnants of these cultures and shares in its historic locale.

The famous French Quarter, with its European charm, antique shops, renowned restaurants, watering holes, and nightclubs, lies in the shadow of the towers of the New Orleans Marriott. From the hotel it is an easy stroll down Royal Street, past the boutiques and cafes, on to the much-photographed Jackson Square and St. Louis Cathedral. Visitors can stop for cafe au lait and beignets at an all-night coffeehouse near the square or turn their way to the bright lights of Bourbon Street to listen to jazz or rhythm and blues. Back at the Marriott it is an equally easy walk past the old mercantile buildings of

Above: Guests in the Marriott lobby enjoy cocktails to the sound of live piano music.

Left: The Marriott features 1,300 comfortably appointed rooms, perfect for relaxation at the end of a full day.

the American sector and the art galleries to the Riverwalk Festival Marketplace, a Rouse development, full of specialty shops and eating establishments located along the Mississippi River.

Offering New Orleans' largest Grand Ballroom, capable of accommodating 3,600 people for receptions or 2,400 for banquets, the Marriott is a meeting planner's dream. With the ability to create 32 function rooms and having an exhibit hall with space for 125 booths, the Marriott puts a total of more than 80,000 square feet of flexible meeting space at the meeting planner's disposal. The large number of spacious rooms affords great flexibility and convenience, and the expertly trained and capable staff members bring a professionalism to their jobs that will put any meeting coordinator at ease.

For the traveling business executive, the Marriott offers proximity to major downtown office buildings, as well as the city, state, and federal court complexes. In-house business services include facsimile transmis-

chine, swimming pool, whirlpool, sundeck, men's and women's saunas, showers, and lockers all await the fitness-minded guest.

Opened in 1972, the Marriott has been through a constant and ongoing transition of refurbishing and redecoration to assure its guests the most comfortable and up-to-date rooms in the city. The addition of another guest room tower in 1979 made the hotel one of the largest in the city and increased its meeting facilities and service areas.

In 1990 the Aquarium of the Americas will open just a few short blocks from the hotel and further enhance the hotel's attractiveness. The new addition to the New Orleans Convention Center will attract even larger conventions, and the large block of rooms offered by the New Orleans Marriott, as well as its central location, will make it one of the most sought after hotels in New Orleans.

The future looms bright indeed for the port city of New Orleans as it approaches the next century and beyond. And the New Orleans Marriott stands ready today to serve in those giant steps forward.

Left: The New Orleans Marriott towers above Canal Street and the bustling French Quarter.

Below: Whether catching sun rays or cooling off, youngsters and grown-ups alike enjoy an afternoon at the pool.

sion, computer access, steno services, and typists.

In addition to the separate banquet facilities, the New Orleans Marriott offers six restaurants and bars, from the rooftop Riverview Restaurant offering a view of the city and the river to the Canal Street Bar with its cosmopolitan panorama which proves ideal for people-watching. And all day long, Cafe du Marche offers American fare and those dishes for which New Orleans is renowned.

For those who want to spend some time working off calories, the Marriott offers a complete health club. Lifecycles, an eight-station weight ma-

WINDSOR COURT HOTEL

UPON CHECKING INTO THE Windsor Court Hotel, it does not take long for discriminating guests to discover that they have landed squarely in the lap of luxury.

Since opening in 1984, the Windsor Court Hotel has consistently placed in the top category of elite hotels throughout the world, outranking such heavyweights as the Bel-Air in Los Angeles, the Ritz-Carlton in Buckhead, and the Halekulani in Honolulu.

Windsor Court's secret, according to managing director Jean Mestriner, is owner Equitable Real Estate's uncompromising commitment to pamper hotel guests. In addition, Mestriner says the staff plays an important role. "How our staff regard themselves and how they regard our guests is essential to our success."

The 23-story, rose-colored granite structure incorporates a perfect blend of old-world elegance and contemporary design, utilizing an exceptional collection of seventeenth-, eighteenth-, and nineteenth-century paintings and furnishings. There are 310 guest accommodations, all of which have a private balcony or bay window overlooking either the Mississippi River or the city of New Orleans.

Of the accommodations, 250 are suites with a separate living room, a petite kitchen or wet bar, and a dressing room adjoining the bedroom and bathroom. The remaining 60 are deluxe guest rooms, and each has a spacious bedroom and Italian marble bathroom.

As well as the other special amenities, every room has three telephones, each equipped with two incoming lines and data ports. There are 53 two-bedroom suites and 15 rooms equipped for the physically handicapped. There are two showcase penthouse suites on the 22nd floor with 2,000 square feet of space and landscaped terraces.

The centerpiece of Windsor Court is the famous Grill Room restaurant. The simple elegance of the Grill Room is visually stunning. Located on the second floor, the Grill Room is open daily for breakfast, lunch, and dinner, as well as for brunch on Saturdays and Sundays. Known for a fine style of New American cooking, this restaurant is a recipient of the

Since opening in 1984, the Windsor Court Hotel has consistently placed in the top category of elite hotels throughout the world. All 310 guest rooms have a balcony overlooking either the Mississippi River or the city of New Orleans.

prestigious Travel/Holiday Award and the Ivy Award, and is the only Five-Diamond-rated hotel restaurant in New Orleans. The Grill Room wine cellar is one of the finest in the region, with an extensive collection of Bordeaux Grand Crus.

Adjacent to the Grill Room on the second floor, the Polo Club Lounge has the ambience of an intimate English club. Open from early morning until late at night, the lounge offers a wide variety of spirits and coffees as well as Louisiana-style snacks.

In a city renowned for its ambience and charm, the Windsor Court Hotel has quickly become an institution admired and respected the world over.

The Grill Room, Windsor Court's restaurant and architectural centerpiece, features a collection of fine art. Open daily for breakfast, lunch, and dinner, the award-winning restaurant serves a variety of New American menu selections.

DELTA QUEEN STEAMBOAT CO.

I N 1812 THE *NEW ORLEANS,* THE first steamboat to travel on America's inland rivers, completed its voyage to its namesake city. Nearly 175 years later the nation's last two overnight steamboats—the *Delta Queen* and *Mississippi Queen*—made New Orleans their home port, keeping alive the city's centuries-old ties to the river and steamboating.

"New Orleans is an ideal city for us," says Delta Queen Steamboat Co. president Patrick Fahey. "It's a warm-weather port with multiple shipyards for maintenance of our boats. It enjoys a worldwide reputation as an exciting travel destination, and, best of all, New Orleans and steamboats share a long and romantic history."

Delta Queen Steamboat Co., the oldest U.S. flag line, was founded in 1890 and has operated steamboats on the Mississippi River system ever since. Of the 11,000 riverboats that once plied the nation's rivers, the

The *Mississippi Queen* (top) and the *Delta Queen* cruise the waterways of America year-round.

company's *Mississippi Queen* and *Delta Queen* are the only two that continue to carry passengers from Pittsburgh to St. Louis, from St. Paul to New Orleans, and many points in between. The boats operate year-round with river cruises ranging from three nights to nearly two weeks in duration.

The *Delta Queen* has been called "the most famous steamboat in the world" and rightly so. Built in 1926 at a cost approaching one million dollars, the *Delta Queen* was listed on the National Register of Historic Places in 1970 and more recently designated as a National Historic Landmark. Reflecting the opulence and craftsmanship of an earlier era, the *Delta Queen* boasts rich hardwood paneling, gleaming brass fixtures, Tiffany stained-glass windows, and a breathtaking grand staircase.

Guests enjoy tea and conversation in the aft cabin lounge aboard the *Delta Queen*.

The *Mississippi Queen* was deliberately designed to be larger and grander than the most fabled steamboats of the nineteenth century. Towering seven stories above the river, it offers passengers a combination of Victorian ambience and up-to-the-minute comforts such as elevators, a sun deck and pool, beauty shop, movie theater, and much more.

In addition to river cruises, Delta Queen Steamboat Co. offers vacation packages that include city stays at the company-owned Maison Dupuy Hotel in the historic French Quarter. "The hotel complements our steamboats and allows us to offer our passengers a holiday much like those taken by southern planters more than a century ago," says Fahey. "Then, as now, people traveled to New Orleans by steamboat just to enjoy the city and all its attractions."

As Mark Twain wrote in *Life on the Mississippi* in 1896, "The finest thing we saw on our whole Mississippi trip, we saw as we approached New Orleans. This was the curving frontage of the Crescent City lit up with the white glare of five miles of electric lights. It was a wonderful sight, and very beautiful."

HOTEL INTER-CONTINENTAL NEW ORLEANS

I N A CITY RENOWNED FOR ITS unique charm and special elegance, there is a hotel which captures the essence and style of New Orleans. The Hotel Inter-Continental. A four-star rated masterpiece, combining Old World charm and Southern grace with European refinements.

The Hotel Inter-Continental New Orleans has been lauded among a select group of hotels with outstanding meeting facilities, luxuriously designed and decorated guest rooms, and consistently high standards of service. For the sixth consecutive year, the Hotel Inter-Continental New Orleans earned the American Automobile Association's four-diamond and the Mobile

Sunday brunch is a festive occasion for both guests and area residents, featuring delights to please the palates of discriminating epicureans.

Located in the bustling New Orleans business district, the Hotel Inter-Continental is poised for the city's tourism renaissance.

Travel Guide's four-star ratings. The hotel's Veranda Restaurant is one of the city's most romantic dining rooms and is locally acclaimed for its regional specialties and continental cuisine under the culinary direction of celebrated chef, Willy Coln.

All that is important to New Orleans radiates from the Hotel Inter-Continental's strategic location on the historic St. Charles Avenue streetcar line, at the center of the city's business, shopping, and entertainment

districts. The world-famous French Quarter, the New Orleans Convention Center, the Superdome, and the new riverfront attractions are within easy walking distance.

Ongoing renovation projects are testimony to the Inter-Continental commitment to excellence. In 1988

Inter-Continental and its co-owner, Pan American Life Insurance Company, invested $3.5 million in the addition of an 11,000-square-foot, state-of-the-art Executive Conference Center, increasing the hotel's meeting space by two-thirds.

The 3,000-square-foot presidential suite, named after Bienville, the city's founding father, is unsurpassed in luxury and is the first of the renovated Governors Suites to be completed. Located on the Executive Floor, each will bear the influences and furnishings of Louisiana's early governors and offer the ultimate in services and amenities.

In celebration of New Orleans' present, specially commissioned works of art, as well as an elaborate sculpture garden, showcase the talents of some of the city's finest artists throughout the hotel.

The Hotel Inter-Continental today is an integral part of this great southern city. Its continuing dedication to the city and its visitors is a clear example of the confidence the hotel has in the future of New Orleans.

The living room of the stunning Bienville Suite, named after the founder of New Orleans.

WEINER CORT FURNITURE RENTAL

THE IDEA OF RENTAL furniture found its way to New Orleans in 1962 thanks to Ben Weiner. In his furniture rental operation lie the roots of Weiner Cort Furniture Rental.

Ten years later, in 1972, Mohasco—a multimillion-dollar, multinational carpet and furniture manufacturer—acquired the growing company, and Weiner's Furniture became Weiner Cort Furniture Rental, a subsidiary of Cort Furniture Rental Corporation. Weiner Cort is now a coast-to-coast furniture rental company with more than 80 showrooms in and around 37 major U.S. cities.

"Our goal is to continue to be the leading provider of high-value rental furnishing services to help solve short- and long-term residential and office needs," says Robert Brandt, district general manager of the New Orleans district. "We accomplish this by utilizing the advantages of decentralized local management to lead the industry in terms of quality products and innovative, responsive customer service."

This philosophy, stressing decentralization, has been instrumental in achieving dramatic financial results for the company—results to the tune of more than $100 million in revenues

Whether for home or office, Weiner Cort Furniture Rental can provide luxurious furnishings for short- or long-term needs.

from the organization's 37 profit centers. These profit centers operate under five regional centers.

Brandt believes that small, entrepreneurial operating units can contribute significantly to an organization's customer service, profitability, and overall effectiveness. Smaller units are more responsive to local needs. They can react to change quicker and can better take advantage of the independence and spirit of people with a sense of pride, ownership, and commitment to their own achievements, Brandt says.

Raised in a family involved in the retail furniture business and groomed with 19 years of experience in the industry, Brandt has noticed that per-

sonal service is the key to keeping customers. The Cort showrooms in New Orleans are able to provide better service to their customers due to their unique situation: Weiner Cort's two showrooms in the parishes of Orleans and Jefferson are large by industry standards, professionally decorated and fully accessorized, and receive their inventory from a massive warehouse at the main Elmwood facility, the third largest in the nation for Cort. Larger-than-average inventory levels for the people of New Orleans mean better personal service for Cort's customers.

Weiner Cort's customers include apartment, home, and condominium dwellers; apartment owners and man-

agers; real estate investors; and office and convention customers.

From its inception back in 1962, Weiner Cort has been committed to service and quality. Today this commitment is clearly visible in the sound, national direction, in the guiding hands of experienced managers, and in the employees who are trained and encouraged to make all decisions with the customer and corporation in mind.

Such values are a source of pride and serve as encouragement for everyone involved—employees and customers alike. Judging from the level of success that Weiner Cort Furniture Rental has enjoyed over the past 25 years, these values seem to be working.

ANTOINE'S

THERE IS SOMETHING ABOUT Antoine's that lends momentum to a lunch or dinner. Every Orleanian knows this and puts the principle to practice whenever an occasion demands an extra measure of celebration and ceremony. They may explore the breadth of the exciting New Orleans dining scene, but for the big holidays, anniversaries, Mardi Gras, corporate parties, and intensely romantic lunches, they come home to Antoine's.

In 1990 enthusiastic New Orleans diners will have been doing that for 150 years. From 1840, when Antoine Alciatore opened the doors, until now, as his great-great-grandson

Bernard Guste welcomes guests today, Antoine's stands as a paragon of culinary continuity. The Antoine's enjoyed yesterday is still there.

These days, when the vogue in restaurants is for constant change, Antoine's holds to a different notion. Just as a Beethoven symphony is as great today as when it was written, so too is classic French Creole-Cajun cuisine—much of which was created in Antoine's kitchen. Antoine's son Jules, one of the greatest creative forces of his time, shaped menus not only at Antoine's but (through their imitations) at other New Orleans restaurants for decades to come.

Jules Alciatore was the man behind

Antoine's most famous dish, oysters Rockefeller. Although it has been copied by restaurants all over the world, the authentic original recipe—a family secret—can be sampled only at Antoine's. (It does not, as many cookbooks report, include spinach.)

The creation of oysters Rockefeller illustrates Jules' culinary genius. One day in the late 1890s he was asked to add a hot appetizer to a private party's menu at the last minute. Jules, a master at not wasting anything, saw some surplus relish trays in the kitchen, and from them improvised a new, rich sauce for oysters. He named it for the then-richest man in the world.

Oysters Rockefeller immediately became a part of Antoine's regular offerings; by 1938 Antoine's had served its millionth order. (The count will pass 3 million on or about the restaurant's 150th birthday.) When guests enjoy oysters Rockefeller as a traditional first course to a grand Antoine's repast, they are reminded to ask the waiter for a card with the number of the order of this true American original.

The end of Jules' tenure as proprietor of his father's restaurant was during Prohibition—a slap in the face of the dining style for which Antoine's is celebrated. But once again Jules' imagination won the day. Trusted friends of the restaurant continued to imbibe their spirits—disguised in cups of coffee. Guests can still savor the special beverage, which evolved after Prohibition into the flaming after-dinner coffee called Cafe Brulot Diabolique.

Some of Antoine's culinary specialties go all the way back to the beginning of the restaurant and beyond. One of those dishes is pommes de terre soufflee—soufflee potatoes, puffed-up, hollow French fries that never fail to delight first-time diners. They were created by accident for King Louis Phillippe of France by a chef named Collinet. Antoine Alciatore learned the trick from Collinet himself. And from that day to this, soufflee potatoes have been an

Antoine's, a New Orleans treasure, celebrates its 150th anniversary in 1990.

Antoine's specialty. Few Antoine's diners would enjoy a meal without them.

Antoine's ample premises include rooms of all sizes for private parties. Many are decorated along unusual themes. For example, the Rex and Proteus rooms have walls lined with the photographs of past Mardi Gras royalty. The Escargot Room is dominated by a large mural of a snail, designed by New Orleans artist John Chase.

Across from the Escargot Room is one of Antoine's unique resources—its 25,000-bottle wine cellar. Temperature and humidity are controlled for the proper aging of the wines, which come from every wine-making region in the world. It was built to this impressiveness during the hegemony of Roy Alciatore; parts of his private wine collection remain untouched in the cellar as a memorial.

Antoine's would not be Antoine's without its distinctive waiters. Experience in the dining room is not measured in years but decades. All the servers worked several years as an assistant to one of their more seasoned colleagues before they started taking orders from customers.

Through this practice the singular Antoine's dining room style is passed on from generation to generation.

The same is true in the kitchen. Antoine's cooks have been on hand as long as the waiters have, moving up through the ranks the same painstaking way. They learn and preserve the classic recipes for future cooks and diners.

With all of the success Antoine's has enjoyed, what is in store for the future? "Every day here presents me

Chef John Deville, who has been with the restaurant since 1963, presents an Antoine's specialty—pommes de terre soufflee.

with a great challenge," says Bernard Guste, fifth-generation proprietor. "The greatest dish—the most delicious dish—has yet to be prepared, and the greatest of all feasts has yet to be served! The finest of all wines may still be on the vine."

A visit to Antoine's for lunch or dinner makes for a special occasion or personal treat. Antoine's welcomes everyone to join in the longest-running joie de vivre in America.

The Antoine's staff. Courtesy of The Times-Picayune, staff photo by Luke Ducote

Proprietor Bernard Guste (right) and waiter Sammy LeBlanc, with Baked Alaska as a centerpiece.

THE GREAT NATURAL RESOURCE

New Orleans and the River Region have been blessed with abundant reserves of natural gas and oil, creating a thriving petrochemical industry.

Photo by Philip Gould

FREEPORT-McMoRan INC.

FROM THE BEGINNING OF TIME Louisiana has been blessed with an abundance of natural resources. Therefore, it is altogether fitting that one of the world leaders in the development of those and other resources be based in Louisiana.

Freeport-McMoRan Inc., headquartered in New Orleans, is a diversified *Fortune* 300 company involved in the exploration, discovery, processing, and development of natural resources. Commodities include phosphate rock, fertilizer, sulphur, oil, natural gas, uranium, copper, gold, and other natural resources. The company also conducts a worldwide exploration program for these and other natural resources.

The name Freeport-McMoRan, originally Freeport Sulphur Company, was organized in 1912 with the beginning of sulphur production in Bryanmound in southern Texas. The firm began operations in Louisiana in 1933 with the development of the Grand Ecaille sulphur mine in the marsh of the Mississippi Delta. After expanding into other areas of agricultural minerals production, oil and gas exploration and production, and precious metals mining, Freeport Sulphur changed its name to Freeport Minerals Company in 1971 to better reflect the diversity of its operations as a mineral producer.

McMoRan Oil & Gas Company was founded in 1969 as McMoRan Exploration Company and enjoyed phenomenal growth as a major independent oil and gas producer during the 1970s. "McMoRan" combines the names of its three founders, W.K. McWilliams, Jr., James R. Moffett, and B.M. Rankin, Jr. Moffett currently serves as chairman and chief executive officer of Freeport-McMoRan, and Williams and Rankin are members of the board of directors. The company's name was changed to McMoRan Oil & Gas in 1979.

The two firms merged in 1981 to become Freeport-McMoRan Inc. This combination resulted in a unified, highly talented entity, superbly positioned in the natural resources industry. The company expanded in new directions, and since the merger Freeport-McMoRan's assets have nearly tripled to almost $4 billion.

Freeport-McMoRan pursues a strategy of continual diversification through aggressive acquisitions and successful exploration. As a result, Freeport-McMoRan is less affected by price volatility for any one commodity than many other natural resource companies.

The firm has been an innovator, particularly in the fields of finance, marketing, mineral processing, and mine construction. It distinguishes itself in the mining industry by its ability to operate in difficult physical surroundings.

One company affiliate, Freeport-McMoRan Copper, in particular stands as a testament to the mining wisdom of the company. Located high in the rugged central mountain range of Pengunungan Jaya Wijaya in Irian Jaya, Indonesia, the copper mining

Located across from the city's famous Superdome, Freeport-McMoRan's headquarters building stands 23 stories tall.

operations are considered one of the world's greatest engineering accomplishments.

The project runs 75 miles into the interior of the island, from crocodile-infested mangrove swamps through upland tropical rain forests into the cold, jagged Jaya Wijaya Mountains. The mine area lies at 12,000 feet above sea level and sits just below a glacial snowcap at 16,000 feet. This region is in Irian Jaya, the eastern-most and largest province of the Republic of Indonesia. Total contained reserves are 8.3 billion pounds of copper, 8 million ounces of gold, and 43.7 million ounces of silver.

Transporting the ore from the mine locations to the ore-processing plant in the valley below presented a monumental engineering challenge. Because the mountains are so steep in this area, no road could be built from the mine level to the processing plant. At first the ore was moved down the steep cliff by means of an aerial tramway. Later, miles of tunnels were added deep inside the mountains to connect the various mines with the processing plant.

The impact of the higher production and expanded geological activities has had a rippling effect through the project, bringing new investment, new construction, added logistical demands, and increased recruiting and new personnel. In addition, Indonesia and Irian Jaya have also benefited greatly from the mine's success. The copper project's taxes and royalty revenues have generated substantial sums for the Indonesian government's development programs.

Freeport-McMoRan's commitment to environmental excellence was first demonstrated in the marshlands of Louisiana more than 40 years ago. It continues today throughout the company's operations and through an environmental and safety department that reports directly to the chairman. A proactive environmental auditing program ensures that the commitment is realized. State and national awards to operating units have acknowledged the results.

In the 1940s, long before there was

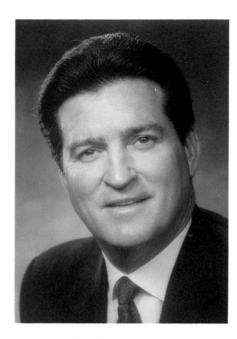

James R. Moffett, chairman and chief executive officer.

general public recognition of the importance of maintaining a quality environment, Freeport-McMoRan conducted bioassay tests to assure that its operations were compatible with the biologically productive marshlands of Louisiana. By the late 1960s the company had an expanded environmental staff working with its sulphur mines and other mineral operations in the United States, including the largest phosphoric acid plant in the world.

As the firm grew in the late 1970s, experienced environmental staffs played key roles in assessing new properties and developing innovative approaches to waste management through recycling. Each new environmental challenge has been met with innovative leadership. For instance, the company's efforts have resulted in awards for reclamation techniques on sensitive national forestlands. In response to the growing concern for wetlands conservation, Freeport-McMoRan has been a pioneer in the creation of man-made wetlands in mined areas and has developed new techniques for expedited reclamation. The National Wildlife Federation, the nation's largest environmental organization, has recognized Freeport-McMoRan's efforts by making the firm

the first recipient of the Corporate Conservation Council Award.

A corporate safety and health policy makes performance in these areas as important as quality, production, costs, and morale. All operating units maintain strong programs in compliance with this policy. A long-term industrial hygiene monitoring program places Freeport-McMoRan at the forefront of this important area. Data collected is used by safety and operating managers with consulting physicians to make work areas safer. Where relevant, operating units have taken the lead in their communities to increase community awareness and upgrade emergency response through literature, training, and mock drills.

Safety programs reach into employee homes periodically with literature, and there is participation by dependents in annual safety contests. These combined environmental and safety efforts help ensure that Freeport-McMoRan provides the positive leadership necessary for a healthy overall human, natural, and business environment.

In addition, Freeport-McMoRan has made it an obligation to be a responsible corporate citizen in the areas in which the company has operating units. Its policy is to support community programs that lead to an improved quality of life for everyone.

Freeport-McMoRan has a generous gift-matching program that is open to employees, retirees, and members of the board. The firm double matches the first $500 gift annually to an individual institution and matches amounts above that figure. It matches employees' gifts up to a maximum of $10,000 annually. Gifts are matched to educational institutions, social service agencies, the arts, environmental organizations, and civic organizations. The firm also has an extensive discretionary giving program that is administered by employee committees.

Freeport-McMoRan encourages its employees to volunteer their services to the communities in which they live. Company workers donate their time to scouting organizations, Junior Achievement, hospitals, schools,

chambers of commerce, United Way, and various social agencies.

The philosophy of the Freeport-McMoRan organization is to give something back to the community. In giving back to the community, the company believes it helps not only those in need, but also its own employees.

This is the reason that Freeport-McMoRan's annual United Way gift is a dollar-for-dollar match of the money donated by its employees. And this is the reason the firm began a teenage suicide prevention program in conjunction with a social service agency in New Orleans. And it is the reason why Freeport-McMoRan employees

Facing: Biological samples are taken from the Gulf of Mexico to monitor the impact of sulphur mining in the area.

Below: Freeport-McMoRan employees practice community support by encouraging students to pursue educational opportunities.

An aerial tramway unloads ore at Freeport-McMoRan Copper Company's mining operation in Irian Jaya.

have gone into the classrooms of schools in low-income neighborhoods and encouraged young students to seek out the brightest future possible.

Freeport-McMoRan has many responsibilities to shareholders, customers, and employees. But no responsibility is more important than the responsibility it has charged itself with in improving the quality of life in the communities in which it operates.

Freeport-McMoRan is an organization that continues to manage the Earth's resources with future generations in mind, an organization that recognizes the role of another important resource—the human resource. More than 6,000 employees help to make the company a leader in the development of natural resources for America, for the world, and for tomorrow.

Freeport-McMoRan, Inc., has never been stronger and more positive about its future or more confident that its leadership role in the global natural resource industry will continue. The company has never been more convinced that, given the proper incentives, adequate supplies of natural resources can and will be produced to sustain the industrialized economies of the world far into the future.

McDERMOTT INTERNATIONAL, INC.

McDERMOTT INTERNATIONAL, Inc., with operations in more than 30 countries and headquartered in New Orleans, is one of the world's leading energy services companies.

About one-third of McDermott's total work force of approximately 30,000 people is engaged in designing, building, and installing offshore platforms, laying subsea pipelines, shipbuilding, other marine construction services, as well as project management. The remaining two-thirds work in the firm's power-generation and defense operations that fall under Babcock & Wilcox, which became a part of the company in 1978.

These operating units have rich and colorful histories. McDermott traces its marine construction operations to entrepreneurial activities associated with the oil and gas industry 70 years ago. During the boom times in the 1920s in the East Texas oil fields, J. Ray McDermott & Co. got its start.

Driven by the energy and shrewd sense of the young R. Thomas McDermott and named for his father, J. Ray McDermott & Co. won its first major contract in 1923, when an East

Texas wildcatter ordered 50 wooden drilling rigs. The 24-year-old McDermott set up the financing and persuaded his father to supervise the construction. The wildcatter struck oil, and McDermott became a business with a future.

Following developments of the oil industry, McDermott moved to south Louisiana in the 1930s, opening the first office in the New Orleans area in 1937 on the Harvey Canal, across the Mississippi River from the firm's present central business district location. Since then, McDermott has shared its fortunes with this unique city, the gateway to the world.

Over the years McDermott has played a significant role in the New Orleans community life as well as in its economy. The company and many of its employees have devoted time and talent, as well as monetary support, to the United Way, the chamber of commerce, Junior Achievement, universities, church-affiliated activities,

Partnerships in Education, neighborhood preservation projects, and many others.

McDermott, as a member of the Business Council, was instrumental in the formation of the Metropolitan Arts Fund, which has injected a new vitality into the city's cultural scene by offering a continuing source of support for local arts organizations, among them the New Orleans Symphony, Opera, and Ballet. The firm has been a major contributor to the New Orleans Museum of Art's expansion program and has locally helped sponsor popular programs such as "Peru's Golden Treasures" and "The Search for Alexander" exhibits.

McDermott was a pioneer in ma-

In stormy or calm seas, McDermott marine construction vessels operate in offshore areas worldwide.

rine construction that began in earnest after World War II, when the first steel template was installed in 20 feet of water in the Gulf of Mexico. In the more than 40 years since then, the technology that began in the gulf has matured and spread to offshore oil- and gas-producing regions throughout the world. And McDermott has led the way.

Over the years McDermott's workers have tackled and solved some of the toughest marine construction problems in the most hostile marine environments. They have laid the deepest pipeline in the Gulf of Mexico and built most of the world's tallest offshore platforms, one taller than New York City's Empire State Building.

Offshore platforms support tons, sometimes thousands of tons, of equipment. They resist constant battering by waves for their 20-year lives. They withstand the corrosive assault of seawater. They prevail against storms, some of immense force.

If all types of structures are included, it is estimated that there are about 10,000 offshore platforms in the world today. Approximately 6,000 of these are considered major structures, half of them in the Gulf of Mexico. Several platforms now operate in more than 1,000 feet of water, and marine construction projects for 3,000-foot depths are now possible. The majority of the world's offshore structures have been McDermott projects.

Strides in many areas of techology and sophisticated new scientific tools have allowed tremendous advances in the way McDermott performs marine construction projects today. Computer technology, automation, improved welding and material-handling techniques, and revolutionary new offshore equipment have transformed every aspect of marine construction—design, engineering, platform fabrication, installation, and pipe laying.

Today McDermott Marine Construction has fabrication facilities and offshore operations in the United States, the Middle East, the North Sea, west Africa, southeast Asia, Australia, Mexico, and Central and South America. Engineering offices overseas are located in London, Aberdeen, and Singapore, and in the United States in Houston and New Orleans. In its offshore operations, McDermott employs a fleet of 200 vessels, including major pieces of marine construction equipment, and offers the industry's widest range of marine construction services.

Advances in technology have led to prosperous diversification in the activities of McDermott Marine Construction. McDermott Shipyard, which traditionally built high-horsepower tugs, push boats, and offshore supply vessels, is now building ships for the U.S. Navy, including prototype SWATH (Small Waterplane Area Twin-Hull) ships and torpedo test craft, as well as going into new lines of shipbuilding. Recent projects have included the building of a ferry and a hopper dredge, and extensively modifying research vessels.

McDermott's new technology now serves government, defense, salvage, subsea markets, and highly flexible software developed to support marine construction. This software, developed to support marine construction, has found a variety of interesting applications outside the industry. Modular construction that is part of efficient construction offshore—in which McDermott is the world leader—may soon be used to support large-scale onshore projects that new units of the company will manage.

McDermott's marine construction

Above: The sun sets upon the "jacket" portion of an offshore platform being built by McDermott.

Right: A McDermott technician works at one of the company's important services—loading and reloading nuclear fuel.

roots developed in the early part of this century, but its power-generation story goes back even further into America's industrial past. Babcock & Wilcox dates back to 1856, when Stephen Wilcox introduced an early version of the water-tube boiler. About 10 years later, in 1867, Wilcox and George Herman Babcock together patented an improved model of the inherently safe inclined water-tube boiler and began their partnership, which was incorporated in 1881.

The year 1881 also marked the beginning of the electrical age—"the age of cities"—when the first central station, Philadelphia's Brush Electric Light Company Station, started producing electricity. It was followed in 1882 by New York City's Pearl Street Central Station. Both were powered by B&W boilers.

Thomas A. Edison ordered the switch thrown to start up the Pearl Street Station. Writing to a friend about to buy a boiler, Edison stated that the B&W boiler "is the best boiler God has permitted man yet to make." B&W is proud of its pioneering role in the power industry, a role that has grown over the years.

B&W built its first marine boiler in 1889. In the 1890s the company received boiler orders from the U.S. Navy. By World War I more than

1,500 B&W boilers had been installed on U.S. Navy and Merchant Marine ships. In World War II more than 75 percent of the major U.S. combat and merchant vessels steamed around the globe powered by B&W boilers.

Realizing the potential of advances made in nuclear energy at the end of World War II, B&W turned its attention to this new source for producing steam. Among the firm's early nuclear achievements was its building of the reactor for the first nuclear-powered merchant ship, the N.S. *Savannah*.

B&W also engineered and fabricated nearly all of the nuclear steam-generator components for the four present U.S. nuclear-powered carriers, the *Enterprise, Nimitz, Eisenhower,* and *Vincent,* and today is involved in the design and construction of components for new nuclear-powered ships. B&W has been a major supplier of nuclear steam systems and fuel for U.S. Navy submarines, and has applied its nuclear experience to

develop other high-precision technologies for the defense industry.

Since its earliest days, B&W has provided pacesetting solutions for the changing needs of its utility customers. The company's 1,300-megawatt, pulverized coal-fired plant for the Tennessee Valley Authority went on line in 1973; it was then the world's largest electrical generating station. The TVA has bought one more 1,300-megawatt unit, and American Electrical Power has bought six similar units, including one being installed in a nuclear plant redesigned to burn coal.

A leader in developing commercial uses of nuclear energy for generating electricity, B&W is a major supplier of fuel and services to existing nuclear power plants. The B&W Fuel Company, a partnership between B&W and three French firms, formed in 1987, refuels nuclear plants built by B&W as well as its competitors. In 1989 B&W and Framatome S.A., the international leader in nuclear power,

McDermott supplies power-generation systems and pollution-control equipment for utilities, such as this plant in Colorado.

formed a partnership to expand the extensive services available to the nuclear industry in this country.

While utilities have provided a major market for B&W boilers, B&W serves other industries as well. It is an important supplier to the North American pulp and paper industry, and the petrochemical and primary metals industries are also major users of B&W boilers designed to burn hydrocarbons. Many industrial units fire process wastes, such as blast furnace gas, black liquor, peanut shells, bagasse, and even coffee grounds.

The burgeoning refuse-to-energy market is dominated by B&W systems. As more and more municipalities look for ways to dispose of waste, B&W's refuse-derived fuel plants provide an efficient method of disposing of garbage and supplying energy that can be converted into electricity.

Along with solving municipal waste problems, B&W has long provided emission-control systems to help industry and utility customers be productive while working in harmony with the environment. Newer systems and much of the firm's research efforts concentrate on perfecting processes that burn fuels cleanly. This technology reduces the need to add emission controls after burning and provides an additional element of security in the quest to preserve the quality of the environment.

In 1881, the very year of its incorporation, Babcock & Wilcox sent an employee to Glasgow, Scotland, to penetrate the first foreign markets in Europe. Canadian-based Babcock & Wilcox International has installed units in 35 countries that generate more than 250,000 megawatts of power. It operates joint-venture fabrication facilities in China, Indonesia, and India and, during the past decade, has performed major projects in Thailand, Venezuela, Argentina, Romania, Saudi Arabia, as well as many other countries. In the more than 100 years since it first established itself as a leader in the energy industry, Babcock & Wilcox has maintained its status as one of the world's foremost names in power generation.

Through its global reach and exceptional combination of resources in marine construction, power generation, and project management, McDermott International, Inc., continues to meet its commitment to be "Where the world comes for energy solutions."

Left: McDermott's power-generation equipment increases efficiency for fossil fuel power.

Below: McDermott has fabricated nuclear steam-generation components and provides fuel for the Navy's Trident submarine fleet. Shown is the USS *Ohio*.

TEXACO USA

THE BEGINNING YEARS WERE busy beyond belief. Nearly 90 years ago a 400-foot Texaco barge plied the Mississippi River on its way to deliver oil to the sugar mills in Louisiana. And Texaco was at Jennings, the state's first oil field in 1902. It was there among the wildcatters at the Caddo Field in north Louisiana in 1906, the Homer Field in 1919, East Hackberry Field in 1929, and the myriad of fields discovered in southern Louisiana's lakes, bayous, and shallow bays.

Texaco became the foremost developer of technology to drill and produce in the wetland areas. The semisubmersible drilling rig, an outgrowth of the submersible drilling barge that was first introduced by Texaco, moved the search for oil out to sea and added vast amounts of petroleum reserves to the world's supply—thanks to technology developed in Louisiana.

Through the years Texaco has been intimately associated with Louisiana's development. From the first corrugated-tin buildings at Amesville and oil fields throughout the state to the modern offices in downtown New

Orleans, generations of Texaco people have both influenced and been influenced by Louisiana.

Today Texaco has operations in more than 140 countries and territories. But the state of Louisiana remains one of its most important areas. Texaco's eastern exploration and producing region, headquartered in New Orleans, encompasses all exploration and producing operations onshore and offshore in the Gulf of Mexico and the Eastern Seaboard. And more than one-third of Texaco's domestic

Texaco sponsors the local Quiz Bowl on WYES-TV.

oil and almost two-thirds of its domestic natural gas are produced in the eastern region.

The Star Enterprise Refinery at Convent, owned by Texaco Refining and Marketing (East), Inc., and Saudi Refining, Inc., has the capacity to process 225,000 barrels of crude oil daily to provide petroluem products statewide, on the U.S. Gulf Coast, and thoughout the Northeast. In addition, Texaco owns a 26.6 percent interest in the Louisiana Offshore Oil Port (LOOP) and is its major user. LOOP is the only offshore port in the United States capable of handling today's very large crude carriers. LOOP brings an average of 777,000 barrels of crude oil per day into the United States for processing.

More than 3,000 people are employed by Texaco with $148 million in salaries paid to Louisianians each year. Nearly 5,000 Louisiana residents own almost 1.3 million shares of Texaco stock, and 8,400 people are royalty owners of Texaco oil and gas production, collecting $40 million each year. More than 900 Texaco and Star Enterprise employees are graduates of Louisiana colleges and universities.

Texaco is the largest oil and gas producer in Louisiana. Gross liquid-petroleum production is 128,000 bar-

Texaco employees enjoy a good old-fashioned Louisiana crawfish boil.

rels per day. At only $15 per barrel, Texaco produces enough oil in less than eight days to equal the Louisiana Purchase price of $15 million.

But numbers alone do not tell the entire story of Texaco USA in Louisiana. What does tell the story are the scenes such as the great industrial complex that stretches along the Mississippi River between New Orleans and Baton Rouge, made possible by Texaco's commitment to a state plan to use natural gas as an economical and efficient source of energy within the state. There is also the giant semisubmersible drilling rig anchored in more than 1,700 feet of water and probing for oil and gas buried beneath the sea floor in the Viosca Knoll area southeast of New Orleans, and a new SYSTEM 2000 station with its bright red-and-white Texaco logo shining a welcome to motorists along the highway.

All are images of the new Texaco.

Texaco USA has long been a major contributor to Louisiana colleges and universities, hospitals, and civic and cultural organizations. And, in a more personal sense, Texaco employees, with company support, reach out directly to their neighbors and the communities in which they live. Texaco volunteers regularly carry out a wide range of civic projects. They adopt

Above: Texaco technicians are always searching for new energy sources.

Left: With a 90-year history in Louisiana, Texaco is the largest oil and gas producer in the state.

families and provide food, clothing, and cheer at Christmastime; paint and repair homes of the elderly and others unable to handle these chores for themselves; and sponsor a Special Olympics for the handicapped with company employees on hand to cheer them on and serve as all-important "huggers" at the finish line. Throughout the state, Texaco and its employees participate with man power and money in activities such as the United Way, Children's Hospital, the Food Bank, the Lighthouse for the Blind, and a host of other projects in meeting both local and statewide needs.

The unique partnership that began at the turn of the century still flourishes—combining resources, people, a mighty river, and a state in a prosperous and growing endeavor.

THE LOUISIANA LAND AND EXPLORATION COMPANY

SINCE ITS CREATION IN 1926, The Louisiana Land and Exploration Company (LL&E) has played a prominent role in the development of oil and gas as a major industry in Louisiana and the world.

Founded as the Border Research Company, LL&E adopted its present name in 1927. LL&E's founders pioneered many of the techniques in oil field geology and engineering that paved the way for the discovery and extraction of prodigious quantitics of oil and gas not only by LL&E but by numerous other producers.

LL&E's fee ownership of more than 600,000 acres of land in southern Louisiana provided the springboard for its future prosperity. By leasing these lands to others for exploration and production and by retaining a royalty interest in the hydrocarbons discovered, LL&E grew into a major royalty company.

During the early years LL&E's operations were concentrated in southern Louisiana. In the early 1960s, realizing that its south Louisiana production would not provide the necessary base for future growth, LL&E's leaders expanded the company's exploration efforts for its own account.

LL&E was an early participant in

The LL&E Tower in New Orleans. Photo by Glade Bilby II

the exploration of the Outer Continental Shelf of the Gulf of Mexico, acquiring important leases in 1962. Petroleum reserves were discovered on many of the leases, some of which are still producing today.

The 1970 discovery of the Jay-Little Escambia Creek Field in Florida firmly established LL&E as a working-interest producer, and in 1971 LL&E's revenues from working-interest production exceeded those from royalty production for the first time.

Today oil and gas exploration and development remain the primary business for this *Fortune* 500 company. However, LL&E's operations are no longer confined to southern Louisiana and the Gulf Coast region. LL&E's oil and gas reserves of 200 million equivalent barrels make it one of America's largest independent oil and gas companies.

Headquartered in New Orleans, LL&E now has division or district offices in Houston, Oklahoma City, and Denver in the United States, and in London, Bogota, and Calgary abroad. In the United States, LL&E continues to be an active participant in exploration and production operations in the Gulf of Mexico. Domestic onshore activities are in the Gulf Coast region, Oklahoma, and Wyoming. In Wyoming, LL&E has a significant interest in natural gas reserves that will produce into the next century. Nearly 60 percent of LL&E's domestic hydrocarbon reserves are natural gas, making this company an important player in an expanding industry.

Approximately 40 percent of LL&E's proved reserves of oil and natural gas are located outside the United States, in the United Kingdom and Dutch sectors of the North Sea, Canada, and Colombia. LL&E's operations are rounded out by its Mobile

LL&E was an early participant in the exploration of the outer continental shelf in the Gulf of Mexico. Photo by Robert Colton

Refinery, which has the capacity to process and refine 80,000 barrels per day of various types of crude oil.

In recent years the firm's executives have restructured LL&E's operations and assets to weather the downturn in the worldwide petroleum industry. Today LL&E is well positioned to capitalize on a healthier market, particularly in natural gas.

The company recently reaffirmed its faith in the future of New Orleans when it agreed to a long-term lease as the major tenant of 909 Poydras, the LL&E Tower. With its headquarters in the LL&E Tower, the firm remains one of the state's more important employers.

In addition, LL&E takes an active role in the civic, cultural, and political affairs of the community. Its employees donate their time and talents to ensuring the success of a wide variety of institutions devoted to the education, health, and general welfare of Louisianians. For instance, LL&E is the

Above: This white alligator is one of 18 found on LL&E property. They are the only known white alligators in the world.

Left: LL&E has oil and gas reservoirs equivalent to some 200 million barrels. Photo by Robert Colton

corporate partner of one of the largest public schools in the city, Alcee Fortier High School.

LL&E has long been a champion of environmentally sound techniques of mineral extraction in the sensitive wetlands of Louisiana, realizing that these fertile nursery grounds are incredibly valuable to the world's food chain and to the survival of many species that contribute enormously to the quality of life on this planet.

More than 35 years ago LL&E recognized that these wetlands were being severely impacted by a combination of saltwater and coastal erosion. Since then, LL&E has been engaged in cooperative programs with federal and state soil conservation and wildlife protection agencies to slow down the pace of coastal erosion. Currently, LL&E is engaged in numerous educational projects designed to acquaint the general public with the value of Louisiana's wetlands to the nation as a whole and the forces that

LL&E has long been a champion of environmentally sound techniques of mineral extraction in the wetlands of Louisiana.

are threatening these wetlands.

The attention of the environmental community was recently focused on LL&E when 18 white alligators were found on the firm's property. These are the only white alligators known to exist anywhere in the world. These charming, blue-eyed flukes of nature can be seen at the Audubon Zoo.

LL&E also has been at the forefront of the BeachSweep Project to clear the Gulf Coast's beaches of litter, much of which is life threatening to water birds. The company is also an exhibit sponsor of the new Aquarium of the Americas.

As a result of many years of thoughtful, creative management, The Louisiana Land and Exploration Company is today respected by shareholders and the financial community and, at the same time, respected by civic and environmental activists as a corporate good neighbor, dedicated to preserving and enhancing the environment in which it operates.

TAYLOR ENERGY COMPANY

PAT TAYLOR IS ONE OF A KIND, described as a maverick by his friends. A self-made millionaire who has already built one of the largest and most profitable independent energy companies in the nation, he is now helping to ensure that tomorrow's generation has the opportunity to obtain a college education.

Taylor earned a scholarship to the prestigious Kinkaid Prep School in Houston, but when he graduated from Kinkaid, he had no funds for college. Learning that Louisiana State University charged no tuition, he successfully enrolled with a loan to pay for room and board. Taylor completed his degree in petroleum engineering in 3.5 years and remained in Louisiana, going to work for John Mecom, Sr.

He and Mecom established Circle Bar Drilling Company, a shallow-water drilling firm. It was sold in 1979 for a $20-million profit. The sale permitted Taylor to form his own exploration and production company, Taylor Energy Company.

In March 1988 Taylor was invited, as a role model, to speak to approximately 180 students who had failed at least two years at Livingston Middle School in East New Orleans and who were not expected to enter high school. Taylor told the assembled kids in that audience that if they stayed in school, maintained a "B" average, took the necessary college-prep courses, and stayed out of trouble and away from drugs, he would "see to it that they went to college."

Since then there have been no dropouts and no drug abusers in this group that calls itself "Taylor's Kids"; one-quarter of them have performed so well that they are in honors programs and advanced courses in high school—proving that the opportunity for a college education provides a positive alternative to drugs, crime, and dropping out.

Subsequently, Taylor researched higher education in Louisiana in depth. Louisiana's public four-year colleges and universities did not require entrance standards, and nearly 70 percent of all students who enrolled were dropping out before

Pat Taylor formed Taylor Energy Company in 1979.

completing a degree. Taylor began promoting his concept that public four-year colleges and universities should require entrance standards of at least an 18 ACT test score, a 2.5 grade point average, and completion of 17.5 credits of college-preparatory classes.

In return, students so qualified, but who were in lower- and middle-income families, could obtain a college education through waivers of tuition and fees. Through Taylor's dogged determination, the idea, called the Taylor Plan, was passed by the Louisiana Legislature and signed into law by Governor Charles Roemer in July 1989.

With the implementation of the plan, some 500 Louisiana youths enrolled in college in 1989 who otherwise could not have. In addition, high school science and math classes are filled with motivated students as never before. Community college attendance and retention figures are considerably increased. An educational awakening has come to Louisiana, the state that took the first step

in offering a college education to all who qualify.

A "60 Minutes" telecast by Mike Wallace in September 1989 highlighted Taylor's Kids and the Taylor Plan. Five states have passed copycat Taylor Plan legislation and another 20 are studying the implementation of the plan in their states. In other words, a national trend is being set, reflecting an educational policy that says public education provided to U.S. students needs to be increased from 12 years to 16 years.

This is a need for the good of society as a whole. Fulfillment of this need will cure illiteracy and wipe out a host of social ills and crimes. It will provide an educated national work force. It will wipe out generational welfare and eliminate what is becoming a permanent underclass. This is the heritage that maverick Patrick F. Taylor created.

CHEVRON CORPORATION

CHEVRON CORPORATION, formerly Standard Oil Company of California, started operating more than 100 years ago. Chevron today is an international energy giant, active in exploration, production, shipping, trading, pipelines, gas processing, refining, and fuels marketing.

Chevron U.S.A., Inc., is the domestic oil and gas subsidiary of Chevron Corporation. The company has approximately 2,000 employees in New Orleans and 4,100 employees and 1,272 retirees in Louisiana.

The Eastern Region Exploration, Land, and Production (EL&P) unit of Chevron U.S.A., Inc., is one of the top oil and gas producers in the Gulf of Mexico, holding more than twice the producing acreage of its nearest competitor. The firm recognizes that its

success also depends on its ability to meet the community's expectations of safety in operations and in the protection of the environment.

In addition to the EL&P unit, which is one of three regional offices for Chevron U.S.A. Inc., Chevron Chemical Company's Oak Point Plant has been operating in Belle Chasse, a community adjacent to New Orleans, since 1943. Operated by the firm's Oronite Additives Division, the plant is one of the world's largest producers of high-quality fuel and lubricant additives, serving both the United States and international markets.

The Oak Point facility is going through one of the largest expansion and modernization programs in its history. The $160-million package of projects will nearly double the facil-

An artist's rendering of Chevron's regional headquarters at 935 Gravier Street in New Orleans.

ity's production capacity of fuel and lubricant additives.

Also, during 1989, the 541 existing Gulf service stations in Louisiana became Chevron outlets, raising the red, white, and blue Chevron hallmark over each business establishment. In all, more than 130 Gulf outlets in the New Orleans metropolitan community made the transition to Chevron.

The brand conversion marked the completion of the merger between Gulf Corporation and Chevron in 1984. Converting Gulf stations to the Chevron brand pumped about $3 million into the local economy. Company officials maintained their commitment to Louisiana saying, "We're proud to make this kind of investment in such an important marketing region. Chevron has a long history of commitment to customers, product quality, and community involvement, and the best parts of our commitment will continue—the same friendly faces and service and the high-quality products that our customers have come to expect."

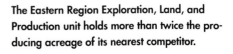

The Eastern Region Exploration, Land, and Production unit holds more than twice the producing acreage of its nearest competitor.

WALK, HAYDEL & ASSOCIATES, INC.

NEW ORLEANS-BASED WALK, Haydel & Associates, Inc., was begun in 1959 by Frank H. Walk and Gerald M. Haydel to provide industries with excellent engineering and project-management services. It would be difficult to find any industrial facilities between the mouth of the Mississippi River and Baton Rouge that have not utilized the engineering expertise of this firm. Walk, Haydel has contributed to the industrial development of the region while growing into a large and diverse engineering firm providing services in all engineering disciplines as well as architectural design, overall project management, and construction management.

More than 3,000 engineering assignments have been completed

The Central Plaza headquarters of Walk, Haydel & Associates, Inc., is located on historic Carondolet Street in New Orleans.

within the New Orleans/ Baton Rouge corridor, ranging from small revamps to projects of national and worldwide importance. Even today, as the firm's staff exceeds 500 people, large and small projects hold equal importance.

Walk, Haydel successfully meets the needs of a broad range of industrial clients by providing quality services at a reasonable price—a reputation that attracts not only private industry, but the U.S. government as well. During the past decade Walk, Haydel served the U.S. Department of Energy's Strategic Petroleum Reserve Program in the design and construction management of salt-dome oil-storage facilities. It was for one of these projects that Walk, Haydel recently received the National Society of Professional Engineers' (NSPE) Award for Outstanding Achievement. The firm also received the NSPE award for engineering excellence in 1981 for the design of the Louisiana Offshore Oil Port.

The types of projects completed by Walk, Haydel range from the design and construction management of refineries to providing architectural, engineering, planning, and construction management services for the outdoor Papal Mass held in New Orleans in 1987.

Other Walk, Haydel projects include marine docks, process unit expansions, fertilizer and pulp-and-paper manufacturing facilities, offshore oil and gas facilities, and various building projects. Walk, Haydel has also carried out projects on five continents.

Walk, Haydel & Associates, Inc., has provided engineering services at this refinery site for more than 10 years. Projects have been as diverse as the design of a distributed control system to the design of a flare gas recovery system.

The large, well-qualified, and dedicated staff enables the firm to handle major projects and offer clients a full range of services. Skilled staff members from three other offices in Baton Rouge, Mobile, and Little Rock often contribute to projects being handled in the New Orleans main office and vice versa.

Walk, Haydel has established itself as a leader in environmental work as a respected consultant to industry and regulatory agencies alike. Private plant owners, the state environmental departments, the U.S. Environmental Protection Agency, and numerous federal departments have all utilized Walk, Haydel's environmental expertise on projects including environmental assessments and audits; permitting (air, water, solid, and hazardous waste); remedial investigations, feasibility studies, and remedial design; design of solid- and hazardous-waste treatment, storage, and disposal facilities; and wastewater-treatment and air-emission control systems.

In the coming years Walk, Haydel & Associates, Inc., will continue to expand on its proven track record for meeting challenging engineering problems with the innovation and responsiveness that have become its trademark.

Photo by Brad Crooks

THE PORT

Millions of tons of cargo cross the wharves of the port of New Orleans each year, placing the city at the forefront of U.S. port activity.

Photo by Brad Crooks

INTERNATIONAL SHIPHOLDING CORPORATION

SPECIALISTS IN WATERBORNE freight transportation, International Shipholding Corporation (ISC) had its beginnings in New Orleans just after World War II as Central Gulf Steamship Corporation, a U.S.-flag vessel owner and operator formed by Niels F. Johnsen (1895-1974) and his sons, Niels W. Johnsen and Erik F. Johnsen, who are currently chairman and president, respectively, of ISC and principal subsidiary Central Gulf Lines, Inc.

Today ISC, through its subsidiaries, is engaged in ocean and inland waterborne freight transportation worldwide. ISC has offices in New Orleans, New York, Washington, D.C., Houston, Rotterdam, and Singapore, while maintaining a network of marketing and operating agents in major world

Above: Charting a course for success at International Shipholding Corporation are chairman Niels W. Johnsen (left) and president Erik F. Johnsen.

Below: The SS *Green Wave,* Central Gulf's first vessel.

Above: An ice-strengthened multipurpose vessel, M/V *Green Wave,* is the fourth company vessel to bear this name.

Below: One of the company's U.S.-flag pure car carriers heads for New York.

cities. The firm's common stock is traded in the National NASDAQ Market System with the symbol INSH.

Major ISC subsidiaries are Central Gulf Lines, Inc., Waterman Steamship Corporation, Forest Lines Inc., and LCI Shipholdings, Inc., who together operate a fleet of 27 modern vessels.

Central Gulf Lines, Inc., is the oldest existing shipping company founded in Louisiana. The firm began operations in 1947 in New Orleans with one war-built Liberty ship and, in less than 20 years, became the

Below: U.S.-flag LASH vessel SS *Green Harbour* sets out from New Orleans.

A giant shipboard crane lifts LASH barges aboard the Waterman LASH vessel SS *Robert E. Lee* at New York.

leading carrier to ports east of Suez.

Recognizing a need to upgrade its liner service with modern shipping technology, Central Gulf had three large U.S.-flag LASH (Lighter Aboard Ship) vessels built and delivered by Avondale Shipyards of New Orleans in 1974 and 1975. The giant barge carriers continue to serve as the vanguard of Central Gulf's American fleet.

Two significant developments in the 1980s underscored Central Gulf's position as a leading U.S.-flag company. In 1982 the firm commenced a

The world's first LASH vessel, M/V *Acadia Forest,* is operated by Forest Lines Inc. in a regular liner service between the United States and Europe.

The 49,500-ton M/V *Probo Gull* is one of two combination bulk/products carriers in company service.

long-term domestic coal-transportation contract for a Florida-based utility. Fourteen towboats and 111 jumbo river barges deliver about 3 million tons of coal annually under the contract. By 1987 Central Gulf had built and begun operating two U.S.-flag pure car carriers (PCCs) for the transportation of automobiles between Japan and North America. Manned by U.S. officers and crews, the PCCs are part of a "historic first" program for the American Merchant Marine.

Central Gulf also operates two ice-strengthened multipurpose vessels and one modern roll on/roll off (RO/RO) vessel under long-term charter to the U.S. Navy's Military Sealift Command (MSC).

The first Central Gulf vessel was named *Green Wave* in honor of Tulane University, the alma mater of N.W. and E.F Johnsen, thus establishing an ongoing pattern for naming all the company's ships—*Green Bay,*

Green Harbour, and *Green Lake.*

Waterman Steamship Corporation is a U.S.-flag owner and operator founded in 1919 in Mobile, Alabama. Its administration and operations offices are situated in New Orleans, while its principal marketing department is located in New York.

Waterman is a subsidized U.S.-flag carrier operating four large LASH vessels in a regular liner service between U.S. Gulf of Mexico and Atlantic Coast ports, as well as ports in the Middle East, India, Pakistan, Bangladesh, and Southeast Asia. The company also operates three RO/RO vessels under a long-term charter to MSC.

The Waterman LASH vessels, named for famous Americans, include the SS *Robert E. Lee,* SS *Sam Houston,* and SS *Stonewall Jackson;* and the RO/RO ships, named for Congressional Medal of Honor recipients, are *Pfc. E.A. Obergon, Sgt. Matej Kocak,* and *Maj. S.W. Pless.*

Forest Lines Inc. has been operating LASH vessels for many years and currently provides a three-ship LASH liner service between U.S. Gulf and the southern Atlantic Coast ports and ports in the United Kingdom and North Europe. The vessels, M/V *Acadia Forest,* M/V *Atlantic Forest,* and M/V *Rhine Forest,* carry LASH barge loads of primarily forest products eastbound and return to the United States with a variety of neo-bulk cargoes.

LCI Shipholdings, Inc., operates LASH feeder vessels, pure car carriers, and combination bulk/products carriers known as PROBOS.

What was started in New Orleans 43 years ago as a new steamship company with one $550,000 vessel is now one of the nation's largest transportation corporations, with assets in excess of $450 million. International Shipholding Corporation maintains offices in the Poydras Center, situated in the heart of New Orleans—America's international city.

BISSO TOWBOAT COMPANY, INC.

THE STORY OF BISSO TOWBOAT Company, Inc., begins with the Mississippi River. It is the story of a family that has known the river well—people who have mastered every wily fluke of its currents, shallows, and deeps.

The company was founded in 1890 by Captain Joseph Bisso. After serving under Admiral David Farragut in the Union navy during the Civil War, Bisso returned to New Orleans, where he acquired property at the foot of Walnut Street near the levee and the river.

In addition to his experience in the navy, Bisso gained valuable knowledge about the tricks of Old Muddy in his first business. He opened a small lumberyard on the river in 1870 and began transporting logs down the river from Natchez, Mississippi, and other points to the north. The logs were made into rafts and piloted down the river by Bisso without the benefit of assistance from any vessel.

As a result, his lumber concern prospered, and he decided to buy a towboat. With the acquisition of *The Leo,* Bisso instituted general towing in the Port of New Orleans. This marked the evolution from a lumber firm to Bisso Towboat Company.

The towing firm, like the lumber

Above: Scott Slatten, secretary of Bisso Towboat Company, Inc.

Left: The owners of Bisso Towboat Company, Inc., Cecilia Bisso Slatten and Captain William A. Slatten, stand in front of a portrait of their ancestor, Captain William A. "Billy" Bisso, in the firm's executive offices.

Below: The tug *Sandra Kay* on her way to meet *Robert E. Lee* in a typical day's work in the port.

company, proved to be a successful operation, and at the time of Bisso's death in 1907, the organization's fleet had grown to include five tugboats and one river steamer. When Bisso died, leadership of the operation passed to Captain William A. "Billy" Bisso.

Like his father, Billy Bisso proved to be an aggressive businessman. In 1908 he formed the New Orleans Coal Company, and, under his guidance, it became the largest ship coaling and colliery business in the port. In 1922 he merged the coal firm with Bisso Towboat Company.

It was the determination of this strong-willed man, in fact, that saw the organization through the Great Depression. By the time World War II broke out, Bisso was the only surviving ship-towing firm in the port. Bisso then entered the war years, towing to safety many American ships disabled by torpedoes in the Gulf of Mexico.

During the immediate postwar years Bisso underwent the traumatic

The tugboat *Capt. Billy Slatten,* so named for the man who has earned the title, "Master of the Rivers."

transition period that faced many maritime firms—the transition from steam to diesel power. The big steam tugs of the prewar years had become too expensive to man and operate. Reluctantly, Bisso heeded the advice of younger minds in the family and gradually began making the move to smaller, more maneuverable, and more powerful diesel tugboats.

Bisso died at the age of 88 in 1963. The firm was reorganized under the leadership of his daughter, Cecilia Bisso Slatten, and his grandson, Captain William A. Slatten.

Realizing that a massive rebuilding and replacement program was necessary if the company was to maintain its competitive position and continue offering its customers first-class service, William Slatten took a fleet that was still only half converted to the modern ways and continued to revitalize it.

Today the Bisso fleet is one of the most modern tug fleets in the world. All vessels are equipped with the finest VHF and radio communications systems, which have a range of 100 miles and operate on a 24-hour basis.

"Master of the Rivers" is the title awarded to the person who has become intimate with the quirks of the Mississippi and other important rivers of the United States. Just as the men of the Bisso family all have been awarded this professional title, the tugs of the modern Bisso fleet all are under the command of those who have earned the right to be called Master of the Rivers, or simply "captain" for short.

Bisso was founded on a philosophy of going where the action is. When lumber was profitable, Bisso was in the lumber business. The same was true with coal. When changing times brought a demand for diesel-powered tugs, Bisso made the transition and captured the business. When it became obvious that customers wanted to be able to get more than one service

from a firm—to avoid a lot of unnecessary middleman red tape—Bisso set out to make it easy on its clients by providing a one-stop maritime shopping center of services for ships and shipowners.

When new trends create new customer demands, Bisso Towboat Company, Inc., will meet those demands because management believes that a customer's requirements, whether routine or of a special nature, are the company's first and only concern. It has been that way for generations.

Bill Slatten, Jr., company treasurer.

LYKES LINES

SINCE THE BEGINNING OF THE twentieth century, Lykes Lines has been a leader among the world's ocean transportation companies. Its growth and development is a fascinating chapter of history—a chapter that spans sail and steam, war and peace, depression and prosperity. Through it all, Lykes has built and maintained a worldwide reputation for service, integrity, and innovation.

Lykes Lines is an integrated ocean transportation company that carries containerized and break-bulk cargoes on trade routes between the United States and its major trading partners.

The range of markets served by Lykes is second to no other carrier that flies the American flag. Utilizing a fleet of 28 American-flag vessels, the company provides ocean transportation services for cargoes in seven principal trade areas: northern Europe,

Lykes operates container vessels with destinations to ports in South America, northern Europe, the United Kingdom, and the Mediterranean.

The Lykes Center in New Orleans, world headquarters of one of the largest American-flag cargo carriers.

the United Kingdom, the Mediterranean, South America, Africa, the Indian subcontinent, and the Far East.

Through connecting carrier arrangements with various railroads and trucking companies, Lykes provides efficient and rapid transportation of cargo to and from inland destinations in all of the regions served.

Headquartered in New Orleans, with offices throughout the United States, the Lykes organization comprises 1,000 employees and agents worldwide that provide competitive ocean transportation services for cargoes moving in international commerce.

Lykes Lines traces its roots to 1900. It was then that Frederick and Howell Lykes, two of the seven sons of Dr. Howell Tyson Lykes, began shipping cattle to Cuba in a 109-foot schooner, the *Doctor Lykes*.

In 1906 the two brothers made the jump from shipping family steers to shipping commercial freight. From Galveston, Lykes began offering general cargo transportation between the West Gulf and Caribbean ports. Soon it was operating 21 chartered schooners, side-wheel steamers, and other craft.

By 1910 four more Lykes brothers—Lipscomb, John, Thompson, and Joseph—had joined the family enterprise, and the corporate structure of Lykes Bros., Inc., came into being.

With the United States' entry into World War I, Lykes made a critical decision that contributed to the company's growth. The U.S. government decided to build a strong U.S. Merchant Marine, and Lykes Bros. agreed to fully cooperate. Lykes abandoned its foreign-flag affiliations and began operating entirely as a U.S.-flag carrier. By 1920 the firm was operating 15 chartered ships, and two years later Lykes purchased five U.S.-flag ships that were built during the war.

The burst of shipbuilding activity during World War I produced several hundred merchant ships. Most remained under government ownership but were chartered to private operators. The intent of the Merchant Marine Act of 1928 was to restore the U.S. fleet to private ownership.

Lykes committed itself to the development of a strong merchant marine. By 1933 Lykes had increased its fleet to 67 vessels. By the mid-1930s the firm's trade routes extended almost as far as today.

During World War II Lykes han-

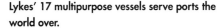

Lykes' 17 multipurpose vessels serve ports the world over.

Lykes Express Class container vessels call the Port of New Orleans home.

dled 60 million tons of cargo. At the peak of fighting, Lykes operated 125 cargo ships of all types. Twenty-two Lykes ships were sunk during the war at a cost of 272 lives.

During the postwar years the company's shipping operations yielded steady profits. Lykes adhered to its conservative policy of paying small dividends and plowing large portions of the profits back into the business.

Lykes participated in a historic event on March 18, 1979, when the SS *Letitia Lykes* became the first U.S.-flag ship to call in a Chinese port since the country's communist revo-

lution in 1949.

The firm opened a new chapter in 1983, when it was purchased by Interocean Steamship Corp., a Florida company whose stockholders included descendants of the original Lykes brothers and members of Lykes management.

Today Lykes' versatility has positioned the firm to greet the 1990s as a major carrier in ocean transportation. With expanded trade-route authority, Lykes container and multipurpose vessels are able to serve not only the most industrialized countries of the world, but also those third-world nations where import and export is dependent on conventional vessel traffic. The company's vast, world-wide intermodal network and state-of-the-art computer and electronic communications systems continue to assure its leadership.

With trade routes extending from the Atlantic, Pacific, U.S. Gulf coasts, and the Great Lakes to the United Kingdom, Europe, the Mediterranean, Africa, South America, the Red Sea, the Indian subcontinent, and the Far East, Lykes Lines looks toward the approaching century with confidence—a confidence earned through decades of experience.

COOPER/T. SMITH STEVEDORING

IN 1842 A YOUNG IRISH immigrant, Terence Smith, settled on the lower Mississippi River. Seeing the demand for his sail-making talents quickly diminish and, with the invention of steam, Terence began work on the waterfront and called his company T. Smith and Son.

Back in the early 1900s young Angus R. Cooper worked for the Munson Steamship Line in New Orleans as its U.S. Gulf superintendent. Later he formed his own business, Cooper Stevedoring Company, and moved its main office to Mobile, Alabama.

Both the Smith and Cooper families became premier stevedoring companies in their own ports. The Smiths stayed in New Orleans primarily and the Coopers operated in Mobile, New Orleans, and St. Louis. In 1983 these two firms joined together to form one of the most powerful stevedoring companies in the United States, operating in 26 ports on all three coasts, America's inland waterway, and abroad. Today it is managed by Angus R. Cooper II, chairman and chief executive officer, and David J. Cooper, president, grandsons of the founder and sole owners of the company.

Many changes have come about since Angus Cooper made contracts on the waterfront in 1905. Back in those days deals were signed and sealed with a handshake, and performance was measured by how well you kept your word. Break-bulk cargo such as bagged goods, lumber, cotton, sugar, and pineapples provided the need for stevedoring services. It is understandable how Cooper became the first to introduce the use of lift trucks in stevedoring. These were platform-type lifts, forerunner of the more efficient forklifts widely used today.

State-of-the-art equipment is one of the well-known trademarks of Cooper/ T. Smith. The firm's large floating derrick cranes are the workhorses used for heavy lifts and midstream operations.

As the export of American agricultural and mining products continues to expand, Cooper/T. Smith is there to meet the demand. Raw grains and grain products move from the grain belt of America's heartland, down the Mississippi River, overseas, and around the world using Cooper/T. Smith innovation. Coal, ores, alloys, and other bulk products are also continuously moved on the Mississippi River and are handled both for export and import by Cooper/T. Smith's midstream operation.

Another product that touches the lives of Americans is steel. Mention steel in the Port of New Orleans and the synonym is Cooper/T. Smith Stevedoring. Steel for cars, drilling pipe, tire rims, and steel-belted radials comes about because one firm has the heavy equipment and technical know-how to handle the product efficiently.

To meet the demands of the contemporary trading business, Cooper/T. Smith combines internationally experienced personnel, computer and communication technologies, the latest in cargo-handling equipment, and an ongoing safety and loss-control program to provide the maximum in service to its customers.

Cooper/T. Smith Stevedoring's young, aggressive management team has built the company into a major player in the maritime industry. Angus Cooper and Terence Smith would take pride in the firm's worldwide operations and reputation for competence.

Cooper/T. Smith operates in 26 ports on three U.S. coasts and in America's inland waterway system with a tradition of personal service and customer satisfaction.

INTERNATIONAL-MATEX TANK TERMINALS

INTERNATIONAL-MATEX TANK Terminals represents an investment from this community of international dimensions—an investment in storage tanks, skilled manpower, and in road, rail, and wharfage infrastructure that provide secure inventory management and transfer capabilities for the major liquid product commodities of international commerce. Consumer access to these products—including fuel products, food commodities, and general chemicals—depends upon port facilities such as these and accompanying modern, environmentally sound storage.

New Orleans provides the headquarters and New Orleanians the leadership for this dynamic company, a partnership with a vigorous Dutch counterpart. The firm conducts its major operations on both the east and west banks of the lower Mississippi River, on the Atlantic and Gulf coasts, in Canada, and in 27 other major ports in Europe, the Pacific, and Latin America.

Where did this service network that now spans the continents get its start? The New Orleans base was established by attorney and New Orleans

native James J. Coleman, Sr., who in 1938 founded International Tank Terminals—an ambitious but prescient name. The firm had grown to six sites in 1975 when it merged with the Van Ommeren group from the Netherlands to form the major international operation it represents today.

The civic leadership that continues to characterize Coleman's commitment to his community is now reflected as well in the efforts and commitment of IMTT's present chief executive officer, James Coleman's son, Thomas B. Coleman. The firm's leadership has been conspicuously committed to the New Orleans image as seen by the rest of the world. The Coleman family has invested substantially in quality office space and hotel housing that serve both executive and tourist visitors to the city.

Right: James J. Coleman, Sr. (right), founder of International-Matex Tank Terminals, with his son, Thomas B. Coleman, the company's chief executive officer.

Below: An aerial view shows the vastness of one of the International-Matex Tank Terminals in New Orleans.

IMTT's leadership also assists in bringing the outside world to New Orleans through service as representatives for five separate nations in the city's consular corps.

When the French built their North American base that extended from Quebec to New Orleans, they envisioned an economic network that was both commercially viable and that also enriched the local quality of life through the exchange that comes with international trade and commerce. Today operations at International-Matex Tank Terminals reflect that same vision.

NETWORKS

New Orleans' network of energy, communication, and transportation providers contributes to its status as a major metropolitan center.

Photo by Brad Crooks

ENTERGY CORPORATION AND LP&L/NOPSI

THREE YEARS AFTER THOMAS Edison developed the first practical incandescent lamp, New Orleans' brilliantly lit waterfront inspired visiting Mark Twain to write, "It is a driving place, commercially, [with] a great river, ocean, and railway business. At the date of our visit, it was the best-lighted city in the union, electrically speaking. The New Orleans lights were more numerous than those of New York, and very much better. One had this modified noonday, not only in Canal and some neighboring chief streets, but all along a stretch of five miles of river frontage."

For a century electricity has fueled New Orleans' growth, and for nearly as long Entergy Corporation and the

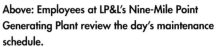

Above: Employees at LP&L's Nine-Mile Point Generating Plant review the day's maintenance schedule.

Left: Representatives of the Middle South Electrical System work closely with commercial and industrial customers.

companies of the Middle South Electric System have supplied the electricity.

Headquartered in the Crescent City, Entergy Corporation is one of nine public utility holding companies and one of the largest electric utilities in the United States. The firm serves 1.7 million retail customers in Arkansas, Missouri, Mississippi, and Louisiana through its operating subsidiaries: Arkansas Power & Light, Mississippi Power & Light, Louisiana Power & Light (LP&L), and New Orleans Public Service Inc. (NOPSI).

The system also includes Entergy Operations, Inc., a wholesale generating company that operates the Grand Gulf Nuclear Station in Port Gibson, Mississippi, Waterford 3 Nuclear Unit at Taft, Louisiana, and Units 1 and 2 at Arkansas Nuclear One at Russellville, Arkansas, and Entergy Services, headquartered in New Orleans, providing engineering and other technical services to the entire system. Final regulatory approval for a new subsidiary named Entergy Power, Inc., was anticipated in mid-1990. Entergy Power, Inc., will market electricity to wholesale customers beyond the Middle South Electric System.

NOPSI and LP&L have provided electric and gas service to the City of New Orleans since the 1920s. NOPSI was organized in 1922, at the recommendation of a federally appointed citizens advisory group, to consolidate the city's numerous and struggling electric, gas, and streetcar operations into one modern public utility. With consolidation, electric, gas, and streetcar service improved, demand rose, and both the city and the corporation flourished.

NOPSI's sister company, LP&L, began its operations in 1927, originally providing electric, gas, water, and transportation services to various parts of Louisiana, including the Algiers community of New Orleans, located on the west bank of the Mississippi River across from downtown New Orleans.

Today NOPSI and LP&L employ some 3,500 Louisiana residents while supplying electricity to 763,700 retail customers. Entergy Services, Inc., adds payroll for another 900 employees to the New Orleans economy. LP&L and NOPSI have a combined generating

Left: Christmas in the Oaks, sponsored by NOPSI, has become a favorite New Orleans tradition.

Below: Entergy chairman and president Edwin Lupberger, with Palmer Elementary School children, demonstrates that supporting public education is a major objective of Entergy.

capacity of almost 6.7 million kilowatts. Service is provided via more than 27,000 miles of transmission and distribution lines, which are part of the 80,000-mile interconnected Middle South Electric System network. The Middle South System, as a whole, has a diversified generating capacity of 15.5 million kilowatts, including more than 60 generating units utilizing coal, gas, nuclear, oil, and some hydro power.

The Middle South Electric System is a recognized partner in the region's economic development—a commitment that dates back to the system's founder, Harvey Couch. Couch was a firm believer that individuals, given encouragement and backing, could create their own opportunities to help themselves.

In the 1930s Couch served as chairman of the Reconstruction Finance Corporation under President Herbert Hoover and President Franklin Delano Roosevelt, distributing public works funds to help the country out of the Depression.

In 1948 the governors of Louisiana, Mississippi, and Arkansas came together on the banks of the Mississippi River to pledge their support of the Middle South. In 1988, 40 years later, the region's three governors reenacted that historic gathering, rededicating their states to work together to improve opportunities in the Middle South. In both instances, the Middle South Electric System supported the efforts of the governors to build regional teamwork for economic development.

The firm has also been an active partner in efforts to promote the region to potential investors domestically and abroad. With the region's governors and other development officials, Middle South Electric System representatives have traveled to Japan, Korea, Taiwan, and Europe, meeting with government officials and corporate executives who have expressed an interest in the Middle South.

System representatives spend time with visiting Korean businessmen at work and at play.

The company also promotes the region through print and broadcast advertising campaigns. A single advertisement in *Fortune* magazine, for instance, generated more than 1,100 responses from interested individuals and organizations. And a company-produced video entitled "NEW Orleans" has enticed investors, visitors, and businesspeople from the world over with its portrayal of the city's resources. The video has been translated into Chinese, Japanese, French, and Spanish and distributed by the New Orleans and the River Region Chamber of Commerce.

Along with its innovations in electricity operations, the firm sponsors a wealth of innovative educational and economic development initiatives that are working.

For example, in Orleans Parish, prison inmates are learning to read

with the help of the PALS (Principle of the Alphabet Literacy System) interactive computer system. Developed by IBM, PALS enables a single tutor to simultaneously teach 16 students to read. Harry, a 27-year-old inmate with 19 months left of a three-year sentence for attempted burglary, recently declined acceptance in the work-release program in order to attend the PALS lab.

"Sure, I could get out of prison for a few hours a day," he explains, "but when I was finally released, I still wouldn't know anything. By staying 'inside' and going to school, I can get a real job on the outside." Many other inmates feel the same way.

LP&L and NOPSI sponsor the prison's PALS lab, with assistance from Entergy Corporation, which also supports PALS laboratories in Monroe, Louisiana; Jackson, Mississippi; and Helena, Arkansas. The companies also fund literacy and high-school diploma equivalency programs, student and educator leadership institutes, and a host of other educational development programs.

The firm's hands-on approach to economic development is also producing results. For example, a company economic development advertisement that ran in a national business publication led to American Fabric's decision to open three divisions in Louisiana. Working with LP&L, the mayor of Bogalusa, and the president of the Washington Parish Industrial Development Foundation, American Fabric opened its lace division in Bogalusa in 1987, added an embroidery division the following year, and a third division in 1989.

In Webster Parish, Louisiana, Standard Manufacturing Company, a division of American Standard, is locating a medium-size facility in the North Webster Industrial Park—another industrial-development project funded by local tax millages and private grants, including a $5,000 grant from LP&L. Standard Manufacturing added approximately 75 new jobs and an annual payroll of between $850,000 and $1.2 million to the Webster Parish area.

Other examples abound. LP&L's

Operation Bootstrap has earned national recognition for its support of local entrepreneurial efforts. Providing start-up support to local developers of new products, Operation Bootstrap is currently helping bring nine new products to market: a baby sling that holds infants upright after eating to avoid digestive problems, a newly designed swimming pool filter, a removable shopping box for wheelchairs, a two-way ratchet wrench for work in tight spaces, a device for building and maintaining pipes, a method for measuring the toxicity of certain substances used by the oil industry to diagnose problems in electric systems, an improved Endo Tracheal Tube for surgical procedures, a piping component with

Advanced electronic intelligence helps dispatchers direct electricity throughout the system's 91,000-square-mile area.

greater durability to withstand abrasive fluids, and a device useful in repair of large natural gas pipelines.

Together, community and company efforts are building a can-do spirit in New Orleans that bodes well for the city's future. In partnership with other organizations and community leaders, Entergy Corporation and the companies of the Middle South Electric System have helped thousands of individuals and created thousands of jobs.

It is an effort that is gathering momentum, as more and more people realize that there is no limit to the power of a good idea, and that ideas are an unlimited resource. Entergy Corporation, Louisiana Power & Light, and New Orleans Public Service are committed to doing their part—continually coming up with new ways to provide electric services at a competitive cost and generating new ideas for development.

SOUTH CENTRAL BELL

TELECOMMUNICATIONS ARE TO *the high-innovation economy what railroads, rivers, canals, and highways were and are to the indus- trial world."*

—David Birch, professor at the Massachusetts Institute of Technology and author of *Job Creation in America.*

All hours of the day and night, South Central Bell people and systems are on the job, providing Information Age ser- vices to the people of New Orleans.

The City of New Orleans is provid- ing governmental services with the help of a recently installed, versatile, 3,000-station ESSX® service telephone system that handles voice and data transmission with ease.

Phones are ringing with distinctive sounds at homes around the city so

South Central Bell account executive Shirley Patron and New Orleans mayor Sidney Barthelemy discuss plans to upgrade the city's telecommunications network as technician Mary Farmer installs equipment.

families can tell before answering whether it is a business or a personal call, thanks to RingMas- ter® service.

People are deciding at the last minute to watch a newly released movie and ordering it automatically from their cable company via TicketTaker® service.

All these services and more are available in New Orleans because of South Central Bell's so- phisticated telecommuni- cations network.

Alexander Graham Bell would be surprised at and proud of all the ways people use the telephone today: to transmit voice and data at the same time on the same line, to send medical test results, to bank from home, to make three-way calls, and more. Most New Orleanians today could not imagine their homes or businesses without modern telecommunications.

"It is clear that the United States is moving into the Information Age very

Long-distance traffic to and from the New Orleans public network passes through this switching center managed by Steve Schneller.

rapidly," says Timothy Ryan, Ph.D., professor of economics and director of the Division of Business and Eco- nomic Research at the University of New Orleans. "Computers have be- come commonplace in almost every office in every type of business. In- formation must be moved between these facilities constantly; you can't wait for tomorrow's mail and remain competitive," he adds.

As a major port, a center for na- tional and international commerce, and a major tourist attraction, New Orleans requires a dependable, state- of-the-art telecommunications system. And South Central Bell delivers by providing a wide range of services, including Lightgate® Service, a high- capacity, private-line, digital commu- nications service with end-to-end fiber-optic technology.

ESSX® Service is a switching-of- fice-based, dependable, flexible sys- tem that provides dozens of optional features such as station hunting, di- rect inward and outward dialing, and station message detail recording. It is updated frequently and monitored around the clock.

Other available services include SyncroNet® Service, a private-line, multipoint or point-to-point data-

Supervisor Paul Helmers inspects fiber-optic cable that quickly and accurately transmits voice and data across the Crescent City Connection Bridge and under downtown streets.

transmission service, and Central Office Local Area Network (COLAN) Service, a service that provides simultaneous voice and data transmission over a single line.

South Central Bell's team of 7,300 Louisiana employees is adept at meeting specialized and reliable day-to-day telecommunications requirements. When the city hosted the 1988 Republican National Convention, several Super Bowls, the NCAA Basketball Finals, and a visit from Pope John Paul II, South Central Bell provided extensive special arrangements for television and radio circuits, as well as thousands of temporary extra phone lines for journalists and visitors.

At the same time the company handled these events, it continued to serve 1.5 million Louisiana customers, who make about 26 million calls per day. The firm has an investment of $3.6 billion in telecommunications equipment in Louisiana and continues to build and modernize the network by investing about $200 million in new capital annually.

South Central Bell was created in 1968, when Southern Bell, which had operated in Louisiana since 1926, was split into two corporations. Southern Bell took over from the pioneering Cumberland Telephone Company, which began providing service in New Orleans in 1879, only four years after the invention of the telephone. For a short time before, the Great

Southern Telephone & Telegraph Company operated an exchange in New Orleans.

Currently part of BellSouth, one of the nation's largest corporations and an international leader in telecommunications and related services, South Central Bell operates in Louisiana, Mississippi, Kentucky, Tennessee, and Alabama. Its Louisiana headquarters is in New Orleans.

Like many other companies in the New Orleans area, South Central Bell supports a variety of community programs through corporate and individual employee involvement. Recognizing that one of the greatest needs is education, the firm has adopted nearly one dozen Louisiana schools, in cooperation with employees and retirees in the Louisiana Telephone Pioneers, part of America's largest volunteer organization. A new program, Volunteer Service Grants, recognizes the value of employees' community activities by enabling them to apply for grants for the nonprofit organizations where they volunteer.

As business and community leaders make progress in diversifying and expanding New Orleans' economic base, modern telecommunications systems become even more vital. "The availability of most modern telecommunications technology is no longer a frill; without this technology, firms simply cannot compete with firms that have it," explains UNO's Ryan.

As New Orleans prepares for the future, South Central Bell's team will remain committed to doing its part to keep the city progressive and competitive for the benefit of all.

DELTA AIR LINES, INC.

DELTA AIR LINES IS NEW Orleans' number-one airline, carrying more passengers there than any other airline and bringing an annual economic impact to the city estimated at $50 million. With 750,000 passengers annually traveling on Delta to and from New Orleans, the airline offers nonstop service to all of its major hubs where passengers will find convenient connections to more than 270 cities served by Delta and The Delta Connection carriers worldwide.

Delta traces its history of passenger service at New Orleans to two major influences. In fact, Delta's heritage can be linked to the cotton fields of Louisiana where the company began

Delta Air Lines leads the industry in passenger satisfaction as the major U.S. airline receiving the fewest number of complaints per 100,000 passengers flown since 1974, according to U.S. Department of Transportation records.

With more than 800 employees at work in New Orleans, Delta is always ready to provide special services for its passengers who need them.

as Huff Daland Dusters, the world's first aerial crop-dusting operation. Chicago and Southern Air Lines (C&S), a struggling new airline (originally known as Pacific Seaboard Air Service), submitted a bid to carry mail over the New Orleans to Chicago route. C&S, which would merge with Delta in 1953, began service from New Orleans to Chicago via Memphis in 1934. Meanwhile, Delta brought its first passenger service to New Orleans in 1943 with a 21-seat DC-3.

More than 800 Delta professionals work in New Orleans in many areas of airline operations. Delta's direct economic impact on the New Orleans area reaches some $50 million annually. Approximately $30 million of this figure is earmarked for salaries, with the remainder used for

items such as landing fees, rental, utilities, passenger food, fuel, and state and local taxes.

In addition to its operations at New Orleans International Airport, Delta operates a district marketing office and reservations center in the city. In addition, 100 pilots and 300 flight attendants are based in New Orleans for the company.

Delta is one of the world's largest airlines, operating 2,400 flights daily to cities worldwide. Carrying 68 million passengers per year, Delta and The Delta Connection carriers serve 270 cities in the United States, Great Britain, West Germany, Ireland, the Netherlands, Japan, Korea, Taiwan, Canada, Mexico, Bermuda, and the Bahamas.

Delta's fleet of 430 aircraft is the youngest of any major U.S. airline with an average age of only 8.4 years. With an investment of $3 billion in new aircraft over the past three years alone,

Delta now has aircraft on order and option valued in excess of $23 billion.

Delta leads the industry in passenger satisfaction as the major airline receiving the fewest number of complaints per 100,000 passengers flown since 1974, according to U.S. Department of Transportation records. Delta is also the only airline ever to be ranked the number-one U.S. carrier for five consecutive years by the readers of the prestigious *Travel & Holiday Magazine.* Travel agents in a survey by *ASTA Agency Management* magazine named Delta the number-one U.S. airline in all categories—best in passenger satisfaction for both business and leisure clients and

The Boeing 757 is one of the more than 400 modern aircraft in Delta's fleet, which is the youngest of any major U.S. airline. Recognized as a leader in the introduction of new aircraft and technology, Delta today has aircraft on order and option valued in excess of $23 billion.

best in service to travel agents.

Delta also leads the industry in schedule reliability, according to a recent study of schedule reliability performance in the airline industry by Dr. Julius Maldutis, a noted airline security analyst with Salomon Brothers, Inc. During the six years covered in the report, Delta was the

only carrier to consistently complete 99 percent or higher of its scheduled flights.

One of the nation's most financially stable airlines, Delta has paid successive dividends to its stockholders every year since 1949 and has been profitable for 41 out of the past 42 fiscal years.

But throughout Delta's history, the company's management has maintained that of all factors involved—routes, equipment, facilities, and employees—its employees have contributed the most to the corporate success by providing the highest-possible standards of service to its customers.

WVUE-TV

MAKING GOOD THINGS Happen." That's the commitment of the television station WVUE, located in the heart of New Orleans.

The ABC affiliate adopted the mission statement in November 1986 and has since proven that a television station can do much more than entertain and inform. Community service is an integral part of WVUE's daily operation.

The station has developed several annual projects under the "Making Good Things Happen" umbrella. Among them is "Making the Grade," a nine-month campaign designed to recognize parents, teachers, and stu-

jobs to fill. As many as 300 applications followed a single "Job Search" report. "Friday Feast" is a weekly food review which presents recipes that viewers can make at home. And "Tuesday's Child" is a weekly report featuring area children who are available for adoption.

While these features help augment the station's mission statement, News 8 New Orleans has been recognized as a leader for day-to-day news coverage. The news team was presented the Best Newscast honor of 1989 by the Press Club of New Orleans, along with the Associated Press' Best Weathercast. And in 1990, WVUE was

chosen Best Newscast in Louisiana by the Associated Press and the Press Club of New Orleans.

WVUE has also expanded its production facilities. The station now hosts many local, regional, and national producers and directors with its state-of-the-art facilities. The station has the area's largest sound stage, measuring 56 feet by 81 feet by 20 feet, with a hard cyc measuring 43 feet by 35 feet by 20 feet. In addition, a 3400 CMX on-line editing suite is interfaced with an ADO 2000 FX unit, 200 GVG switcher, and various interformat VTR equipment to allow for specialized post production.

Under the direction of Burnham Broadcasting Company, WVUE in New Orleans is dedicated to quality in television broadcasting. It is a station committed to the growth and development of the community. In short, WVUE is a television station that is making good things happen in New Orleans.

Left: WVUE Channel 8, the ABC affiliate in New Orleans, makes good things happen in the community.

Below: Many local, regional, and national producers and directors take advantage of WVUE's expanded, state-of-the-art production and post-production facilities.

dents who are making a difference in education. During prom and graduation season, the station launches "Operation Prom Grad," a campaign against drinking and driving. And, in May, the station salutes high school valedictorians for their academic excellence with its annual "Best of the Class" campaign.

News 8 New Orleans, in addition to reporting the breaking news of a growing city, also subscribes to the station's "Making Good Things Happen" spirit. A series of news-you-can-use features appears daily in the station's 5, 6, or 10 o'clock newscasts. "Healthwatch" offers viewers a dose of medical news five days per week. "Call Eight" solves viewer problems and offers consumer information. "Job Search" reports on companies with

Photo by Brad Crooks

BUSINESS AND PROFESSIONS

Greater New Orleans' business and professional community brings a wealth of ability, expertise, and service to the area.

Photo by Bob Rowan/Progressive Image Photography

FIRST NATIONAL BANK OF COMMERCE

LIKE THE GRAND CITY OF NEW Orleans, First National Bank of Commerce was born on the Mississippi River, bred on commerce, and bent on tradition.

Its history is as inseparable from New Orleans as Mardi Gras, sweet honeysuckle in bloom deep in the Garden District, and the streetcars that travel down historic St. Charles Avenue.

First National Bank of Commerce (First NBC) began in 1831, only 16 years following the Battle of New Orleans and 28 years after the Louisiana Purchase, with the birth of its predecessor, the New Orleans Canal and Banking Company.

The Canal Bank's charter provided that it would construct a canal from Lake Pontchartrain at West End into the business district; its terminus was located at the site of the present Louisiana Superdome. The New Basin

First NBC customers take care of financial needs at the bank's main lobby at 210 Baronne Street. This ornate building, erected in 1927, remains a distinctive architectural landmark.

Canal has long since been filled in, but for more than a century it served the city as an alternate water route from the Gulf, relieving the Mississippi of much of its traffic. When the project was completed, the Canal Bank had a first-year profit of $405,563.

The bank's balance sheet has changed tremendously since the early years. It is now a multibillion-dollar institution. First NBC's assets, however, have not changed its principle of getting involved in community projects.

First NBC's tradition of caring for the people of New Orleans and the River Region has remained an integral part of the bank's 159-year-old philosophy. Just as the bank's ancestors took a lead role in establishing an important city waterway, the bank today follows the same community philosophy. Evidence of that can be found throughout the city. Bond financing through First NBC helped create the New Orleans skyline, the Louisiana Superdome, the Mississippi River Bridge construction, and the Greater New Orleans Expressway.

More important, First NBC doesn't

just help in the construction of buildings and highways, it also helps to build community pride and educate future leaders. First NBC is the first corporate sponsor of the nationally recognized Habitat for Humanity Program in New Orleans. By aiding Habitat, First NBC helps elevate low-income families out of project housing situations and places them in homes that have been revitalized. Unique to First NBC, everyone—from the bank's board of directors to hourly employees—spends time doing whatever else needs to be done to ready the structures for occupancy.

And there are still other volunteer programs. Five schools in the greater New Orleans area have been adopted by First NBC. Under the program, the bank helps to meet the financial and educational needs at the facilities. Employees volunteer their time tutoring students, teaching classes, and acting as role models for the students, many of whom come from financially depressed neighborhoods.

The bank also takes part in a nationally applauded program, Inroads Incorporated, whereby minority students are selected to work at the bank during the summer months to gain banking skills and work experience. Upon graduation, these students are also considered for full-time employment with the bank. With these education-related programs, it is no wonder that First NBC is the largest financier of education in Louisiana.

First NBC believes its greatest earnings opportunity comes from the level of convenient, quality service it provides to customers. Service is a key element that separates First NBC from the rest. It aggressively pursues the available market with top-of-

Above: Students at Walter Cohen High School get helpful financial advice from First NBC vice president Millicent Jones.

Left: Bank employee Karl Sanders brushes on a new coat of paint for a house being renovated for a low-income family.

businesses to the shipping industry. Its Trust Division has been identified in the top 10 stock managers for the past 10 years, as cited by *Pensions and Investment Age* magazine.

International banking has been a part of First NBC since its inception, due to the major trading post of New Orleans. With correspondents in more than 100 countries worldwide and, in particular, expertise in Latin America, First NBC actively assists international commerce in the Gulf South region.

First NBC is the Gulf South's leading correspondent bank, offering clients an array of services from highly competitive prices to personal computer-based wire links to the bank.

Individual service is the hallmark of First NBC's Private Banking Department. It is designed to address the special needs of high-profile businesspeople in the community, such as doctors, attorneys, and other professionals. The Private Banking staff is a group of highly trained professionals with enhanced lending authority and the direct support of specialists in trusts and investments.

First National Bank of Commerce is the flagship bank of First Commerce Corporation, also headquartered in New Orleans. First Commerce Corporation has five banks throughout Louisiana that all share the same philosophy: community commitment.

Nine-year-old Michael Davidson gets early financial direction from First NBC branch manager Rene Oubre.

ment to the community and its staff of professionals help to make it happen.

First NBC's Retail Division is rated number one in customer service and efficiency. A multimillion-dollar branch expansion project has made it the fastest-growing bank in the greater New Orleans area, with 35 full-service locations.

The bank's First BankCard Center is the largest credit card issuer in the Gulf South. It was recently awarded a government contract to provide both bankcard and proprietary/private labeling processing services for the U.S. Air Force Logistics Command on six military bases.

First NBC's commercial lending leads the region, from oil-related

the-line banking products backed by a strong record of financial performance and knowledgeable, friendly employees.

At the same time, the bank encourages each of its full-service branches to develop and implement programs in the local communities where they serve. Whether it's helping a boy who needs a heart operation or assisting the family of a local sheriff's deputy who died of a terminal illness, First NBC rises to the occasion. First NBC continues to flourish, and its commit-

THE CHAMBER/NEW ORLEANS AND THE RIVER REGION

THE CHAMBER/NEW ORLEANS and the River Region is the largest business and professional organization in southeastern Louisiana. Its membership of more than 3,000 businesses comprising some 7,000 volunteers stretches over seven parishes (counties) and several hundred square miles.

Founded in 1913 to serve as an arbitrating body for settling disputes in foreign commerce transactions, The Chamber has remained at the forefront of the metropolitan business community. Throughout the twentieth century The Chamber has been responsible for a variety of projects that have dramatically improved the quality of life in New Orleans and the surrounding region.

The Chamber formed the Community Chest (later to become the United Fund, now the United Way)

Above: The chamber's main office is located at 301 Camp Street in the heart of the city's central business district.

Left: Members view a live, interactive teleconference at the chamber's Teleconferencing Center.

in 1923 and issued its first appeal for $50,000. Other reminders of chamber projects go by such names as Tulane College of Commerce, the Southern Regional Research Hospital, the Southern Baptist Hospital (for which the chamber was instrumental in acquiring the land), the Veterans Hospital, Municipal Auditorium, the Industrial Canal, the Better Business Bureau, the Westbank Expressway, the Greater New Orleans Tourist and Convention Commission, and reforms in workers' compensation and unemployment compensation.

During the past decade The Chamber continued to lead the business community to a number of historic firsts. Anticipating the communications revolution, the organization became one of only two chambers of commerce in the country to begin teleconferencing operations. The chamber became a leader in the fight against crime by establishing and sponsoring one of the few chamber-sponsored crime-abatement programs in America.

The New Orleans Chamber was also chosen as the administrator of the United States' first tax-free shopping program. Patterned after the highly successful value-added tax rebate found in Europe, chamber officials hope to increase the number of international visitors coming to Louisiana. By marketing New Orleans to international visitors, The Chamber is demonstrating its commitment to one of the city's fastest-growing industries.

Justifiable pride can be taken by chamber members in their many notable achievements over the years. The Chamber/New Orleans and the River Region has provided and will continue to provide the vision and the resources necessary for the New Orleans metropolitan community to obtain the jobs and quality of life that its citizens so richly deserve. It is a commitment backed by years of experience.

WORLD TRADE CENTER OF NEW ORLEANS

THE WORLD TRADE CENTER OF New Orleans is a private, non-profit organization of 2,700 members founded in 1943 as International House and in 1945 as International Trade Mart, its two predecessor organizations. WTC New Orleans was the first of more than 200 World Trade Centers in 49 countries that today comprise the World Trade Centers Association (WTCA). The WTCA was founded in New Orleans in 1968.

WTC New Orleans operates two office buildings in the downtown area: the 33-story World Trade Center at 2 Canal Street on the riverfront, and the 11-story International Building on Gravier Street in the heart of the central business district. Each building has a private dining club for WTC members and their guests.

Tenants in the two buildings are engaged in a full range of international trade activities and include foreign consulates and trade offices, the

Above: The World Trade Center of New Orleans stands at 2 Canal Street on the Mississippi River. Photo by David Harvey

Left: The WTC's second facility is the International Building at 607 Gravier Street.

headquarters for the Port of New Orleans, federal and state trade agencies, and more than 100 export/import companies, steamship lines, freight forwarders, international attorneys, banks, travel agencies, maritime insurance brokers, and other internationally oriented firms.

Membership advantages of WTC New Orleans include use of the Plimsoll Club and the International

House Club, plus reciprocal rights with other WTCs and clubs around the globe; information and counseling on exporting and importing; enrollment in foreign trade conferences, training courses, language classes, overseas missions, and trade shows;

use of the WTC's international trade library, containing 10,000 volumes, trade journals, and periodicals; free enrollment in NETWORK, a worldwide electronic telecommunications system for instant trade leads among all WTCs; and subscriptions to special publications on international trade produced for the WTC membership.

Through these and other programs, WTC New Orleans serves as a catalyst in furthering trade and other ties between the nations of the world and bringing together international buyers and sellers.

BUSINESS COUNCIL—NEW ORLEANS AND THE RIVER REGION

AT THE HEIGHT OF THE economic depression that gripped New Orleans and the surrounding area during the 1980s, approximately 50 local chief executive officers banded together to provide the necessary leadership and resources required by the community.

Formed in 1985 under its first chairman, James R. Moffett, who was also chairman of the board and chief executive officer of Freeport-McMoRan, Inc., the Business Council—New Orleans and the River Region has amassed an impressive list of accomplishments in its short history.

Almost immediately after its formation, the Business Council contributed $250,000 to operate the city's public libraries until a mill tax was passed to provide permanent funding. Just after averting the potential library crisis, the organization contributed one million dollars to operate the city's public recreation facilities and day camps. In addition, member companies also visited day camp settings to provide adult role models with face-to-face in-

teraction with the children.

The second chairman of the Business Council, Ronald W. Jones, president and chief executive officer of Louisiana Coca-Cola Bottling Company, Ltd., has continued the leadership established by the early organization's leaders. To his credit, he has kept the Business Council's focus on issues relating to economic development, education, and budget and tax reform.

Several members of the Business Council formed a committee to study the financial and accounting procedures of the city. This effort required the extensive pro bono time of nine major accounting firms, an estimated $500,000 value. This expertise was then offered to the city in an effort to streamline and improve its accounting practices. The Business Council paid for the project and offered to provide

The Business Council—New Orleans and the River Region was formed in 1985 to provide the New Orleans area with the leadership and resources necessary for a bright future.

a manager to implement the system audit recommendations.

In order to provide a stable source of funding and management resources to arts organizations such as the New Orleans Symphony, Ballet, Opera, and Arts Council, the Business Council established a centralized pool of $10 million over a five-year period. This fund, Metropolitan Arts Fund, Inc., is the largest pool of funding for the cultural and performing arts in the United States.

Finally, the Business Council, in conjunction with the chamber of commerce and other civic groups, has formed the Metrovision Task Force, a committee designed to assess and evaluate the current economic situation in the New Orleans metropolitan area and prepare a far-reaching and long-range strategic plan for the economic development of the area.

This essay provides only a brief list of accomplishments as the Business Council—New Orleans and the River Region continues to provide the leadership and resources that are needed.

HOWARD, WEIL, LABOUISSE, FRIEDRICHS, INC.

MOST PEOPLE CAN TELL YOU what happened," says William H. Walker, president of Howard, Weil, Labouisse, Friedrichs, Inc. "But people pay us to tell them what's going to happen."

Begun in New Orleans in the latter part of the nineteenth century, Howard Weil merged with Legg Mason Wood Walker, Inc., in 1986 to further expand its resources and better serve its clientele. The Howard Weil/Legg Mason merger resulted in a nationwide network and a capital base that ranks the firm near the top of investment banks in the country. Howard Weil/Legg Mason has more than 800 registered representatives with 132,000 retail accounts. In addition, the merger allows the firm to manage funds of up to one billion dollars.

Says Walker, "We're a full-service investment banking operation but, at a time when many investment bankers are increasingly transaction oriented, our firm's investment banking activities are relationship driven and result from a coordinated effort between

The presence of Howard Weil's analysts in the Sun Belt has helped the firm gain a worldwide reputation in energy research.

corporate finance and research professionals. They perform in-depth analyses of client companies and provide them with financing alternatives and valuable options."

Howard Weil is widely recognized as the premier energy investment bank in the United States, with capital market sales and research devoted primarily to the energy industry. The primary focus of the firm's investment banking activities is buying the stock of client companies. Corporate finance personnel work with research analysts to structure financial alternatives to maximize shareholder value. The company believes that the key to effective investment banking services is the integration of proposed transactions with a thorough understanding of the trading dynamics of a client's securities.

A tangible dividend of this dynamic philosophy is the Annual Institutional Energy Conference, sponsored by Howard Weil and now entering its third decade. The conference brings together hundreds of chief executive officers from hundreds of the top energy-related companies in the United States and puts them in touch with institutional investors from major domestic and international money-management companies. The resulting interaction has been very successful.

John Levert, chairman, sums it up this way: "We provide a service. We want the people from the money-management companies to see the color of the eyes of the man or woman that they're buying stock in. We want them to experience the flavor of management of any given company before they give them any money."

After spending a few minutes with the people of Howard Weil, Labouisse, Friedrichs, Inc., it is easy to see that the company does not just tell a client what is going to happen, they help a client understand why it is going to happen that way.

Technological competitiveness and depth of trading experience have enabled Howard Weil to maintain long-term relationships with institutional and individual clients.

ALERION BANK

SUCCESS IS BUILT ON fostering a corporate culture that demands integrity, and rewards and promotes leadership, innovation, and performance." This is just a glimpse of the mission that Alerion Bank, formerly American Bank & Trust Co., has set for itself in the 1990s. After a decade in which the City of New Orleans has undergone enormous economic crises, the 1990s hold the promise once again of growth and prosperity for everyone. Alerion is preparing for this new day with anticipation and action.

Recent changes both in ownership (the bank is now wholly owned by the Ferruzzi family of Ravenna,

Above: Alerion Bank has long been active in the international banking community.

Left: Recent changes at Alerion Bank have allowed the bank to concentrate on a decade of growth ahead.

Italy) and in management have enabled the bank to reassess its course and plan for a decade of growth. Thomas S. Mabon, an expert in international finance, joined Alerion Bank in May 1989 as president and chief executive officer. Veteran bankers Gerald Gilbert and Barry Schlaile also joined the bank as executive vice presidents of banking and administration, respectively.

"We couldn't be more enthusiastic about the possibilities ahead in the 1990s," Mabon says. "The year 1989 was an investment year for our organization. We are looking forward eagerly to the 1990s. Our biggest challenge won't be finding opportunities—it will be choosing among them."

Long active in international banking, Alerion views the 1990s as an opportunity for continued growth in the international arena. There is also a demonstrated potential for expansion within the bank's metropolitan branch network. Personalized customer service combined with an eye toward building strong, competitive banking products round out the key

elements of Alerion's plans.

People, both customers and employees, have been critical to Alerion's success in this marketplace since its founding in 1917 as American Bank. One of only two banks in the city to survive the national banking "holidays" of 1933, the bank has consistently enjoyed a loyal customer base and a strong corps of employees. The institution's management sees this kind of loyalty and pride as one of its most important assets. It is management's plan to continue cultivating and strengthening those loyalties.

"We've spent a lot of time and effort building the kind of management team it will take to lead the bank into the future, and we think that it is paying off," Mabon says. "We believe

People—both employees and customers—have been critical to the success of Alerion Bank.

we've got some of the best people in banking, from our board of directors on down the line. Three key ingredients—leadership, innovation, and performance—are paving the way for Alerion's success into the 1990s."

WHITNEY NATIONAL BANK

■N 1883 NEW ORLEANIANS HEARD the first female telephone operators at The Great Southern Telephone and Telegraph Company. They took the first passenger train from New Orleans to California. And they formed the first lines in front of the teller cages at the new Whitney National Bank.

Gone are the horses that patiently waited for their masters outside the Whitney on Gravier Street. One could probably hear the steamboat calliopes on the river a little bit clearer from the steps of the Whitney in those days, but one thing has remained the same—the Whitney's dedication to serving the people of the Crescent City.

There was good news and bad news for Louisiana at the time the Whitney opened for business in 1883. On the one hand, Captain James Buchanan Eads had completed his jetties at the river's mouth and the port of New Orleans was born again. The state legislature had moved back to Baton Rouge. And New Orleans was busy planning the

The Whitney's Poydras Street branch opened its doors on October 1, 1920.

Promotional materials used by the Whitney in the early 1900s used humor to generate new accounts.

Cotton Centennial Exposition.

On the other hand, a representative of the gas company called at city hall to say he would have to turn off the streetlights if the long-overdue gas bill wasn't paid. At the same time, newly elected Mayor William J. Behan was at his bank making a personal loan of $100,000 to meet the city hall payroll. And, across the state, Louisiana was recovering from one of its worst floods.

Perhaps the founding fathers of the Whitney might have chosen a more auspicious time for their bank's beginning. But the performance of this solid financial institution has proven very good news for the people of Louisiana—people it has served so long.

With little notice, the Whitney opened on November 5, 1883, with 11 employees in rented rooms at 637 Gravier Street. From the very beginning it competed successfully with a dozen already established and prospering banks. One of the Whitney's first stockholders was Edward Douglass White, who went on to become chief justice of the Supreme Court of the United States. The other stockholders, including George Q. and Maria Louise Whitney, were at the entrepreneurial center of economic affairs of the city.

Over its first 100 years the Whitney's main office could always be found in the 600 block of Gravier Street, although its third home—the present main office—would list its post office address as 228 St. Charles Street. Built in 1911, this large structure absorbed the first address, near

Today the Whitney is proud to serve Jefferson Parish with 14 branches including the Lakeside branch, opened in 1988.

the present bank's Gravier Street entrance. The Whitney's second home, prior to 1911, still exists at 619 Gravier. It is an outstanding example of neogothic architecture with its Egyptian-influenced frontal decoration. Today it functions as the safe deposits division of the main bank.

The Whitney has had a proud past. It was the only major bank in New Orleans that kept its doors open during the Depression. In fact, the bank grew from $67 million of deposits in 1929 to $79 million in 1933.

During World War II employees accepted for military service had any reduction in their earning capacities reimbursed by the bank. The bank set up a separate department to handle ration book accounts covering gasoline, sugar, processed foods, meats, fats, shoes, and other consumer goods. In addition, the bond department devoted most of its time to the issuance of war bonds. The Whitney

takes pride in the fact that every employee of the bank participated in the Defense Bond Program.

Throughout the years the Whitney has always had strong ties to the community. In 1988, when the Cabildo was struck by a tragic fire, the Whitney started the Cabildo Rebuilding Fund to finance repairs and new exhibits not covered by insurance. To date, the fund has generated more than one million dollars in donations and is still growing.

Following the advent of statewide banking in 1983, the Whitney expanded beyond the city limits. By 1990 the Whitney could count 36 addresses, including locations in Baton Rouge, Lafayette, Slidell, Convington, Mandeville, and Nassau, Bahamas.

Today Whitney customer services include credit cards, personal checking accounts, special checking accounts, the Now Account, money market deposit accounts, savings accounts, certificates of deposit, bonds, IRAs (individual retirement accounts), SEPs (simplified employee pensions), automatic transfers, Christmas savings accounts, personal money orders, cashiers checks, drafts, safe deposit boxes, bank by mail, automatic social security and government agency deposits, freight payment, trust management, and currency exchange. When it comes to international banking, the Whitney has established relationships with banks worldwide to facilitate funds transfers.

As it begins its 107th year, Whitney National Bank is well prepared to meet the challenges of the economy and is ready to take on the growth opportunities of the twenty-first century.

HIBERNIA NATIONAL BANK

ON SEPTEMBER 1, 1870, THE Hibernia Bank and Trust Company opened for business in New Orleans, thus joining the ranks as one of only a handful of courageous banks seeking to survive the devastating aftermath of the Civil War. Three years later the company joined the National Banking System and became Hibernia National Bank.

Hibernia, a Latin term meaning "Ireland," was established by a small group of New Orleans businesspeople, led by Patrick Irwin, the bank's first president.

For this group of financial pioneers, Hibernia meant stability, strength, and promise—the promise of improved economic conditions, innovative products, and services backed by intelligent, caring professionals.

Over the years Hibernia prospered and merged with other banks, and by the early 1920s it had outgrown its facilities. Plans were launched to build a 20-story, high-rise building in the center of downtown New Orleans, equipped with the city's first tower. Although no longer open to the public, the Hibernia tower remains a beacon to American free enterprise and a promise for results—a Hibernia tradition.

In the spring of 1973 Hibernia established a standard of operating as an earnings-driven, not size-driven, organization with a clearly defined corporate objective: "To maximize shareholder wealth by meeting customer needs and providing opportunities for employee achievement and reward."

Hibernia set a new standard for identifying and satisfying customers' needs—and doing it profitably. Since the spring of 1973 Hibernia's people have delivered what customers want in banking services, and the bank's market share has risen steeply, while results for customers, shareholders, and staff alike have been a three-way win.

Today Hibernia is the largest and most profitable bank in Louisiana and one of the top regional banks in the nation. A distant third-place competitor in the city of New Orleans in

Although no longer open to the public, the Hibernia tower (with the Louisiana Superdome in the background) remains a beacon to American free enterprise and a promise for results—a Hibernia tradition.

1973, Hibernia is today the market leader in the state, with 46 percent of the loans and 41 percent of the deposits among key competitors in its service areas.

In 1973 Hibernia Corporation had $500 million in assets. Today Hibernia has more than $7 billion in assets. Employment since 1973 has moved from 713 employees at 12 branches in one market, New Orleans, to more than 3,000 employees serving customers in 170 locations in Louisiana and Texas.

In addition, since 1976 Hibernia's dividend has been raised 18 times and has increased almost eightfold.

Hibernia shares are held nationwide and in Western Europe. Hibernia has developed a national reputation as an aggressive, yet prudent, financial institution. Unlike its major Louisiana competitors, Hibernia has recorded profits in good and bad times alike.

Hibernia's exceptional performance has been the subject of articles in several national publications, including *Forbes Magazine, The New York Times,* the *Wall Street Journal,* and *Barron's.*

Since multiparish banking legislation went into effect in 1985 and interstate banking legislation went into effect two years later, Hibernia has been very deliberate and studied in its merger/acquisition strategy. Its aggressive, yet careful, strategy has paid off, as Hibernia is the largest bank in Louisiana in assets, loans, deposits, and trust operations.

Still, Hibernia's commitment to New Orleans and the rest of Louisiana is unwavering. The bank makes more loans to businesses and individuals statewide than any other Louisiana bank.

Despite its longtime status as the largest and most profitable bank in Louisiana, Hibernia people are careful not to get complacent. The company's philosophy of "running scared" and

never getting overconfident is embraced by everyone who works at Hibernia.

Hibernia employees are leaders in many civic and public improvement projects. In New Orleans, for example, Hibernia people participate in the Partnerships in Education program to

help students in Orleans Parish public schools. Employees are also active in Louisiana Special Olympics, Junior Achievement, the March of Dimes, the United Way, the Boy Scouts of America, The Chamber/New Orleans and the River Region, and the New Orleans Ballet. As a member of the chamber, Hibernia regularly participates in discussions and plans to identify and stimulate business opportunities in all segments of the local economy.

Hibernia's overall objective is to serve every community that it enters by providing superior products and customer service. The bank's people realize that the only way to accomplish this objective is through teamwork and a commitment to excellence.

Built in 1870 on the principles of stability, strength, and promise, the Hibernia National Bank of today more than fulfills the promise of those early ideals.

PAN-AMERICAN LIFE INSURANCE COMPANY

A+ IS WIDELY ACKNOWL-edged to be the mark of excellence, a sign of superior effort, and a stamp of unquestioned approval. It is also the designation given to Pan-American Life Insurance Company by the A.M. Best Company, the longtime independent analyst of the insurance business. Best's rating measures the performance of each company in such vital areas as competency of underwriting, control of expenses, adequacy of reserves, soundness of investments, and capital sufficiency.

An A.M. Best report states, "The company, which is purely mutual, has been most ably managed in the interest of its policyholders. Pan-American Life currently ranks among the 40 largest mutual life insurance companies in the nation from the standpoint of both admitted assets and total life insurance in force."

Says John K. Roberts, Jr., FSA, president and chief executive officer, "We were obviously very pleased with the Best rating, which is recognized by the industry as the mark of excel-

lence. The designation was consistent with the vision of this company, and that is to be one of the highest-quality, more profitable insurance companies in the industry."

Roberts goes on to point out that quality can be found throughout the Pan-American organization through a combination of service, products, and prices for customers; compensation, benefits, and a good working environment for employees and agents; and service to the communities that Pan-American serves.

"Profit is needed to sustain high-quality benefits for our customers, employees, agents, and communities," says Roberts. "We will achieve this high quality as ethics permeate our individual actions throughout the organization and our measurable performance is in the top quartile of our competition."

Founded in New Orleans in 1911, Pan-American Life is licensed to operate in 35 states, the District of Columbia, eight Latin American countries, Puerto Rico, and the Virgin Islands. Operations are conducted on the personal-agent system in the United States and on the branch-manager plan in Latin America through nearly 5,200 agents and brokers.

In 1972 Pan-American established a new International Operations Division that is responsible for total administration and service of all business outside the continental United States. In addition, the corporation formed a subsidiary domestic life company, International Reinsurance Company, for the purpose of providing reinsurance facilities for various associated firms. Pan-American moved to its present location on Poydras Street in 1980, and the following year it formed a subsidiary domestic life insurance company, Pan-American Assurance Company, for the principal purpose of marketing universal life coverages.

Roberts cites Pan-American's responsiveness in dealing with the

The Pan-American Life Center adds beauty and dimension to the New Orleans skyline.

meeting areas such as the Executive Conference Center and a 260-seat auditorium with front- and rear-screen projection facilities. Opened in 1984, the Hotel Inter-Continental is 71 percent owned by Pan-American Life.

Roberts sums up his vision of the company this way: "Pan-American will continue to be dedicated to quality—quality in the design of our products and quality in the services we provide our policyholders. This can only be accomplished through quality people—our directors, officers, employees, agents, and sales representatives."

Whether overseeing a life insurance company or co-managing a major hotel, the management at Pan-American Life Insurance Company extends to the policyholder and the visitor alike its commitment to quality. The result is an "A+" in anyone's grade book.

The interior atrium at the Pan-American Life Center provides an open, relaxing environment for businesspeople.

volatile, ever-changing world of underwriting and investment as a reason for its success. He says, "Being responsive in today's market requires the ability to accurately evaluate trends and react quickly and effectively to grasp opportunities while they exist. A company must be lean and flexible and yet have the market muscle to turn an idea into profit."

The market muscle that Roberts refers to has definitely been felt in the New Orleans community, where Pan-American contributes a $27-million annual payroll to the local economy

and has invested more than $130 million. Among the more high-profile investments of the company is the Hotel Inter-Continental New Orleans.

Designed to complement the adjacent Pan-American Life Center, the hotel is a 14-story glass and granite structure. The courtyard between buildings is an aesthetic oasis featuring a quiet garden spot where visitors are serenely serenaded by a giant musical sculpture designed by six New Orleans artists.

Together, the hotel and Pan-American Life Center offer executive

LISKOW & LEWIS

WHAT HAD MODEST beginnings in 1935 in the southwestern Louisiana city of Lake Charles has evolved into one of Louisiana's premier law firms. A relatively young firm by New Orleans' standards, Liskow & Lewis has become firmly entrenched in the community and has gained national standing in its practice of law.

Housed in the top two floors of One Shell Square, the city's tallest building, Liskow & Lewis is comprised of 77 attorneys—48 partners, 26 associates, and 3 are of counsel. Of this number, 21 attorneys staff an office in Lafayette, Louisiana.

Founded by Cullen Liskow and Austin Lewis, and now headed by Gene Lafitte, the firm opened its New Orleans office in 1959. The firm has expanded its practice over the years to include admiralty; antitrust; banking; commercial litigation; oil and gas;

corporate; environmental; federal, state, and local taxation; negligence; products liability; probate and real estate; and security law. The firm litigates in all of these areas in trial and appellate courts and before administrative bodies, and in arbitration and other forums of dispute resolution.

In the environmental area, the firm counsels with and represents in litigation members of the oil and gas industry. These projects, some of which are national in scope and significance, relate to the exploration and production of oil and gas as well as its transportation, processing, and refining. The firm also represents industrial clients in toxic tort litigation and with respect to hazardous waste discharge,

Frank Massengale (left), partner in general litigation, and J. Berry St. John, head of the environmental section, discuss a case.

and advises real estate clients with respect to environmental problems in the acquisition, development, and financing of projects.

The admiralty section handles maritime and offshore litigation, including collision, personal injury, property damage, offshore blowouts, maritime liens, and marine insurance and contracts. This section also drafts and negotiates offshore contracts and charter agreements. The firm has been involved in a number of internationally recognized cases arising from major maritime disasters, including the sinking of the semi-submersible drilling rig *Ocean Ranger* off the coast of Newfoundland, the M/V *Testbank* collision in the Mississippi River Gulf outlet, and the 1988 *Piper Alpha* explosion in the North Sea.

Liskow & Lewis also specializes in the defense of casualty, products liability, and toxic tort cases, both in state and federal courts. Its lawyers have defended cases arising out of chemical spills, chemical exposure, and injuries caused by allegedly defective machinery in work areas. These lawyers have also represented drug manufacturers in personal injury litigation resulting from

Gene Lafitte, head of Liskow & Lewis, and attorney Kathleen Ketchum leave One Shell Square for an appointment.

Partners in the business section include (seated, from left): Marguerite Noonan, Bruce Oreck, Thomas Getten, Marilyn Maloney, and Blake Bennett. Standing are Leon Reymond (left) and Richard Anderson.

the ingestion of drugs.

The firm's commercial litigation includes cases dealing with securities fraud, antitrust law, lender liability, and bankruptcy. It has represented the FSLIC, FDIC, and Resolution Trust Company in connection with receiverships and conservatorships of failed institutions and in director and officer liability suits. The efforts of the firm have resulted in the recovery of substantial sums to reimburse the FSLIC and FDIC for losses in closed

Liskow & Lewis attorneys at work in the firm's library. Clockwise (from top) Robert Theriot (on ladder), Cheryl Cunningham, Scott Seiler, Cheryl Kornick, and Oswald Sobrino.

banks and savings and loan institutions.

Historically, Liskow & Lewis played a major role in the development of mineral law in Louisiana. Beginning with Cullen Liskow and Austin Lewis, firm attorneys have handled many of the landmark cases in the mineral law of Louisiana. The oil and gas section continues the firm's representation of clients engaged in the exploration, production, and marketing of oil, gas, and other minerals. These attorneys also do extensive work in matters with or before the Louisiana Office of Conservation and the Louisiana State Mineral Board.

Attorneys in the business section handle commercial matters of all types, including general corporate problems and corporate acquisitions and mergers. They represent local and out-of-state banks in making loans on Louisiana property. In the real estate area, attorneys represent real estate developers, lenders, and investors in real estate development, financing, and joint ventures. The firm is qualified in all federal and state tax matters including estate planning, but it has particular expertise in the state sales, use, severance, income, and franchise tax areas.

Liskow & Lewis has achieved significant growth over the years, largely as a result of providing quality legal services to a diverse group of clients. Since 1979 the number of attorneys in the firm has more than doubled. However, the firm still maintains its high standards of excellence. The majority of Liskow & Lewis attorneys graduated in the top 10 percent of their law school classes, qualifying for Order of the Coif or other academic distinctions. Most were editors or members of the law review at their respective institutions.

The firm attracts lawyers not only from Louisiana law schools such as Tulane, Louisiana State University, and Loyola, but also from such institutions as New York University, Vanderbilt, Georgetown University Law Center, University of Virginia Law School, Cornell, and Boalt Hall School of Law (University of California, Berkeley).

Specializing in maritime and offshore litigation are (from left) David Leefe and Gene Fendler, admiralty partners, and Donald Abaunza, head of the admiralty section.

Liskow & Lewis attorneys have achieved national prominence and recognition in the profession. Two members of the firm have filled the office of president of the prestigious American College of Trial Lawyers. Austin Lewis was president in 1974 while Gene Lafitte served as president in 1984-1985. J. Berry St. John served as chairman of the Natural Resources Law Section of the American Bar Association. On the local level, Charles Gremillion is a former president of the New Orleans Bar Association.

From modest beginnings the law firm of Liskow & Lewis has built a solid reputation of quality service while fulfilling the needs of local, national, and international clients.

DEUTSCH, KERRIGAN & STILES

AGGRESSIVE, WELL PREPARED, and cost effective are what the lawyers of Deutsch, Kerrigan & Stiles believe their clients want their attorneys to be. The firm strives to fulfill that expectation.

DK&S recognizes that lawyers have joined other professionals as public whipping boys. Lawyers are now perceived as synonymous with dilatoriness, lack of trust, insincerity, and extraordinary expense. These are attributes that DK&S neither likes nor condones.

DK&S has been one of New Orleans' major law firms since its founding more than 60 years ago. Begun in 1927 by Eberhard Deutsch and R. Emmett Kerrigan and joined in 1940 by Harry Stiles, DK&S continues today with the same basic organizational structure that evolved during the earlier life of the partnership. Each of the firm's four departments—civil litigation, business, construction, and admiralty—has a department head who is responsible for the work of that department.

In contrast to the public's perception of law firms in general, DK&S is committed to providing quality legal services in a responsive, cost-effective manner. A customized program is designed for every client, with a senior attorney designated as the responsible attorney for each file. The responsible attorney is the liaison with the client. He or she knows the status and contents of each file and ensures that each client's work is handled at the most effective and efficient level. The responsible attorney may be the sole attorney for the client or may organize a team of lawyers with the proper level of experience to serve the client's needs. In order to do this, the attorney may draw from the expertise of the entire firm, using lawyers from other departments and sections. The responsible attorney assures that the client is promptly advised of any changes in the status of the file. In order to personalize the client/attorney relationship even further, every attorney assigned to a file is available to the client at all times, and clients are provided with the

Above: Victor Stilwell (left) and Frederick Bott review a pending case.

Right: Robert Kerrigan is one of more than 60 attorneys at Deutsch, Kerrigan & Stiles.

home telephone number of each attorney.

DK&S's departments are subdivided into specific sections. The admiralty department, which established its reputation in the marine industry during the 1930s, is one of the oldest admiralty practices in New Orleans. The department performs all types of maritime matters, involving extensive federal court litigation, as well as arbitration and administrative practice with various marine-related federal agencies, including the U.S. Coast Guard, the U.S. Customs Service, the National Transportation Safety Board, and the Federal Maritime Commission. The department also handles virtually every type of maritime-related matter, including vessel construction, shipping, longshore work,

and the offshore-petroleum industry in the Gulf of Mexico.

The civil litigation department provides consultation and litigation services for all types of tort and insurance matters. While most of the work performed by this department is de-

Above: DK&S is located in the restored La Belle Creole Cigar and Tobacco factory in downtown New Orleans.

Below: Former governor David Treen conducts a legal seminar at DK&S.

all phases of litigation. Several of the attorneys in this department are architects and engineers by original training.

The business department is engaged in all aspects of commercial and corporate banking law extending into tax-related services, estate planning, real estate, and labor law, as well as litigation in these fields.

DK&S represents local, national, and international businesses, nonprofit organizations, and individuals. Clients range in size from *Fortune* 500 companies to new businesses. They include insurance underwriters, agents, brokers, airlines, architects, engineers, contractors, domestic and foreign manufacturers, companies engaged in dredging and in oil and gas exploration and production, marine-service businesses, real estate developers, government contractors, and financial institutions.

In 1983 DK&S took a bold step in moving its main office from the heart of the central business district to the restored La Belle Creole Cigar and Tobacco factory in the historic Lafayette Square district. At that time tax laws were extremely favorable for refurbishing old, historic buildings. DK&S remodeled in accordance with federal historic guidelines, obtaining U.S. Department of Interior certification and an architectural award for its renovation in this culturally rich warehouse district in New Orleans. The firm utilized the expertise of its attorneys in finance, real estate, and construction to obtain the industrial revenue bond financing, tax-qualified rehabilitation, and office space for its own use. Today the building stands as one of the best-preserved examples of factory architecture from the late nineteenth century.

fense oriented, DK&S also represents individual and corporate plaintiffs.

The firm's reputation in construction-related litigation has been earned through its long-standing representation of contractors, sureties, owners, architects, engineers, and insurers in

ADAMS AND REESE

AT ADAMS AND REESE WE respect tradition, but we aren't tied to it. We feel the community views us as a prestigious law firm, but that's not our major concern. Our one concern is to meet the needs of our clients—to be progressive and service-oriented. That might not sound too glamorous, but perhaps it explains our rapid growth," says Thomas J. Wyllie, senior partner at Adams and Reese.

Numbering more than 100, the lawyers at Adams and Reese have their eyes on the future—for their clients and themselves. They recognize, however, that the future is shaped by the past.

The firm traces its roots to St. Clair Adams, a sole practitioner who hung out his shingle at the turn of the century and rapidly established himself as one of Louisiana's most distinguished trial attorneys. Adams was later joined by his son, St. Clair Adams, Jr., and in 1943 the firm's other namesake, W. Ford Reese, joined the practice. For more than 40 years the firm has been known simply as Adams and Reese. The current partners have chosen to retain this name, not only out of respect for the founders, but as a tangible symbol of the firm's collegial spirit and stability.

Its stability, however, is not at the cost of flexibility. Adams and Reese prides itself on being able to adapt to its clients' ever-changing needs. These clients range from small financial institutions to large pharmaceutical companies, privately owned maritime concerns to major oil and gas companies. In addition, a large part of its practice involves defending professional liability suits and serving as counsel to numerous professional organizations and boards.

As its clients' needs change, so too does the firm. A few years ago the firm recognized that its industrial clients were feeling increased pressure from a multitude of new state and federal environmental regulations. In response, Adams and Reese developed an environmental law practice to offer these clients services in hazardous waste litigation and management, with emphasis on coordinating environmental regulatory compliance.

Anticipating the needs of its clients was the same force that led the firm to establish its governmental relations practice. "Our clients' legal problems don't occur in a vacuum," says Adams and Reese's E.L. Henry, a former speaker of the Louisiana House of Representatives and former Louisiana Commissioner of Adminstration. "Laws on the local, state, and federal level have a drastic impact on the business climate in which our clients operate. For that reason, we feel it is necessary to represent their interests before lawmakers."

Just as governmental action can shape the legal problems and strategies of a business, so too can public perception. A big courtroom victory is hollow if a company's public image is destroyed during the litigation process. Adams and Reese has a marketing person on staff to advise its clients on how to approach public relations issues.

It is this team approach which characterizes Adams and Reese's law practice.

Perhaps no area of litigation requires as much teamwork between the client and lawyer as products liability. The firm's attorneys who handle general products liability cases, as well as pharmaceutical and medical device litigation, recognize that a law-suit of this nature is not an isolated legal problem. Every case is evaluated in terms of the impact it will have on each client as well as the industry as a whole. The firm works in cooperation with attorneys around the country to ensure consistency and continuity of representation.

Understanding technical matters is critical to the successful defense of a products liability suit. Adams and Reese's experience in handling this type of case has allowed it to develop departments with attorneys having backgrounds as pharmacists, engineers, and registered nurses. The attorneys work with an extensive support group of independent consultants to prepare a case for trial and construct a defense which will be understandable to a lay jury, should a case ultimately be tried.

In addition, the firm has computer specialists to assist lawyers in the handling of complex litigation and to ensure that a client's dollars are spent on true legal services, rather than repetitive administrative tasks.

While its legal practice is national in scope, Adams and Reese is committed to the community in which it is based, notably exemplified by its community service program called HUGS (Hope, Understanding, Giving, Support). Each month the members of HUGS work with a different needy group of individuals in the community. One month it might be repairing homes for the poor; the next month it might be serving food to the homeless or hosting receptions for the mentally handicapped. It is a commitment not only of money, but also of human resources.

With an office already in Baton Rouge and a tradition of representing national concerns, Adams and Reese is poised for geographic expansion that will be based on the same criterion as its diversification into new practice areas: client need, not expansion for its own sake.

The firm's roots, however, are in New Orleans and, while planted at the turn of the century, they are strong enough to propel the firm smoothly into a new century.

STONE, PIGMAN, WALTHER, WITTMANN & HUTCHINSON

A HIRING POLICY THAT selects only top law school graduates, selective client screening, and work on matters of national significance has enabled New Orleans' 68-lawyer Stone, Pigman, Walther, Wittmann & Hutchinson quietly to build a practice comparable to many 200-lawyer firms in New York, Chicago, and Los Angeles.

It all began in 1929. John Minor Wisdom and Saul Stone, both top graduates of the Tulane Law School, turned down offers from New Orleans' most prestigious firms and started their own firm instead. Wisdom & Stone hired its first associate in 1947, when Paul O.H. Pigman, ranked first in his Tulane class, joined the firm. In 1957 Wisdom was appointed to the United States Fifth Circuit Court of Appeals.

In keeping with the principles established by its founders, the firm grew carefully and slowly. Its practice broadened to include all areas of commercial concern; it developed a solid reputation for excellence and success in the courtroom and at the negotiating table; and its name evolved to Stone, Pigman, Walther, Wittmann & Hutchinson.

The firm's attorneys are selected

(From left) David L. Stone, Phillip A. Wittmann, Paul O.H. Pigman, Saul Stone, Ewell P. Walther, Jr., and Campbell C. Hutchinson.

for superior performance in law school or in postgraduate experiences such as judicial clerking, law teaching, and graduate studies. More than three-quarters served on the law reviews of their schools, and most graduated in the top 10 percent of their classes.

The firm's litigation section has extensive experience in all types of commercial cases for a variety of clients. Much of the representation is high-stakes, one-of-a-kind litigation, such as the firm's representation of several major oil and gas companies in successful marine construction antitrust litigation. The firm has also represented many of the major motion picture antitrust cases throughout the southeastern United States. The firm's antitrust practice includes both civil and criminal representation. Several lawyers in the firm are highly skilled in the representation of the unique interests of major

publishing and communications firms.

Stone, Pigman represents a number of national and regional securities firms in cases involving federal and state corporate and securities laws and in brokerage litigation. The firm has also developed a substantial banking and loan workout practice, representing both the FSLIC and the FDIC in matters arising from the failures of financial institutions in the southeastern United States.

The business section of Stone, Pigman is also talented and highly diverse. In the corporate and securities fields, members of this group have extensive experience representing lenders, borrowers, issuers, and underwriters in all types of financing and equity transactions, public offerings, private placements, and the filing of regulatory submissions with the Securities and Exchange Commission.

The firm has devoted continuing attention to real estate development and financing for many of the major builders and developers in the com-

The entrance to 546 Carondelet Street at dusk.

The offices of Stone, Pigman, Walther, Wittmann & Hutchinson are located at 546 Carondelet Street, the former city hall annex. Originally built in 1910, the historic building was renovated in 1984 for the firm's offices.

munity. The tax group includes lawyers who are designated as Board Certified Tax Attorneys and several who hold the Certified Public Accountant certificate. Members of the firm have considerable experience in matters involving the health care industry and the construction industry. The business section has developed expertise and recognition in the retirement plan and welfare benefit plan areas under ERISA. Another specialty within the business section is trusts and estates, including estate planning, tax, and probate.

Several Stone, Pigman lawyers practice in the area of oil and gas law through the representation of both exploration and operating companies and large landowners in transactions and litigation. The firm also provides services to clients in the increasingly important areas of pre-acquisition and pre-merger environmental law, environmental cleanup, and federal and state environmental litigation.

Members of Stone, Pigman's bankruptcy section have extensive experience in all aspects of bankruptcy practice and litigation. The firm has recently combined its expertise in oil and gas and bankruptcy to represent the State of Louisiana and the State Mineral Board in complex litigation arising from the Texaco bankruptcy.

A practice area of the firm that deserves special mention is the field of utility regulatory law. The firm has long represented the Louisiana Public Service Commission, and lawyers in this section of the firm have attained national recognition in this very specialized area.

Stone, Pigman, Walther, Wittmann, & Hutchinson

is retained often by law firms, judges, and individual attorneys to handle their personal legal work, earning the firm the reputation as "lawyers' lawyers." Providing the highest level of service to clients has earned the firm a reputation for excellence, both locally and nationally.

The second-floor landing leading into the offices of Stone, Pigman, Walther, Wittmann & Hutchinson. The building's monumental staircase and black-and-white slate floor duplicate materials used in Gallier Hall, the former city hall.

JONES, WALKER, WAECHTER, POITEVENT, CARRERE & DENEGRE

JONES, WALKER, WAECHTER, Poitevent, Carrere & Denegre is the largest law firm in Louisiana today, with more than 160 attorneys. A major force in the business affairs of Louisiana and the surrounding region, the law firm is young, dynamic, and aggressive. The firm has offices in New Orleans and Baton Rouge, Louisiana, and in Washington, D.C.

Founded in 1937—very young by New Orleans standards—the firm mirrors the recent history and growth of the city. A quarter-century ago the firm was one of the major tenants in the city's first modern building, 225 Baronne. In 1985 the firm relocated its principal offices to the top six floors of the 52-story Place St. Charles, a stunning new skyscraper dominating the skyline of the city's financial district. The firm's continuing growth reflects the success in achieving its principal goal—service to the client.

Jones, Walker's areas of practice include a wide variety of federal, state, and local law matters. The varied fields of practice reflect the diversity of its clients and their requirements. The firm represents a great many of the major enterprises headquartered in Louisiana. In addition, Jones, Walker represents the Louisiana interests of many national and international enterprises: *Fortune* 500 companies, worldwide financial institutions and insurers, and world-class health care institutions. The firm is routinely called upon to participate in matters of regional,

Above: Jones, Walker is the largest law firm in Louisiana.

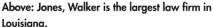

Below: Although Jones, Walker was founded in 1937, it is still young by New Orleans standards.

national, and international scope.

Individual clients and smaller business enterprises also are an integral part of the firm's eclectic practice as are the handling of industrial and maritime disasters, bank mergers, corporate and securities matters, tax and complex estate matters, litigation, and complex financings. Jones, Walker strives to strike a delicate balance between the more traditional one-on-one relationship of lawyer and client and the exigencies of today's increasingly more complex legal problems that often demand a team of lawyers with experience in a variety of disciplines.

A progressive leader in the communities where it maintains offices, Jones, Walker is involved in a number of civic projects.

The plethora of talent and energy embodied in Jones, Walker professionals also is employed to improve the overall quality of life in metropolitan New Orleans. One major, innovative step was the formation of the Young Leadership Council (YLC), which Jones, Walker encouraged and continues to support. Open to professionals under the age of 42, the YLC was primarily responsible for placing the decorative lighting on the Crescent City Connection, the bridges over the Mississippi River uniting New Orleans' East and West Bank communities.

The firm has also been integrally involved with Tulane University, Tulane Medical Center, the New Orleans Symphony, the New Orleans Museum of Art, the Audubon Zoo and Botanical Gardens, the recently completed Aquarium of the Americas on the riverfront, the New Orleans and the River Region Chamber of Commerce and the Business Council of the City of New Orleans, the Council for (Louisiana) Fiscal Reform, and Partners in Education.

The firm backs up its lawyers with a full and talented paraprofessional complement, highly qualified support staff, a 28,000-volume law library, computerized research and document retrieval systems, in-house computers, and the most advanced word-processing systems.

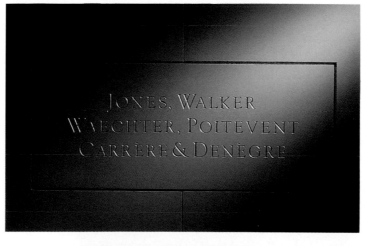

Organized into seven sections, attorneys of the firm are grouped according to experience in casualty litigation, corporate and securities matters, general business (financing) and energy matters, general litigation, maritime litigation and financing, mineral law, and taxation and estates law.

Although the firm is organized by sections, lawyers from multiple sections often combine to satisfy intricate client requirements. The firm also has special intersectional teams that address such matters as white-collar crime; sports, arts, and entertainment law; family and domestic law; health care law; toxic tort litigation; corporate mergers and acquisitions; and secured lending transactions.

The firm occupies the top six floors of the 52-story Place St. Charles.

MILLING, BENSON, WOODWARD, HILLYER, PIERSON & MILLER

WHAT BEGAN NEARLY A century ago has evolved today into Milling, Benson, Woodward, Hillyer, Pierson & Miller, one of the largest law firms in the South.

Built on the precept that the firm would provide the highest quality in legal services promptly, efficiently, and effectively, Milling, Benson represents major business, financial, and commercial concerns, including the Whitney National Bank, Chevron Oil Company, McDermott International, The Louisiana Land and Exploration Company, The Kansas City Southern Railway Company, Louisiana & Arkansas Railway Company, Louisiana Power & Light Company, and New Orleans Public Service Co., Inc.

Near the turn of the century the Louisiana Railway & Navigation Company persuaded Robert E. Milling to open a New Orleans office. Milling, a former district attorney of Winn Parish, Louisiana, brought the firm of Milling & Sanders into New Orleans, setting up an office in the old Godchaux Building on the downtown riverside of Canal and Chartres streets, where the New Orleans Marriott stands today.

Through the early 1900s the firm went through numerous name changes and moved its location, sometimes by choice, other times by necessity, such as in 1915, when a storm literally blew the firm out of its Godchaux location. After the

storm Milling, Benson took up residence in the original Whitney Bank Building.

Subsequently, the firm began to build a practice based principally in real estate, oil and gas, corporate, and railroad law. One of its largest clients, The Louisiana Land and Exploration Company, was formed from interests in the Timken estate, which had vast land holdings in southern Louisiana and elsewhere. The firm also represented other substantial land companies such as the Miami Corporation, Continental Land & Fur Co., Inc., and

Milling, Benson's tastefully decorated reception area reflects the firm's century-old legal tradition.

the La Terre Co., Inc. The firm continues to represent the owners of approximately 2 million acres of Louisiana land.

The Louisiana Railway & Navigation Company, the firm that had a hand in the formation of Milling, Benson, had been acquired by The Kansas City Southern Railway Company. These developments and representation of the New Orleans, Texas & Mexico Railway, later acquired by the Missouri Pacific Railway, increased the firm's railroad practice.

During its early years Milling, Benson's growth was slow but steady. The firm has more than quadrupled its size since 1950, presently comprising 42 partners and 31 associates. In 1987 the firm moved from the Whitney Bank Building into the newly constructed LL&E Tower on Poydras Street.

Throughout the early history of the firm, most of the senior partners have considered themselves to be generalists and client oriented, rather than confined to any speciality. The fact that partners were, of necessity, becoming specialists in many areas of the law, however, led to dividing the firm into seven departments: admiralty; commercial litigation; labor and employment law; corporate, banking, and business law; natural resources, energy, and environmental; tax, trusts, and estates; and casualty. Departmentalization does not, however, restrict any lawyer's ability to practice in a desired area.

Milling, Benson is governed by a three-member management committee. Other standing committees are responsible for recruiting, training, evaluation, and professional development of new and summer associates. Ad

hoc committees of partners, and sometimes associates, are appointed to deal with particular problems as they arise.

Each attorney is assigned to a primary and secondary department. Each of the seven departments has a chairman and, in some instances, a vice chairman. The members of each department determine how that department shall operate, subject to review. The chairmen's duties are largely administrative. They attempt to even out work loads by suggesting voluntary work shifts among attorneys in their departments and by assigning new work. They coordinate meetings and education within their departments, give and receive advice as to matters being handled, and provide information to the management and

practice committee on administrative matters relating to their respective departments.

Throughout its history Milling, Benson, Woodward, Hillyer, Pierson & Miller has continually striven to achieve excellence in the practice of law, including the highest level of technical competence, constant loyalty, and dedicated service to the firm's clients and a scrupulous adherence to ethical rules that govern the legal profession. The firm also considers it important to maintain excellent working relationships and an atmosphere of collegiality, as well as respect, confidence, and trust, among the firm's partners, associates, and other professionals. In essence, the firm represents a century-old tradition of providing the highest-quality legal services available.

INDUSTRY

New Orleans' location and qualified work force draw manufacturers, distributors, and high-tech industries to the area.

Photo by Brad Crooks

TEXTRON MARINE SYSTEMS

IT MAY BE ONE OF THE BEST kept secrets in the country, but John J. Kelly wants to change all that.

Kelly, who is president of Textron Marine Systems (TMS), says, "We believe that New Orleans can be the center of advanced marine technology. The type of work that we do either meets or surpasses work standards anywhere in the country."

Specifically, the kind of work that Kelly and his company does is the design, construction, and testing of several different types of state-of-the-art military and commercial marine vessels. In short, TMS is the U.S. leader in air-cushion technology and special-purpose marine craft. TMS' technical advancements have produced unique craft, unlike any previous sea/land vessels for the U.S. Navy, U.S. Marine Corps, the U.S. Coast Guard, and commercial industries.

TMS technology has produced an extraordinary string of historic firsts, including the first surface effect ship to exceed 100 miles per hour, the first air-cushion vehicle to carry a 60-ton

Textron Marine Systems' modern complex incorporates both manufacturing and warehousing operations.

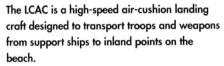

tank from sea to land, the first air-cushion vehicle to engage in combat by U.S. forces, the first commercial utility air-cushion vehicle to serve the U.S. oil industry, and many, many more.

In addition, the cost-effective application of TMS technologies is resulting in the production of new, higher-performance craft for the U.S. military, the Coast Guard, and commercial industry.

For the military, TMS has produced the Landing Craft, Air Cushion (LCAC),

The LCAC is a high-speed air-cushion landing craft designed to transport troops and weapons from support ships to inland points on the beach.

an amphibious vehicle that is supported primarily by a cushion of air between the vehicle and the surface of the water. Lift fans are used to supply air under pressure to the air cushion, which is contained by use of a flexible seal, or skirt, around the entire periphery of the hull, thereby making it amphibious. Air propellers are used in place of water propellers. Being amphibious, LCACs are designed to skim over a variety of surfaces: water, land, ice, snow, and marsh.

The LCAC represents one of the most sophisticated and capable improvements in U.S. landing craft since World War II. The ability of the LCAC to provide high-speed, ship-to-shore, and over-the-beach amphibious capabilities in the transport of personnel and equipment provides the Navy and Marine Corps with a new dimension in projecting combat power ashore.

The Lighter Amphibious Air-Cushion Vehicle (LACV-30), designed and constructed by TMS for the U.S. Army, is an innovative solution to logistics over-the-shore missions. The LACV-30 is a proven, reliable lighter-age that travels at more than 40 miles per hour over water, land, ice, and marginal terrain. The vehicle does not require fixed ports and supporting fa-

cilities and can use 70 percent of the world's beaches as compared to 17 percent with conventional craft. The LACV-30 operates independently of tides, reefs, mudflats, water depth, or underwater obstacles.

In addition to craft built for military use, TMS Surface Effect Ships (SES) are increasingly being used commercially in support of offshore oil and gas exploration. They are used as high-speed crewboats and personnel transportation boats. The excellent seakeeping, speed, and reliability of SESs have proven them superior to any other boats or ships operating in the oil fields. The air cushion maintains a smoother and better ride with almost none of the slamming characteristics typical of conventional hulls and catamarans.

The SES' sidehulls have a unique configuration, developed over many years of TMS research and development. The revolutionary hullform provides good handling qualities at sea. The unique combination of stability and maneuverability of the SESs makes them capable of successfully interfacing with a wide variety of personnel and equipment transfer in virtually all sea and wind conditions.

TMS maintains its shipyard operations for air cushion, surface effect ships, and other shipbuilding activities at its facility in eastern New Orleans. This site is located on 25 acres of land adjacent to Bayou Sauvage, which provides easy and direct access to the Intracoastal Waterway, the Mississippi River, and the Gulf of Mexico.

The modern complex incorporates manufacturing and warehouses/storage. Covered building areas of more than 270,000 square feet are used with room for expansion as program requirements dictate. Modern production assembly lines, manned by highly skilled and trained workers, ensure efficiency and quality through every phase of the modular construction process. Knowledgeable and experienced manufacturing supervision strictly adheres to the specifications and manufacture of high-quality products. Officials at TMS are proud of the total team interface methods used by its manufacturing staff in its accomplishment of all facets of craft construction.

The tradition at Textron Marine Systems combines its experienced, professional engineering and manufacturing staffs with the latest in equipment for effective shipbuilding management, manufacturing, and support needs—for today and tomorrow.

Textron Marine Systems maintains its manufacturing operations in eastern New Orleans.

MARTIN MARIETTA MANNED SPACE SYSTEMS

SINCE THE EARLY DAYS OF the United States' space program, New Orleanians have played an important part in the nation's exploration and utilization of space. Today Martin Marietta Manned Space Systems is proud to carry on that tradition.

The National Aeronautics and Space Administration (NASA) occupied the sprawling Michoud Assembly Facility in eastern New Orleans in 1961. The 832-acre tract had been the site of defense-related manufacturing during World War II and the Korean War. The facility boasts one of the world's largest buildings, with 43 acres under one roof, and deepwater access for the transport of space structures by barge to Florida launch pads. In short, the entire configuration of Michoud made it ideally suited for the manufacture of large space vehicles.

The first NASA project at the Michoud facility was the design and assembly of the first stage of the powerful Saturn launch vehicle, which propelled Apollo crews on their journeys to the Moon. Following the success of the six Apollo lunar landing missions, NASA officials considered future forms of manned spaceflight. The reusable Space Shuttle resulted from those studies.

Work on the Space Shuttle began locally in 1973, when the Martin Marietta Corporation was selected to design and assemble 59 external tanks, the only nonreusable major shuttle component. At that time some 200 Martin Marietta employees relocated to New Orleans and the Michoud facility to begin development on the shuttle's massive fuel tank.

The external tank provides propellants to the shuttle's three main engines and serves as the structural backbone of the entire shuttle stack. At launch, the 154-foot-long, 28-foot-

diameter tank carries more than 1.6 million pounds of liquid oxygen and liquid hydrogen, and supplies propellants to the main engines at a rate of 1,035 gallons per second. At that flow rate, the external tank could fill an average-size swimming pool in less than 30 seconds.

In 1987 Martin Marietta Manned Space Systems received the first annual NASA Excellence Award for Quality and Productivity, acknowledging the company and its 3,500 New Orleans-area employees above all other NASA contractors for outstanding performance on the Space

The Space Shuttle *Atlantis* lifts off en route to outer space. Martin Marietta's external tank supplies propellants to the three main engines and serves as the shuttle's structural backbone.

Shuttle program.

Today the firm's shuttle role continues. In 1989 NASA awarded Martin Marietta a $1.8-billion contract for the assembly of an additional 60 external tanks, which will increase employment and guarantee tank production through 1997.

The economic impact of the external tank project reaches far beyond New Orleans. Suppliers from virtually every state in the union support Martin Marietta on the project, including hundreds of Louisiana suppliers.

Several future projects are under study by Martin Marietta engineers. One such project is the proposed unmanned, cargo-carrying Shuttle-C. The Shuttle-C would consist of Space Shuttle solid rocket boosters, the external tank, and a new cargo carrier. Controlled from Earth, the Shuttle-C will be capable of transporting as much as 150,000 pounds of payload into near-Earth orbit. In the future, Shuttle-C also could carry elements of a lunar colony or components of a manned mission to Mars.

Another concept under study is a recoverable propulsion/avionics (P/A) module. The most expensive elements of any launch vehicle are the engines and avionics equipment. Those components, incorporated into the P/A module, would be utilized

An external tank, 154 feet long and 28 feet in diameter, dwarfs a passing bicyclist.

during a launch and then returned to Earth for reuse on another launch vehicle.

The liquid rocket booster (LRB) is under study as a possible replacement for the solid rocket boosters now used on the Space Shuttle. The LRB offers a versatile, reliable, low-cost alternative to the solid rocket booster. Special features would include an emergency shutdown capability, increased performance, and the potential for eliminating environmental contamination.

Currently, each external tank reenters the Earth's atmosphere and is destroyed after its role in a Space Shuttle launch is completed. But in the future, external tanks may be used as work platforms in space. One such scenario envisions using the tank as a gamma-ray imaging telescope, carried into orbit along with the shuttle's orbiter. Astronauts would enter the external tank and prepare it for its new role as the host of an inflatable telescope that will observe the universe in the gamma-ray-wavelength spectrum.

Building on the solid foundation of the Space Shuttle's external tank,

Martin Marietta Manned Space Systems explores the frontiers of space, bringing with it advanced technology and skilled jobs for this and future generations of New Orleanians. As launch vehicles continue to lift off from the planet Earth, major components will bear the label "Made in New Orleans."

Personnel at work inside an external tank's liquid oxygen tank, which holds more than one million pounds of liquid oxygen at launch time.

E.I. DU PONT DE NEMOURS AND COMPANY

LOCATED IN THE HEART OF the River Parishes, in the area once known as the German Gold Coast, Du Pont's Pontchartrain Works manufactures a range of quality products that make a contribution to improving the quality of life for consumers worldwide.

Its highest volume product, neoprene, a synthetic rubber, is used in automobile belts and hoses, adhesives, and road surface materials. Another product, PPDA (paraphenylenediamine), is a basic ingredient for Kevlar® aramid fiber, which annually protects thousands of police officers in

"Continuing as a good neighbor into the next quarter-century," as Du Pont's theme states, the company maintains active environmental and worker safety standards at the Pontchartrain Works manufacturing plant.

soft body-armor protection, reinforces radial tires, and assures stability in aircraft. Dytek A, a third product, is used in some polyurethane coatings, textile fibers, epoxy floor coatings, and fluorescent dye resins. Agriculturally-related products include OPDA (orthophenylenediamine), an intermediate chemical used in the production of Benlate®, a fungicide used by farmers to grow better fruits and vegetables that ultimately end up on dining-room tables, and HMI, which is used in a rice herbicide to control weeds in commercial fields.

In operation since 1964, the plant employs just under 600 people. Like other Du Pont facilities worldwide, Pontchartrain Works employees are active members of their community.

The plant supports many charitable, civic, and other worthwhile organizations in the community through direct financial support and employee participation. Annually, Pontchartrain Works employees support activities and organizations such as the United Way, St. John Theater, Junior Achievement, and the Audubon Zoo.

Science teachers from area public schools in the River Parishes attend the National Science Teachers' Association as a result of funding provided by Pontchartrain Works. The plant also has adopted East John High

School as a part of the statewide Adopt-a-School program.

Pontchartrain Works also joined with other area industries to develop the St. John Parish Community Awareness and Emergency Response (CAER) program. CAER is a joint community/industry effort to integrate all area emergency plans and services into a single, cohesive emergency plan.

In addition, a number of Pontchartrain Works employees are involved in local, parish, and state politics, and many others devote hours of personal time as scout leaders, working with church groups, local hospitals, and other community service-oriented organizations.

Annual employee wages, salaries, and benefits at Pontchartrain Works average about $30 million, and Du Pont pays an average of $20 million per year in state and local taxes. In addition to its 600 full-time employees, the plant also provides jobs for another 100 to 200 contract workers, and spends more than $200 million annually on local purchases of goods and services.

Safety, health, and environmental excellence are major thrusts at Pontchartrain Works. As a result of its emphasis on safety, Du Pont consistently has one of the lowest accident rates among all industries. Further,

An eight-foot-wide film of neoprene comes off a "freeze roll." Film is washed, dried, and gathered into a rope, and then cut into "chips" for packaging.

This commitment to employee health and safety is manifested in a stable work force, with a very low turnover rate.

For more than 25 years Du Pont's Pontchartrain Works has been a positive force in the community. When the plant celebrated its 25th anniversary in 1989, about 20 percent of all its employees also celebrated 25 years of service.

But Du Pont employees are not willing to rest on their laurels or point to past achievements. Rather, they are eagerly looking forward to the next quarter-century of service. In fact, the theme for their 25th anniversary celebration was "Continuing as a good neighbor into the next quarter-century."

Pontchartrain Works has been honored by the Occupational Safety and Health Administration as "the safest plant in Louisiana," among all industrial sites in the state. The plant consistently ranks among the top Du Pont plants in terms of safety records. But safety records, in and of themselves, are not the primary concern of Du Pont management at Pontchartrain Works—it is the people themselves who matter most, as the company places a very high value on its human resources.

It is these same people who share with all Louisianians the strong desire and determination to maintain both a high quality of life and the scenic beauty of the state's natural environment. Pontchartrain Works, to date, has spent $38 million to build state-of-the-art environmental facilities to ensure proper handling of waste materials generated in the processes used to manufacture its products—products that ultimately end up being used almost daily by the average U.S. citizen. The site spends an additional $13 million annually operating these environmental facilities.

And while the plant keeps a close

eye on the environment at all times, it places equal emphasis on employee health and safety. All equipment and processes are designed so that employees are not exposed to chemicals. Most areas and employees are monitored for the chemicals they work with on a regular basis. In addition, employees are scheduled for routine physicals annually or biannually, depending on the age of the employee.

An aerial view of the Pontchartrain Works, situated in the heart of the Louisiana River Parishes.

The future for Pontchartrain Works is a bright one, indeed. Employees can look forward to job stability with a company that cares—about its people, its product, its customers, its community, its state, and the environment—a company intent on being a good neighbor.

McILHENNY COMPANY

HERE'S A FORMULA FOR world conquest: Forget all the unpleasant business with armies, politics, bureaucrats, and the like. Just develop an extraordinary pepper sauce and let the waves of history wash it around the world.

Not the sort of thing that gets told in song and story, perhaps, but the sun that turns the air sultry over tiny, remote Avery Island, in south Louisiana, never sets on the Tabasco sauce domain that was born there. The fiery red (and fiery hot) blend of capsicum peppers, vinegar, and salt has found its way into the drink mixes, stews, sauces, and hearts of more than 100 countries since its invention more than 120 years ago. And its world is expanding still.

Post-*perestroika* Russia is being reintroduced to Louisiana's most famous seasoning, which it hasn't seen since the days of the czars. A new Italian Tabasco sauce cookbook is being circulated (confirming the Japanese perception that it is just the thing for pizza and spaghetti). The West Germans continue to savor it (though just where it appears in the cuisine of *Wurst and Kartoffelsalat* is still an open question around McIlhenny Company's Avery Island headquarters), and a liking for Tabasco sauce remains one thing, at least, that the Arabs and Israelis have in common.

Tabasco sauce has been to Khartoum with Kitchener, to King Tut's tomb with Carter, to Mount Everest with Hillary, and to outer space with Skylab.

But though it ranks in ubiquity with any edible item on earth and dominates sales in its category by a sizable margin, Tabasco sauce is not driven across the world by a high-

pressure marketing program—not yet, anyway.

"We've spent the past four generations proving that quality sells," observes McIlhenny president Edward McIlhenny Simmons. "Now we're going to prove that quality *and* marketing sell even more."

Those words sound a little strange in the surroundings in which they're spoken. Avery Island and McIlhenny Company are about as remote from the concrete-and-glass sterility of corporate America as one can get. Avery Island, 120 miles southwest of New Orleans, is an odd dome of solid ground in the midst of the southwest Louisiana marshes—the cap of a subterranean salt mountain whose base lies 50,000 feet below the surface. Part of the island's 2,500 acres is given over to a wildlife preserve and botanical garden that bespeaks the Avery and McIlhenny families' conservationist tradition. Then there are the fields of bright red peppers, surrounded by moss-draped oaks. The company office and plant are architecturally compatible and properly proportioned to this idyllic setting.

The attention to life and beauty may be an outgrowth of the grim days of Reconstruction following the Civil War, when patriarch Edmund McIlhenny cultivated a few special capsicum peppers in the plantation's vegetable garden and began the experiments that led to his development of the pepper sauce that would make the name "Tabasco" a

also moral outrage. It is simply unthinkable to the management of this fourth-generation, family-run company that anyone might be deluded into believing that something is a Tabasco-brand product that has not passed beneath the critical eye of a senior member of the McIlhenny family.

There is more to pass beneath their eyes these days—and more yet to come. What was once a single-product company now has expanded its line to include a successful Bloody Mary mix, a picante sauce, an add-your-own-ground-beef bottled chili mix, and a still top-secret addition to the line that everyone in management loves referring to and no one will describe.

trademark known from the Thames to Tokyo.

It's a fiercely protected brand, too. Few companies are more zealous in guarding their trademarks, copyrights, and patents than McIlhenny Company. Encroachers upon the Tabasco name and the slim, diamond-labeled bottle design and logo have found themselves hauled into court the world over and obliged to cease and desist. A rogue's gallery of defunct, would-be Tabasco clones is arrayed on shelves at McIlhenny Company headquarters.

There's more than protection of a valuable property behind this determined defense of the name. There's

That expansion into other products, along with the growing demand for Tabasco sauce, may pick up the genteel pace around the island. But it won't change the nature of things. "We're a family business," says Ned Simmons. "That's a plus—and a permanent reality. There'll still be a McIlhenny inspecting every barrel of mash that goes into Tabasco sauce in 2089, just like there was in 1889 and 1989."

Brave words in an era of food industry mega-mergers. But the McIlhenny clan has already turned down some lucrative offers for what a food industry source once described as "a real jewel of a company." And in a world of soulless super-corporations, one has to hope that they make it.

CRESCENT DISTRIBUTING COMPANY

THE ENDING TO THIS STORY hasn't been written yet," says Stanley S. Scott, owner and operator of Crescent Distributing Company, in obvious satisfaction with his latest venture. The story that Scott refers to is his life, a remarkable odyssey of public- and private-sector achievements. By becoming his own boss, the 56-year-old Scott sees the culmination of a fortunate and exciting career.

Scott's domain is the 21-acre Miller beer-distributing facility in Harahan, Louisiana. With more than 200,000 square feet under one roof, Crescent ranks as one of the 10 largest beer-distribution outlets in the country. In 1989 Crescent sold more than 5 million cases of beer and controlled some 38 percent of the New Orleans metropolitan market. It stocks nine different varieties, including Miller Lite, Miller Genuine Draft, Miller High Life, and Lowenbrau.

Scott, who is black, is in select company. Of Miller's 740 independent distributorships, only five are black owned. There are 11 minority-owned distributorships in all.

How did Stan Scott grab the brass ring? He credits Hamish Maxwell, chairman and chief executive officer at Philip Morris Companies Inc., and

The management team looks over the company's latest marketing plans with Stanley Scott (second from right).

Miller brewery president Leonard Goldstein, who looked at Scott's successful track record and opened the door of opportunity when he knocked.

Scott, formerly a vice president and assistant to the chairman of the $45-billion Philip Morris Companies Inc., which owns Miller Brewing Co., views his role in the community as a return on investment. Taught from an early age that it is not enough just to consume in a capitalistic society without giving back something to the community, Scott is very active in civic and social activities. Scott was appointed by Louisiana Governor Buddy Roemer to the state's Economic Development Corporation. He is a member of the New Orleans Audubon Commission, the New Orleans branch of the Federal Reserve Bank, and the Urban League of Greater New Orleans.

Scott, a former journalist whose family publishes the *Atlanta Daily World,* the nation's first black-owned daily newspaper, managed a $200-million budget and 500 employees as an assistant administrator of the

State Department's Agency for International Development during President Gerald R. Ford's administration. He also served as special assistant on domestic affairs to presidents Nixon and Ford from 1972 to 1974. A man of many talents, Scott, as a UPI reporter, was also nominated for a Pulitzer Prize for his eyewitness account of the assassination of Malcolm X.

Undoubtedly, Scott will draw from this reservoir of experience and talent to accomplish his goals for the distributorship. Explains Scott, "I'm in a state and an area that's been hit hard by the oil slowdown, and it's my challenge to continue to maintain our market-share in New Orleans." Since taking over in the spring of 1988, Scott has made it a point to meet the community and political leaders. "I'm an outgoing, gregarious type of guy. And besides, you can't sell beer sitting behind a desk," he says.

Scott says that marketing goals are right on target. His next goal is to go one step further with his dream and become a diversified entrepreneur. The ending to his story hasn't yet been written.

Stanley S. Scott, owner and operator of Crescent Distributing Company.

BARQ'S, INC.

ONCE EVERY THREE WEEKS or so, John E. Koerner III drives an hour and a half from his downtown New Orleans office to the Mississippi Gulf Coast to mix another batch of the secret formula for Barq's Root Beer.

When Koerner and his partner, John F. Oudt, bought the company from the Barq family in 1976, they received little more than that secret formula. There was an outdated bottling plant in Biloxi that still managed to service the brand's remarkable 20 percent market share (second only to Coca-Cola), but, more important, the pair bought worldwide rights for Barq's Root Beer.

Former classmates at Tulane University, Koerner and Oudt (who is chairman of the board) grew up drinking Barq's, and they set their sights on the company because they liked the taste of Barq's Root Beer. "We figured that if we could give Barq's nationwide only a fraction of the success that the brand enjoyed along the Mississippi coast, we would be immensely successful," says Koerner, president of Barq's, Inc.

Looking back, the seasoned busi-

Below: Barq's is the second-largest-selling root beer in the world.

nessmen are amused at their naivete. "If we had known the soft drink industry when we bought the company, we probably never would have dreamed of national expansion," says Koerner. "We didn't know it was 'impossible.'"

Now on the downhill slide of achieving that "impossible" national status, the success of Barq's has been beyond phenomenal. At the time of the acquisition, the Barq's (pronounced "Barks") bottler network comprised 19 bottlers scattered across the country. Most were near-bankrupt Barq's-only bottlers left over from the explosive growth in the soft drink industry following World War II. The pair canceled most of these remaining franchises and began anew, licensing rock-solid Coca-Cola and Pepsi-Cola bottlers to produce and distribute Barq's Root Beer.

Barq's now operates in 45 states through hundreds of franchised bottlers, making the brand available to about 75 percent of the U.S. population. In fact, after just 12 years under Koerner and Oudt, Barq's emerged as the second-largest seller of root beer—only behind nationally distributed A&W.

Koerner and Oudt's choice of New Orleans as the company's corporate headquarters was far from simply homing instinct. For marketing and public relations reasons, they retained the brand's original plant in Biloxi for manufacturing. But the headquarters move to New Orleans brought with it added benefits: convenient travel connections, a strong draw in recruiting executive talent, a cooperative financial community, and, of course, the brand's favorite-son status among local "po-boy" fans.

Standing at Jackson Square are John Oudt (left), chairman of the board, and John E. Koerner III, president, of Barq's, Inc.

As one of the only national consumer packaged-goods makers headquartered in New Orleans, Barq's, Inc., finds benefits in the city other companies might overlook. "Our business depends a great deal on our relationship with our customers," Koerner says. "Between the food, boating, Mardi Gras—the fun—there simply isn't a better place than New Orleans to entertain clients."

And customers seem to understand when Barq's offices close on Mardi Gras day. Koerner says, "It reminds them we are a unique company to do business with."

KENTWOOD SPRING WATER

Kentwood Spring Water, based in New Orleans, Louisiana, has enjoyed steady growth—expanding from a modest 5 routes in the beginning to more than 140 routes today.

Begun in 1965 by the Levy and Rosenblum families in New Orleans, Kentwood Spring Water has been the focal point of 25 years of success as consumers and connoisseurs alike become aware of the need for purer quality drinking water.

The complete dedication of past and present employees and the superb quality of its product and customer service has today earned Kentwood Spring Water the reputation of being the number-one fastest growing bottled water company. Kentwood ranks as one of the most pure waters in America, according to the International Bottled Water Association, which honored Kentwood Spring Water with membership in the IBWA Top Twenty-Club—an honor that recognizes superior standards for quality control. To make it to the Top Twenty, Kentwood had to be rigorously inspected according to federal, state, and IBWA regulations. Kentwood Spring Water is the only bottled water company in Louisiana and Mississippi to receive this honor.

These brief comments testify to the dramatic present successes of activity of the company. What really stirs the imagination, however, is the story of how it all began.

Bill Roohi, vice president and general manager of Kentwood Spring Water, explains that the company founders, Edward Levy and Julius and Paul Rosenblum, assumed as a personal quest to find the purest source for a quality bottled water.

In the piney woods of Kentwood, Louisiana, some 98 miles north of New Orleans, they found what they were looking for flowing from one of the world's finest, deep, underground springs. Kentwood prides itself in supplying a natural spring water, just the way Mother Nature produced it.

"Yes, there are other bottled water companies that get their water from the same Kentwood source, but it is the high level of quality control and supervision that Kentwood Spring Water takes that makes the difference between the quality of Kentwood Spring Water and other bottled waters," says Roohi.

Basically, the bottled spring water that is delivered to the customer's door or purchased at the retail store is delivered spring fresh, the day after it is taken from the spring. The spring water is pumped from the natural deep-water artesian springs into Kentwood's own stainless-steel tankers and then directly transported to its New Orleans bottling facility. These carriers are used exclusively by Kentwood Spring Water and are meticulously maintained and inspected. "They carry only our water," exclaims Roohi, "so there's no chance of contamination from another liquid." Kentwood's team of full-time, certified Quality Control Specialists run a series of hourly tests to ensure that nothing interferes with the fresh, clean taste of Kentwood Spring Water. From there it is run through Kentwood's own filtration and ozonation process. No chemical is ever used in or around Kentwood Spring Water. It is further tested by independent testing laboratories and surpasses all state and federal standards for bottled water. These measures are a part of Kentwood's commitment to quality control.

Today Kentwood Spring Water produces Artesian, Distilled, and Fluoridated spring water in five gallon and half gallon bottles for home delivery service and 10-ounce bottles, one-liter bottles, two-and-one-half-gallon bottles, and one-gallon bottles for supermarkets, drugstores, and mass merchandise and convenience stores. Also available in 10-ounce and one-liter bottles is Kentwood Sparkling Water, a soft-carbonated water which can be used as a mixer or as a spritzer all by itself and is most commonly used in restaurant and hotel bars. Kentwood also produces 10-K, one of the leading isotonic beverages on the market today. "We have also expanded branch offices in Venice, Baton Rouge, Lafayette, Houma, Morgan City, Lake Charles, and Jackson, Mississippi," says Roohi.

"Eight is great!" proclaims the International Bottled Water Association, referring to the needs our bodies have for 8 full glasses of water each day in order to maintain a perfect balance of health. "Over a quarter of a million people in southeastern Louisiana and Mississippi drink and cook with Kentwood Spring Water. One fact remains—the source of the success of Kentwood Spring Water. "Our 400-plus employees are the force behind the tremendous success that we've experienced. The close working relationship shared by all employees serves as a shining reflection of caring, sincere service to our customers—and our customers are the V.I.P.s of this company."

Natural, great-tasting Kentwood Spring Water helps customers throughout southeastern Louisiana and Mississippi maintain good health.

Photo by Philip Gould

QUALITY OF LIFE

Medical and educational institutions contribute to the quality of life for New Orleans area residents.

Photo by Philip Gould

OCHSNER MEDICAL INSTITUTIONS

OPENED JUST AFTER THE start of World War II, the Ochsner Medical Institutions soon earned a position as a leader and innovator among medical centers. Today Ochsner enjoys a broad patient base, serving the Gulf South and Latin America, and has expanded with a growing commitment to community-based primary care.

A symbiotic relationship between quality medical care and innovative delivery methods is cultivated at Ochsner. More than 4,200 employees support the efforts of 315 Ochsner physicians working within a highly refined medical system. What this means to a patient admitted to the Ochsner Medical Institutions is an administratively efficient system loaded with consumer conveniences that produces spectacular results.

In addition to being the second-largest nongovernmental employer in Jefferson Parish, with a payroll exceeding $110 million, Ochsner attracts more than 170,000 visits each year from patients who reside outside the greater New Orleans area. The facility trains physicians by conducting the second-largest nonuniversity-based medical program in the United States. More than 200 young men and women are in training each year at Ochsner. The Ochsner School of Allied Health conducts 14 different medical technology programs providing high-technology career opportunities.

Among its many achievements in medicine and research, Ochsner has earned a worldwide reputation for treating cardiovascular problems. A tiny fiber-optic device called an angioscope, developed by two Ochsner cardiologists, promises to eliminate the remaining uncertainties in the nonsurgical treatment of coronary artery blockages—the cause of or type of blockage. The angioscope travels to the heart arteries by catheter used in angioplasty and provides the cardiologist with a view inside the coronary artery, helping determine what treatment is most appropriate. The Ochsner Medical Institutions was the first facility in the United States to

Above: Day or night, the Ochsner Medical Institutions is well equipped and ready to serve the medical needs of the community. Photo by Jackson Hill

Right: Ochsner has a long-standing reputation for excellence in surgical procedures. Photo by Jackson Hill

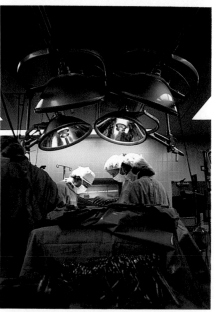

use the angioscope in a beating heart artery.

The surgery department is a leader in the Gulf South in providing comprehensive critical care. Recent advances in research and expansion of the surgical staff have provided tremendous advances in cardiac, vascular, and cancer surgery. Highly successful programs are now established in liver, heart, and kidney transplantation.

Ochsner heart surgeons have begun using an ultrasonic device to clear away calcium deposits that can clog the body's heart valves. The condition narrows the heart's aortic valve, frequently necessitating the replacement of the valve with an artificial one. The ultrasound device uses a vibrating metal probe that pulverizes the calcium deposits on contact, leaving healthy tissue intact. This new technology allows surgeons to repair rather than replace the heart valve

and further reduces the length of the operation. Laser angioplasty is being used for the management of localized vascular blockage.

Ochsner Foundation Hospital is one of eight medical centers nationwide testing the effectiveness of a surgical sensing device to detect cancer cells in concentrations too small to be seen or felt by the surgeon. The probe detects very low-level radiation from a monoclonal antibody with an affinity for cancer cells. Once the visible or palpable tumors are removed

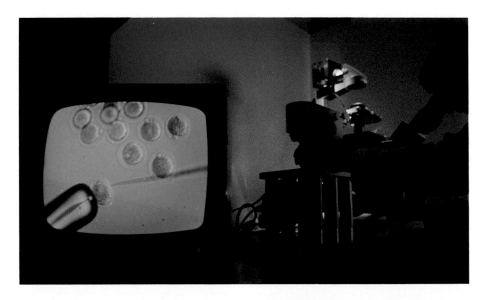

Research at Ochsner provides patients with the latest treatments available. Photo by Jackson Hill

medical care, a number of the neighborhood clinics will expand to accommodate growing patient volume.

On the Ochsner campus, the radiation oncology pavilion has been updated and expanded to reinforce its commitment to state-of-the-art cancer care.

The commitment of the community and the region to the center and its research was seen in a successful capital campaign that provided funding for the new Ochsner research center.

The center provides additional laboratories and the latest technology to promote the continued expansion of medical research.

The explosive growth in clinic patient volume has necessitated major expansion of physician offices and examination and treatment areas. The new structure will also include additional clinic and foundation offices and will be integrated into the existing campus buildings by a five-story, climate-controlled atrium containing a retail medical mall.

The final phase of this construction plan involves a new critical care tower incorporating a new emergency room, plus new and larger specialty care areas including medical/surgical, coronary, pediatric, and neonatal intensive care units.

The Ochsner Medical Institutions continues a tradition of excellence that is known worldwide and is generations deep, providing valuable contributions to the quality of life. The Ochsner commitment to that quality and to the New Orleans metropolitan area is evidenced by its human and financial investment, which assures that the facility will continue to be a preeminent provider of health care well into the twenty-first century.

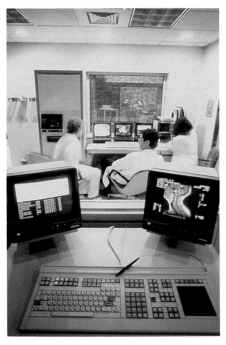

Above: A statue of Alton Ochsner, M.D., one of five founders of the Ochsner Medical Institutions.

Left: Ochsner is known throughout the state for its leadership in diagnostic capabilities.

during surgery, the surgeon examines the surrounding tissues with the probe, which beeps when it encounters any remaining cancer cells.

Research at Ochsner consists of both basic science and clinical elements. The Ochsner molecular biology laboratories are conducting forefront research into the mechanisms by which cancer develops and progresses.

Ochsner has recently established a Laboratory of Cellular Immunology that is devoted to the understanding of the mechanisms by which cellular factors regulate the growth and development of the immune system.

Research in cellular and molecular biology and the efforts of the immunology laboratory are easily translated into patient use such as the recent establishment of lymphokine-activated killer cell/Interleukin-2 cancer therapy, with encouraging results.

To meet the medical challenges of tomorrow, plans call for expansion and modernization of the facility with activities that will continue throughout the decade of the 1990s.

As a result of the well-received neighborhood clinic concept, which provides more convenient primary

SOUTHERN BAPTIST HOSPITAL

SOUTHERN BAPTIST HOSPITAL, an Uptown New Orleans landmark on Napoleon Avenue since 1926, is one of the largest private hospitals in Louisiana. Established by the Southern Baptist Convention, the hospital currently operates independently of the convention as a private, not-for-profit institution. However, in keeping with its heritage, Baptist continues its commitment to provide the highest-quality medical care in an atmosphere of Christian concern.

The hospital completed the largest building program in its history, dubbed Project 2000, with the opening of the Clara Wing in 1985. Though no additional patient beds were added during the project (SBH is licensed for 533 beds), expansion provided space to accommodate patients in more comfortable rooms and to relocate some departments for more convenient and efficient service.

Project 2000 also provided a modern garage that is connected via secure, air-conditioned second-story bridges to the Clara Wing, the McFarland Center, and the Napoleon Medical Plaza. And finally, the project included total replacement of the hospital's power plant and installation of a clean, fuel-efficient waste-disposal system that meets all EPA standards.

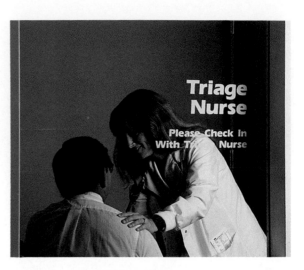

The hospital's emergency center provides quick, expert care in times of crisis.

Proud of being a good neighbor, SBH has taken responsibility for maintaining the neutral ground in front of the hospital on Napoleon Avenue. Every year during the Christmas holiday season, trees on the hospital campus and on the neutral ground are lighted (courtesy of the SBH League) for a sparkling Christmas greeting.

The McFarland Education Center is a seven-story, 84,000-square-foot facility that is home to William Carey College School of Nursing, Baptist's 50,000-volume capacity Learning Resource Center, and the hospital's education, human resources, pastoral counseling, and public relations departments. A 350-seat auditorium and meeting rooms have been host sites for many community events, including health fairs, recitals, public school awards programs, and gubernatorial debates. Also located in the center are rooms that are rented at reasonable rates to family members who need to stay close to hospitalized patients.

While patients undoubtedly appreciate Baptist's attitude of civic responsibility and the comforts modern buildings provide, it is the quality of the SBH medical and nursing staffs that continues to hold the hospital in its favorable position in the hearts and minds of New Orleanians. More

Southern Baptist Hospital has been an Uptown New Orleans landmark on Napoleon Avenue since 1926.

than 450 highly qualified physicians in every major specialty have met the rigorous requirements for admission to the SBH medical staff.

Responsible for the hands-on, minute-to-minute care of patients, SBH nurses are famous for their warmth and professionalism. In a time of chronic nationwide nursing shortage, SBH attracts and retains nursing's best with competitive pay scales, a career-ladder program, and a supportive work environment rich in professional opportunity.

Long known as the birthplace of New Orleanians, SBH continues to build on its established reputation for excellence in women's and children's services. Education programs for every member of the expectant family are offered, as are pre- and postnatal exercise classes for mothers. Perinatal specialists, the most modern monitoring equipment, and Baptist's Neonatal Intensive Care Unit provide the specialized high-tech, high-touch treatment necessary for low-weight premature or high-risk babies to survive and thrive.

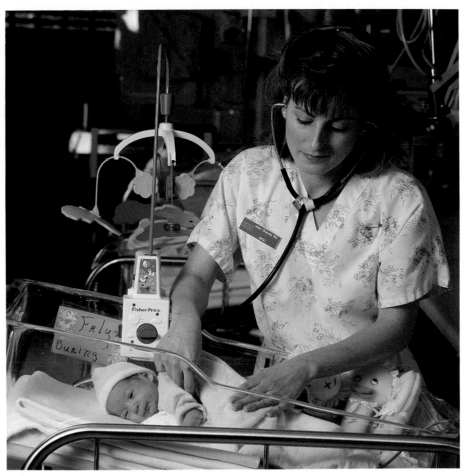

Aquatics classes for persons with arthritis are offered through Baptist's Arthritis Center.

Recent additions in surgical and cardiovascular services continue the SBH history of providing state-of-the-art technology to improve patient care. Advanced laser technology is used in some procedures, allowing patients to recover and return home more quickly than was possible with traditional surgical methods.

Baptist's excellence in sports medicine has welded its longtime special relationship with the New Orleans Saints. But students and amateur athletes also benefit from Baptist's years of experience at getting injured athletes back in the game. To complement the excellent orthopedic services that historically have existed at the hospital, the Human Performance Center recently expanded its fitness assessment, preventive exercise, and post-injury rehabilitation services.

The SBH Executive Wellness Program provides comprehensive physicals and follow-up to executives throughout the greater New Orleans area.

No commentary on SBH would be complete without a word about the long-standing tradition of pastoral

Baptist's Neonatal Intensive Care Unit provides the high-touch, high-tech care required by low-weight, high-risk babies.

care. In 1988 the hospital's chaplains made more than 38,000 visits to patients, family members, and employees. Students, parish clergy, chaplains, foreign students, and members of religious orders participate in the hospital's continuing education program for pastoral care.

Faithful to its special mission in New Orleans as envisioned more than 60 years ago by the men and women who founded it, Southern Baptist Hospital continues its commitment to deliver the highest-quality service at a reasonable cost in a safe and comfortable environment and in a friendly and compassionate manner. Further, it is committed to promote healthful living, educational advancement, and spiritual care through pastoral guidance, education and counseling, health promotion, and community outreach.

LOUISIANA STATE UNIVERSITY MEDICAL CENTER

WHEN THE LOUISIANA STATE Medical Center (LSUMC) was founded in 1931, the New Orleans *Item-Tribune* headlined its story, "New LSU Medical Center Finest of Kind in Country." In the years since, LSU has more than lived up to its top billing.

LSUMC now comprises six professional schools—two schools of medicine, a school of nursing, a graduate school, the state's only schools of dentistry and allied health professions, a university hospital in Shreveport, and the Pennington Biomedical Research Center in Baton Rouge. In addition, there is also the world-renowned LSU Eye Center, Kresge Hearing Research Laboratory, Southeast Regional Food Science Nutrition Center, Neuroscience Center, Human Development Center, and the International Center for Medical Research Training in Central America, all of which are components of the present-day LSUMC.

Patients from all over the world are referred to the center's outpatient clinic for expertise and the very latest treatments in a broad range of medical and surgical specialties. In addition, LSUMC maintains affiliations with more than 100 hospitals statewide and with research entities that span the globe.

As an economic force, few in the New Orleans region have as positive or as influential an impact as LSUMC. Providing jobs for 7,000 people, LSUMC's annual operating budget is approximately $300 million, with only about one-third of that coming from the state. LSUMC is the state's largest single holder of federal grant money, receiving about 50 percent of the state's National Institutes of Health money annually, with a total of $25 million to $30 million in sponsored research each year.

The center enjoys a national as well as international reputation for excellence in education with both professionals and students coming from all parts of the world. The mission of LSUMC is threefold. The first responsibility is to educate and train the health care professionals of tomorrow. Equally important, however, is the second charge—to conduct research. It is only through research that mankind can continue to improve the quality of life. To fulfill this endeavor, LSUMC

Above: The Infant Services Program of LSUMC's Human Development Center serves children (birth to age three) with developmental disabilities. Through early intervention, specialists in a variety of areas work with the parents to help these children reach their fullest potential. Photo by Robert John Reinhard

Left: LSUMC's faculty provides expertise and advanced care to patients as well as quality education to the next generation of health care professionals. Photo by Lisa Candelario

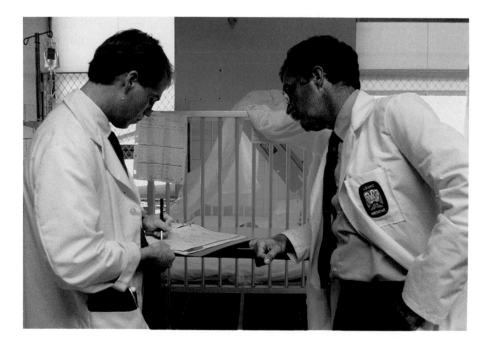

has dedicated approximately 350,000 square feet to research activity. In addition, an Office of Technology Transfer has been established to translate ideas from the laboratory to the marketplace. The third and final responsibility is that LSUMC is a service organization serving the needs of a worldwide community.

Scientists and physicians at LSUMC have been at the forefront of research efforts for many years, earning international acclaim in a variety of disciplines for their efforts. Their

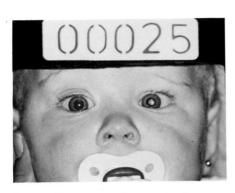

If eye problems are not diagnosed early, correction may not be possible. LSU Eye Center's Dr. Keith Morgan helped develop the VISISCREEN 100 Ocular Screening System from NASA technology to screen children too young to read. A camera takes photos that reveal eye problems. Here, the left eye shows a cataract. Photo by Maxine Haslauer

contributions will continue to make significant changes in the way people live their lives. For example, Dr. Gerald Berenson's Bogalusa Heart Study, an ongoing, multidisciplinary project, has gained worldwide distinction and has yielded the world's largest collection of data on childhood cardiovascular risk factors. It was this study that provided the knowledge that cardiovascular disease can begin in childhood and provided the intervention technique to avoid it.

Dr. Conrad Gumbart performed Louisiana's first bone marrow transplant, and his program remains the region's premier transplant program.

Also, Dr. Jack Strong has studied atherosclerosis since the 1960s and was the first person in the world to link the progression of this major cause of heart disease to smoking. At the Department of Ophthalmology's internationally recognized Eye Center, the Excimer Laser—a laser that works without heat to eliminate vision problems and the need for corrective lenses—was the first in the nation to receive FDA approval for testing on sighted patients.

Dr. Pelayo Correa, a highly respected epidemiologist and an expert on cancer etiology, is conducting two landmark studies. The first is an international study of gastric carcinoma.

Among the factors examined in this multidisciplinary project is the role salt plays in carcinogenesis. The second study involves LSUMC as one of only five centers in the country participating in the largest case-control study of the effects of passive smoking. This research project, the largest of its kind ever conducted, will examine the risk factors of lung cancer in nonsmoking women exposed to secondhand tobacco smoke.

Other important contributions from LSUMC are the development of a non-A, non-B hepatitis vaccine; the development of hydroxylapatite, which allows bone to actually bond to dental implants and bone grafts; the development of a reciprocating brace that allows paraplegics to walk; DNA fingerprinting; and the list goes on and on.

Louisiana State University Medical Center has an eye toward the future. It will continue to grow and fulfill its threefold mission—in education, research, and service—to fully realize its potential so clearly seen by its visionary founders in 1913.

In a perfect example of successful technology transfer, the LSU Reciprocating-Gait Orthosis makes it possible for paraplegics to walk, one foot in front of the other. Patients around the globe are walking with the help of this device, developed and patented by LSUMC. Photo by Robert John Reinhard

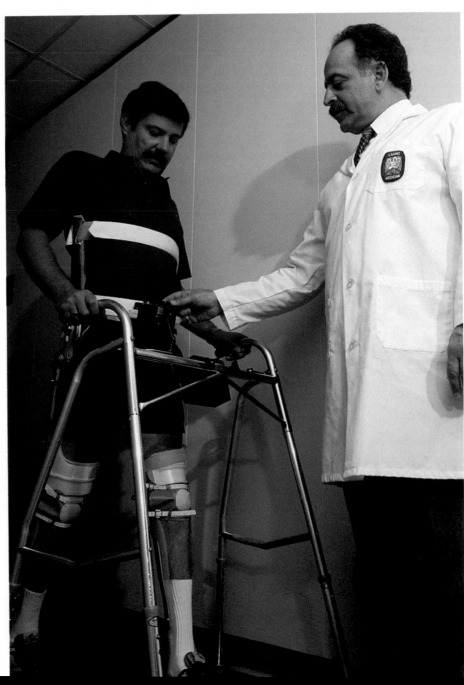

LOYOLA UNIVERSITY

LOYOLA UNIVERSITY IN NEW Orleans—the Jesuit University of the South—is the largest Catholic university in the southern region of the United States from the western border of Arizona and east to Florida. It was founded in 1912 by the Society of Jesus as an institution dedicated to the Jesuit academic tradition of contributing to the liberal arts education of the whole person.

Today, as the annual home of about 5,000 students, 360 faculty, a dedicated support staff, and an active Jesuit community, Loyola still operates under its founding principles of offering a liberal arts education to all who seek knowledge and truth.

Loyola consists of four undergraduate schools and a School of Law. Academic divisions include the College of Arts and Sciences; the Joseph A. Butt, S.J., College of

The student-faculty ratio at Loyola is maintained at about 15 to one, providing an ideal learning experience.

Business Administration; the Loyola City College; and the College of Music (nationally acclaimed for its outstanding music education and performance programs and as the only college of music among America's 28 Jesuit colleges and universities).

Loyola is a university where current and future growth is viewed in terms of increasing numbers of learning opportunities, not substantially increasing enrollment numbers. The student/faculty ratio is maintained consistently around 15 to one to ensure that each student receives a personalized educational experience.

Loyola is located in the historic Uptown University district, overlooking Audubon Park, and the campus is

only a streetcar ride away from the French Quarter. The 19-acre main campus is a collection of Tudor, Gothic, and modern architecture. Two blocks up St. Charles Avenue, the university's Broadway campus offers four additional acres, which is home for the Loyola Law School, the Institute of Human Relations, the Visual Arts Department, the Institutional Advancement Office, and a residence hall.

Beyond its active participation with the city's other fine colleges and universities in improving the educational climate in New Orleans, Loyola's programs add significantly to the city's cultural life, and its students and faculty annually add more than $250 million to the local economy. In addition, the university's more than 25,000 alumni reside in all 50 states and in 50 nations worldwide.

Acting as a concerned and committed institutional citizen of the city, the state, and the nation, Loyola has included in its mission statement an extraordinarily strong affirmation of involvement in community service, asserting that "Loyola stands ready to do whatever is in its power as an independent Catholic university to solve the problems of American society today."

Loyola University in New Orleans is the largest Catholic university in the southern United States.

TULANE UNIVERSITY

TULANE UNIVERSITY BEGAN 155 years ago, when seven young New Orleans physicians launched the Medical College of Louisiana to train doctors to fight the yellow fever that plagued the area. Since then, the university has played a central role—economically, culturally, medically, and educationally—in the life of the New Orleans community. At the same time, Tulane's activities in all four areas extend worldwide.

Tulane is among the major research and teaching universities in the nation. It is one of only six southern institutions invited to belong to the prestigious Association of American Universities, a group of 58 major American and Canadian universities.

More than 11,000 students are enrolled in Tulane's 11 schools and colleges. Undergraduate studies in liberal arts and sciences, architecture, engineering, and business make up approximately two-thirds of the total enrollment. The final third is comprised of graduate students enrolled in law, business, social work, medicine, public health and tropical medicine, or liberal arts and sciences.

Freshmen provide just one example of the university's quality: The typical first-year student ranks in the top third of his or her high school. To ensure the continuing presence of good students, Tulane's financial-aid

Tulips and azaleas grace the front of Tulane's administration building, constructed in 1894.

budget has increased sixfold in nine years, to reach almost $40 million. Over the past six years, three Rhodes scholars have been selected from Tulane. Only five other schools in the nation—Harvard, Princeton, Stanford, Yale, and Georgetown— boast more Rhodes winners during that time.

The university, with its medical center, is the largest private employer in Orleans Parish, with almost 6,100 employees and a payroll of $145 million. Directly or indirectly, Tulane is responsible for almost 10,500 jobs, almost $400 million in expenditures, and more than $16 million in government revenues in the New Orleans region every year.

In addition to their reputation for excellence, Tulane students have a tradition of concern for the local community. The Community Action Council of Tulane University Students (CACTUS), which celebrated its 20th anniversary in 1989, involves more than 350 volunteers each semester in one or more of 20 projects. Organizing food drives, planning recycling programs, tutoring children in need, and providing medical and legal advice on the streets at Mardi Gras are only a few examples. Tulane Law School was the first in the nation to require its students to complete work pro bono—in the public interest—before they graduate, setting an example for schools nationwide.

Above: Casting glass into art is a specialty of the Newcomb Art Department.

Left: Jogging and basketball are just two of the activities available at the Reily Student Recreation Center.

UNIVERSITY OF NEW ORLEANS

T HE UNIVERSITY OF NEW Orleans, Louisiana's major urban university, is rapidly moving into a new era, one that will assure it a leadership position in the public/private growth of the metropolitan area.

Chancellor Gregory M. St. L. O'Brien thinks UNO has the potential to be the best major urban university in the nation. "Being the best means extending the range and depth of the university's partnerships. UNO is a valuable resource for the city itself and is destined to become a major factor in the economic development of the region," he says.

Long known for academic excellence—reflected in its noted researchers, authors, and top-notch graduates—the university has now immersed itself directly into the economic, social, cultural, and civic communities it serves. These efforts are producing tangible results in areas as diverse as economic development and the study of jazz.

To keep pace with the 1990s, major public urban universities such as UNO offer a variety of disciplines inside the institution as well as topical research

The University of New Orleans Performing Arts Center is home to the school's departments of music, drama, and communications. Jazz great Ellis Marsalis heads the unique Jazz Studies program.

and public service programs. The university's 16,000 students in six senior colleges and graduate schools can earn bachelor's degrees in 60 fields, master's in 50 fields, and doctorates in 12.

The college boasts the largest College of Business and the only College of Urban and Public Affairs in the state. Its School of Hotel, Restaurant & Tourism Administration serves as a resource for New Orleans' tourism industry and its scores of hotels and restaurants. Recently, jazz great Ellis Marsalis (father of Wynton and Branford) returned to head the newly created Center for Jazz Studies.

UNO's College of Engineering boasts the School of Naval Architecture and Marine Engineering. The college is housed in a $20-million, nine-story facility.

The Metropolitan College, comprised of four downtown and suburban centers, is the university's largest and delivers courses and seminars near home and the work place. It also houses the university's Center for the Pacific Rim. Within the College of Business, there are six areas currently providing research services and professional consultation to business, industry, and governmental entities.

The College of Engineering has been awarded a $2.2-million grant through its Center for Urban Waste Management to assist local jurisdictions in upgrading solid-waste management.

Five other colleges and divisions are working on programs linked to bringing the university closer to the city and, in turn, are helping the area compete in the global marketplace.

"What an exciting opportunity," says O'Brien. "We're making the future happen right here."

Photo by Bob Rowan/Progressive Image Photography

FROM THE GROUND UP

Developers, contractors, and realtors all help to shape the New Orleans of tomorrow.

Photo by Bob Rowan/Progressive Image Photography

WESTMINSTER CORPORATION

WESTMINSTER CORPORATION traces its origin in New Orleans to the turn of the century and continues to grow in stature as one of the largest developers and managers of office space in the southern United States.

Westminster was founded by Harry Latter, who organized Latter & Blum, Inc., a commercial real estate brokerage firm, with Joseph Blum in 1915. Harry Latter, his son Shepard, and now a third generation, Lee Schlesinger, have developed and managed commercial properties for the Latter-Schlesinger family under the Westminster umbrella. Westminster management operations have expanded to over 60 properties; over half are owned by Westminster and its affiliates. Since 1980 the company has also managed properties owned by other investors.

Westminster has developed over 4 million square feet of office space for its own account and advises others on over 2 million square feet. Westminster also operates over 1,000 multifamily residential units and some 10,000 parking spaces. Westminster has properties and management offices in Baton Rouge, Louisiana; Lafayette, Louisiana; San Antonio, Texas; and Chicago, Illinois, in addition to New Orleans. The tenant list, exceeding 300 companies, includes Exxon, McDermott International, Freeport-McMoRan, Chevron, IBM, Tulane University, Metropolitan Life Insurance, The Travelers, Xerox Corporation, Whitney National Bank, G.D. Searle, Hibernia National Bank, and the First National Bank of Commerce. Tenants range in size from New York stock exchange company world headquarters requiring several hundred thousand square feet to sole legal practitioners and snack shops utilizing only a few hundred feet.

Westminster's philosophy is based on tenant service and long-term ownership. This orientation pervades all phases of operations, dictating a hands-on approach with personal attention to detail. Westminster provides a full range of in-house services to lease, maintain and operate each

property efficiently. A full-time security staff monitors each property and the surrounding areas to present a safe environment. The engineering department is responsible for all aspects of operating the buildings' physical plants on a daily basis. Scheduled programs for periodic inspections, preventative maintenance, and long-term capital improvement forecasts are routine. The engineering staff's responsibilities go far beyond operating equipment efficiently to include labeling mechanical rooms with color-coded piping, assisting with ac-

The 1010 Common Building, home of Westminster Corporation.

quisition evaluations, to providing continuing education on topics such as asbestos abatement and researching alternate cooling mediums to replace certain varieties of freon that the EPA is phasing out.

Over the years, Westminster has built a reputation for solving complex management, operational, and investment problems. One of its more ambitious projects was the complete rehabilitation of the 300,000-square-

Above: The Westminster City Center Properties buildings are immediately adjacent to the Louisiana Superdome.

The Westminster City Center Properties complex by day (right) and at dusk (below).

natural gas made the system obsolete and uneconomical. It needed to be replaced without closing the building. Over the three-week installation period for the new electric chillers, the Westminster engineering staff lifted 1.2 million pounds of ice to the roof cooling towers to keep the building and its tenants comfortable. The transition was virtually transparent to the tenants.

Development of Westminster City Center Properties on Poydras Street, across from the Louisiana Superdome, began in 1978. The complex includes three highrise buildings with over 1.5 million square feet

foot 925 Common Building, the former New Orleans headquarters for Shell Oil, and subsequently Exxon. Beginning in 1982, all building components were upgraded to state of the art. Tenant finishes are now the same as those used in recently completed buildings. The facade, lobby, and sidewalks were redesigned and replaced. The classic stainless steel and brass elevator cabs remain, but a new Westinghouse computer controller

sees that they provide fast, trouble-free service for demanding tenants. The 38-year-old building is now over 90 percent leased.

A fully occupied building with mechanical problems presents an entirely different challenge. When the Saratoga Building was built for Gulf Oil Company in 1957, the cooling system ran on Louisiana's abundant supply of cheap natural gas. By the early 1980s the price and short supply of

of office space and 1,500 parking spaces. Westminster City Center Properties is the western anchor of the Poydras corridor and a focal point for visitors entering the Central Business District from Interstate 10.

Creativity in the marketplace, combined with a long-term attitude toward tenants, positions Westminster Corporation to develop, own, and manage properties well into the next century.

HISTORIC RESTORATION, INC.

PIONEERING IS RISKY business. After all, they buried La Salle on the banks of the Mississippi River," says developer Pres Kabacoff, comparing risks taken by the French explorer with his own bold venture into historic renovation and restoration. In the spirit of the seventeenth-century explorer, Kabacoff, along with codeveloper Ed Boettner, formed Historic Restoration, Inc. (HRI), in 1982.

Together they saw an opportunity to build elegant, affordable apartments using abandoned warehouses in an area adjacent to downtown New Orleans. Says Kabacoff, "Our model was the SoHo neighborhood in Manhattan where they've been converting warehouses into apartments for quite awhile. The physical characteristics such as the high ceil-

ings and large windows as well as the building materials utilized were far beyond what you see in conventional apartments."

The so-called Warehouse District is a 400-acre tract, roughly the same area as the more famous French Quarter, and is situated upriver from the central business district. Today the

An interior view of one of the Henderson apartments.

location and the original adventurous idea are proving to be more than ideal for the young professionals and others working in the downtown area.

Using the impetus of the 1984 World's Fair, which created a public recognition of a viable, exciting downtown area coupled with the installation of infrastructure and utilities specifically for the fair, HRI began its ambitious project. Investment tax credits were very important to the project since they provided money in the way of tax incentives necessary to restore and develop the historic properties. Kabacoff says, "These projects are very expensive to do, and if it hadn't been for the tax credits and groups like the Preservation Resource Center, we would have never seen the dream through to fruition."

Today the warehouse district serves as home to some 1,200 people living and working in the downtown area. Nearly 850 residential units have come on line since the inception of the project. In addition, the area has become an art district as well with 14 art galleries and the Contemporary Arts Center—all located within easy walking distance of one another.

Business and commercial ventures, while slow during the 1980s, have begun increased activity due to the increase in residential and tourist traffic flow in the area. Several law firms and professional agenices have moved their offices into the heart of the Warehouse District. A list of HRI developments includes a building that is today The Woodward Historic Riverfront Apartments, which was built in 1912 as a new home of the Woodward, Wight and Co. With more than 40 different floor plans, each with its own character and design, the apartments are built to fit into the existing structure of an old southern warehouse.

The Henderson Historic Apartments reflect the craftsmanship of a charming historic building renovated in superior style. From conception to construction, each luxury apartment is a unique blend of original architectural details, efficient space planning, designer finishes, and modern amenities.

The central atrium of The Woodward Apartments features an old box chute that has been refurbished as a work of art.

In 1988 HRI Management Corporation re-created the ambience of the original St. Mary's Market. With a lush tropical greenhouse, spouting water fountains surrounding 105 luxury apartments, and a magnificent walkway lacing back and forth, the new St. Mary Apartments are one of the best deals in town.

And finally, the Federal Fiber Mills, the original concept, creation, and completion of warehouse living, offers 130 individual units from which to choose. Some of the apartments offer breathtaking views of the city skyline, while others look out over the reawakened riverfront and the banks of the Mississippi River. It is an altogether fitting view for the developers and residents of the Warehouse District.

LANDMARK LAND COMPANY OF LOUISIANA, INC.

NEW ORLEANS IS DESTINED to become great again," predicts Gerald G. Barton, chairman and chief executive officer of the California-based Landmark Land Company, Inc. "That's because, among other reasons, New Orleans is the smallest of the great port cities of the world that sits on a major river."

Landmark Land is a diversified real estate developer with offices in Louisiana, Florida, Oklahoma, California, and South Carolina. The company is primarily involved in the development of planned real estate golf communities, industrial parks, shopping centers, and office parks. The company is the developer of Oak Harbor Golf and Waterfront Neighborhood in St.

The recently opened Oak Harbor Golf and Waterfront Neighborhood in Slidell is a prime example of Landmark's dedication to quality.

Tammany Parish and the Belle Terre Country Club and subdivision in St. John the Baptist Parish. Oak Harbor is currently selling home sites, and its championship golf course will open in October 1990. In addition, the company owns the Oak Tree Savings Bank in New Orleans.

Why would a real estate company invest millions of dollars in the New Orleans region? Barton provides a list of reasons why he believes outside investors should take a strong look at New Orleans. Among the many reasons are natural resources—energy, seafood, farming, and timber—but above all else is the Mississippi River, a conduit for agri-

Belle Terre Country Club in La Place is one of Landmark Land's major commitments to Louisiana.

cultural products from America's heartland. In addition, there are the human resources of a good work ethic and friendly spirit.

The city also has unique financial resources, including a banking community whose major players are all in good health.

Says Barton, "As many investors take a shorter and shorter view, preferring investments that do not require intensity of management, the opportunity for creation of value by combining Landmark's resources and management talents in long-term real estate projects becomes greater and greater."

Landmark Land Company's commitment to the creation of value has long been a tradition. That tradition continues in New Orleans and its surrounding community.

The beautiful St. Andrews golf community.

CHARBONNET CONSTRUCTION COMPANY

JOHN D. CHARBONNET KNOWS his business, and he makes it a point to pass that knowledge on to his clients.

Since 1973 Charbonnet has owned and operated Charbonnet Construction Company, a medium-size, design/build construction firm that specializes in meeting its customers' expectations and bottom line.

"We take time to understand what an owner really wants, because a general contractor truly affects an owner's occupancy costs. If you double the capital investment, then you are, in effect, doubling the occupancy costs down the road," says Charbonnet.

Having a hand in the success of a business from the ground floor up is a responsibility that the employees at Charbonnet Construction Company do not take lightly. That is because much of the firm's business is provided by repeat customers who have been thoroughly satisfied by the work done by this conscientious organization over the years.

Charbonnet categorizes his customers as the typical New Orleans client base. While specializing in the construction of strip shopping centers, flex space, and warehouses, the company has also built office space, plumbing supply houses, lumberyards, electrical wholesale facilities, and distribution centers. The firm has worked on multimillion-dollar deals to small jobs that were cemented with a simple handshake. The company services an area of roughly 100 miles in and around the New Orleans area.

A native New Orleanian, Charbonnet has a master's degree in structural engineering from Tulane University. In addition to overseeing his construction company, Charbonnet has been a leader in the civic community of New Orleans and the surrounding region.

He has served as President of the Board of Trustees of the Academy of Sacred Heart and on the Advisory Board of Jesuit High School. Charbonnet also holds seats on the boards of Loyola University, the First National Bank of Commerce, and the Ear, Nose and Throat Hospital of New Orleans. He served as chairman of The Chamber/New Orleans and the River Region in 1989.

In 1988 Charbonnet was chosen Rex, King of Mardi Gras, an honor he acknowledges was the civic high point of his life. Says Charbonnet, "New Orleans has been very good to me and my family, and that's why I remain active in community affairs— to give something back. But the crazy thing about this city is that it always seems to be one step ahead in returning my investment."

Charbonnet Construction Company gives its time and expertise and, in return, its customers are all the better for it.

John D. Charbonnet, owner of Charbonnet Construction Company. Photo by Donn Young

GERTRUDE GARDNER REALTORS

■ N A POLL BY *MONEY* magazine, New Orleans was ranked near the top as one of the best places to live in America. This rating was based on a variety of variables, with one of the most important factors being the amount and diversity of affordable housing in the metropolitan area.

It is Glenn M. Gardner's job to see that customers looking for nice, affordable housing or commercial buildings—either to rent or to buy—get what they are looking for. Gardner is president of Gertrude Gardner Realtors, a three-generation real estate agency that was founded in 1943 by Gardner's grandmother, Gertrude.

"To help people thinking of relocating to the Greater New Orleans area," says Gardner, "we're tied into a national statistical data base that compares housing costs, utilities, tax cost, and other pertinent factors so that our clients can see for themselves what a great buy they're getting in this area. The data base includes 270 metropolitan areas in all 50 states, some 2,200 communities, and nearly 20,000 neighborhoods."

Gardner oversees a company of several hundred Sales Associates with a managerial and clerical support staff of another 60 full-time employees. Gertrude Gardner Realtors operates residential, commercial, and industrial sales, leasing, and property management services for its clients. The agency has 14 offices strategically located throughout the metropolitan area. Says Gardner, "The greatest strengths of our company are its excellent people, our ongoing training, and our national relocation network of more than 36,000 Sales Associates.

"For example, our sales managers have an average of 18 years of real estate sales and management experience. We learned a long time

ago that no commission is worth the reputation of our company. We practice the 'Golden Rule' and treat people the way we'd like to be treated.

"Over the years that personalized, professional approach has paid off with a lot of repeat business and referrals from a loyal clientele who know we will treat them fairly and honestly."

The company conducts special courses throughout the year for its sales associates and managers on a variety of subjects, including financing, new marketing ideas, appraising, and new computer programs. "It keeps us on the cutting edge of a very competitive business," says Gardner.

Being on the cutting edge persuaded the U.S. Department of Housing and Urban Development (HUD) to choose Gertrude Gardner

Right: Posing at yet another successful sale are (from left) Glenn M. Gardner, president; Lynda Nugent, director, Career and Education; and Scott Brown, director, Relocation and Corporate Services.

Below: The top management of Gertrude Gardner Realtors (from left): Glenn M. Gardner, president; Gertrude Gardner, chairperson; Jerry Berry, director of administrative affairs; Frank Trapani, director, Commercial Industrial Division; and Bob Kilinski, director, Branch Affairs.

Realtors as one of only six companies in America to assist in a special pilot program. HUD selected the agency to help move a large portion of HUD's inventory of FHA foreclosures through Gertrude Gardner's advanced management, marketing, and sales techniques.

Meeting the needs and wants of potential home buyers and sellers, training hundreds of very successful sales associates, assisting in local and national relocation, securing commercial and industrial space, performing quality property management, helping lenders with their repossessed real estate, and giving simple, straightforward information are what Gertrude Gardner Realtors is all about.

PATRONS

The following individuals, companies, and organizations have made a valuable commitment to the quality of this publication. Windsor Publications and The Chamber/New Orleans and the River Region gratefully acknowledge their participation in *New Orleans: America's International City.*

Adams and Reese*
Alerion Bank*
Antoine's*
Barq's, Inc.*
Bisso Towboat Company, Inc.*
Business Council—New Orleans and the River Region*
Charbonnet Construction Company*
Chevron Corporation*
Cooper/T. Smith Stevedoring*
Crescent Distributing Company*
Delta Air Lines, Inc.*
Delta Queen Steamboat Co.*
Deutsch, Kerrigan & Stiles*
E.I. du Pont de Nemours and Company*
Entergy Corporation and LP&L/NOPSI*
First National Bank of Commerce*
Freeport-McMoRan Inc.*

Gertrude Gardner Realtors*
Hibernia National Bank*
Historic Restoration, Inc.*
Hotel Inter-Continental New Orleans*
Howard, Weil, Labouisse, Friedrichs, Inc.*
International-Matex Tank Terminals*
International Shipholding Corporation*
Jones, Walker, Waechter, Poitevent, Carrere & Denegre*
Kentwood Spring Water*
Blaine Kern Artists, Inc.*
Landmark Land Company of Louisiana, Inc.*
Liskow & Lewis*
The Louisiana Land and Exploration Company*
Louisiana State University Medical Center*
The Louisiana Superdome*
Loyola University*
Lykes Lines*
McDermott International, Inc.*
McIlhenny Company*
Martin Marietta Manned Space Systems*
Milling, Benson, Woodward, Hillyer, Pierson & Miller*

New Orleans Convention Center*
The New Orleans Hilton Riverside and Towers*
New Orleans Marriott*
Ochsner Medical Institutions*
Pan-American Life Insurance Company*
South Central Bell*
Southern Baptist Hospital*
Stone, Pigman, Walther, Wittmann & Hutchinson*
Taylor Energy Company*
Texaco USA*
Textron Marine Systems*
Tulane University*
University of New Orleans*
Walk, Haydel & Associates, Inc.*
Weiner Cort Furniture Rental*
Westminster Corporation*
Whitney National Bank*
Windsor Court Hotel*
World Trade Center of New Orleans*
WVUE-TV*

*Participants in Part Two of *New Orleans: America's International City.* The stories of these companies and organizations appear in chapters 12 through 19, beginning on page 155.

INDEX

GENERAL INDEX
Italicized numbers indicate illustrations